A Home for All Jews

The Schusterman Series in Israel Studies

EDITORS · S. Ilan Troen · Jehuda Reinharz · Sylvia Fuks Fried

The Schusterman Series in Israel Studies publishes original scholarship of exceptional significance on the history of Zionism and the State of Israel. It draws on disciplines across the academy, from anthropology, sociology, political science and international relations to the arts, history and literature. It seeks to further an understanding of Israel within the context of the modern Middle East and the modern Jewish experience. There is special interest in developing publications that enrich the university curriculum and enlighten the public at large. The series is published under the auspices of the Schusterman Center for Israel Studies at Brandeis University.

For a complete list of books in this series, please see www.upne.com

Brandeis Series on Gender, Culture, Religion, and Law

EDITORS · Lisa Fishbayn Joffe · Sylvia Neil

This series focuses on the conflict between women's claims to gender equality and legal norms justified in terms of religious and cultural traditions. It seeks work that develops new theoretical tools for conceptualizing feminist projects for transforming the interpretation and justification of religious law, examines the interaction or application of civil law or remedies to gender issues in a religious context, and engages in analysis of conflicts over gender and culture/religion in a particular religious legal tradition, cultural community, or nation. Created under the auspices of the Hadassah-Brandeis Institute in conjunction with its Project on Gender, Culture, Religion, and the Law, this series emphasizes cross-cultural and interdisciplinary scholarship concerning Judaism, Islam, Christianity, and other religious traditions.

For a complete list of books in this series, please see www.upne.com

ORIT ROZIN

· ·

A Home for All Jews

CITIZENSHIP, RIGHTS, AND NATIONAL IDENTITY IN THE NEW ISRAELI STATE

· ·

Translated by
HAIM WATZMAN

BRANDEIS UNIVERSITY PRESS

Waltham, Massachusetts

BRANDEIS UNIVERSITY PRESS
An imprint of University Press of New England
www.upne.com
© 2016 Brandeis University
All rights reserved
Manufactured in the United States of America
Designed by Eric M. Brooks
Typeset in Garamond Premier Pro by Passumpsic Publishing

For permission to reproduce any of the material in this book,
contact Permissions, University Press of New England, One Court
Street, Suite 250, Lebanon NH 03766; or visit www.upne.com

Research funded by the Israel Science Foundation (934/09)

Chapter 2 is based on two previously published articles by
Orit Rozin from 2010, "Israel and the Right to Travel Abroad, 1948–1961,"
Israel Studies 15 (1): 147–76; and 2011, "Negotiating the Right to Exit
the Country in 1950s Israel: Voice, Loyalty, and Citizenship,"
Journal of Israeli History 30 (1): 1–22.

Library of Congress Cataloging-in-Publication Data
NAMES: Rozin, Orit, author. | Watzman, Haim, translator.
TITLE: A home for all Jews: citizenship, rights, and national identity
in the new Israeli state / Orit Rozin; translated by Haim Watzman.
DESCRIPTION: Waltham, Massachusetts: Brandeis University
Press, 2016 | Series: The Schusterman Series in Israel Studies |
Series: Brandeis Series on Gender, Culture, Religion, and Law | Includes
bibliographical references and index. | Description based on print version
record and CIP data provided by publisher; resource not viewed.
IDENTIFIERS: LCCN 2015048850 (print) | LCCN 2015048041 (ebook) |
ISBN 9781611689518 (epub, mobi & pdf) | ISBN 9781611689495
(cloth: alk. paper) | ISBN 9781611689501 (pbk.: alk. paper)
SUBJECTS: LCSH: Israel.
CLASSIFICATION: LCC DS126.5 (print) |
LCC DS126.5 .R6913 2016 (ebook) | DDC 323.095694—dc23
LC record available at http://lccn.loc.gov/2015048850

5 4 3 2 1

To my wonderful sons,

YUVAL AND YOTAM

CONTENTS

· ·

ACKNOWLEDGMENTS
· ·

Perhaps not surprisingly, like most authors I can honestly say that during the writing of this book I experienced long bouts of frustration punctuated by moments of elation and discovery. In the real world — away from my books and my computer — I was looking for a tenure-track position. Many academics today share this quest, which only seems to be getting more protracted and harder. In 2011 I found a home at Tel Aviv University in the Department of Jewish History, and I am thankful to all who made this possible. There were dark days of despair while reading reports about girls who were forced into premature marriages; about people separated from their loved ones overseas; about the plight of immigrants. And then there were the demons of doubt and the hours of perplexity. True, the perspective from the swimming pool often saved me, suggesting insights as I plowed through the water.

Fortunately, I have gifted and caring colleagues. Assaf Likhovski suggested that I write this book. He commented on preliminary drafts and offered valuable advice; Pnina Lahav opened her Boston home to me and has been a keen supporter of this research project up until its final draft. Avital Margalit and Yael Darr read earlier drafts of some chapters and otherwise spent time discussing this project with me. Moshe Elhanati added a sober perspective, great theoretical advice, and wonderful home-cooked meals. I am grateful to Derek Penslar for his comments and suggestions on the final draft and for being the mensch that he is.

Anita Shapira read various drafts and kindly offered generous support with the substance and in spirit. Establishing and heading the researchers' forum at the Chaim Weizmann Institute for the Study of Zionism and Israel, she nurtured a community of scholars, of which I am happy to be a member. I am grateful to all, and especially to Avi Bareli, Meir Chazan, Orna Cohen, Uri Cohen, Ruth Ebenstein, Danny Gutwein, Paula Kabalo, Nir Kedar, Nissim Leon, Tali Lev, Itamar Radai, Zohar Segev and Anat Stern.

When embarking on a new project, there are always essential data to gather, secondary research literature to cull through, and theoretical perspectives to consider. Many colleagues assisted me willingly. I am thankful to

Yaacov Shavit for generously sharing his vast knowledge with me and for relentlessly encouraging me along the bumpy road. Yael and Eviatar Zerubavel provided both intellectual and emotional support. I am grateful to Moussa Abu-Ramadan, Jose Brunner, Yoav Gelber, Itamar Even-Zohar, Motti Golani, Michael Feige, Menachem Hofnung, Liat Kozma, Ruth Lamdan, Bat-Sheva Margalit-Stern, Menny Mautner, Esther Meir-Glizenstein, Jacob Metzer, Amihai Radzyner, Yoram Shachar, Margalit Shilo, Bernard Wasserstein, and Laura Weisman. Omer Aloni, David Bassoon, Jonathan Bensoussan, Yael Braudo, Nomi Levenkron, and Guy Seidman shared archival material and assisted in other ways.

Archivists and librarians are the gatekeepers to history's treasures. My curious and diligent research assistants Ilit Gamerman and Eitan Rom spent many days in libraries and archives. I wish to thank Gilad Livne, Michal Saft, and Helena Vilensky at the Israel State Archives, Leanna Feldman and Hanna Pinshow at the Ben Gurion Heritage Institute Archives, Gilad Nathan at the Knesset Archive, Doron Aviad at the Israel Defense Forces and Defense Ministry Archives, Batya Leshem at the Central Zionist Archive, Michael Polishchuk and Haya Seidenberg at the Moshe Sharett Labor Party Archive, and the staff of the Pincas Lavon Institute for Labour Movement Research.

Zohar Shavit approached me while I was still working as an adjunct professor at Tel Aviv University and encouraged me to apply for funding from the Israel Science Foundation. The foundation's generous grant made this project possible. Ilan Troen and the Schusterman Center for Israel Studies at Brandeis University provided financial support and much encouragement. Lisa Fishbayn-Joffe at the Hadassah-Brandeis Institute offered additional funding. Tel Aviv University supported this project generously: I wish to thank the Minerva Center for Human Rights at the Law Faculty, the David Berg Institute for Law and History at the Law Faculty, the Yaniv Foundation at the Chaim Rosenberg School for Jewish Studies, and Dean of Humanities Eyal Zisser.

My editors Sylvia Fuks Fried at Brandeis University Press and Phyllis Deutsch at the University Press of New England helped shape this book and, most important, helped me find my own voice. Translator Haim Watzman's queries made me think again.

I am thankful to my friends, many of whom are listed above, and to Michal Ben-Jacob and Orly Krinis for lifting my spirits on bad days and for celebrating the joyous moments of life with me. While I was writing this book's concluding chapter, during the summer of 2014, sirens tore through the silence of my otherwise tranquil study. Before the ceasefire agreement was reached, I left Israel for Canada to finish working on the manuscript on the shores of Bella Lake in the serene Billie Bear resort. What for many Canadians was an ordinary summer was for me, coming from nerve-wracking Israel, a paradise on earth. I am grateful to Audrey Karlinsky for inviting me and for reading and commenting on parts of the manuscript, and to Richard Anderson, my favorite cook, for feeding me his Southern delights.

Over the past three years I have lost two outstanding scholars and friends. Ilan Gur-Zeev passed away in 2012; his thoughts and his firm spirit inspired me in many ways. Eshel Ben-Jacob died in May 2015. For decades he brought sheer intellectual joy to my life. With them I could converse about life, the universe, and (almost) everything.

My mother Lea Asia and my mother-in-law Arnona Rozin kept the Jewish calendar and its festive meals, while I was busy writing. My thoughtful sons Yuval and Yotam cheered me up when I was low and provided love and hope. I am forever committed to Gezer for all that he is and all that he does for me. And to my beloved four-legged feline friends who make me get out of my chair.

Some of my compatriots have forgotten the true value of democracy to humanity at large and to Israelis in particular. I hope that this book will remind them that the freedoms and rights, recognition, and sense of belonging that are so hard to achieve should never be compromised.

A Home for All Jews

· ·

Creating Citizenship in the New State

O N MAY 14, 1948, a Palmach (the elite fighting force of the
Haganah, the underground army of the Jewish community
in Palestine) soldier stationed at the Kalia Hotel, on the
besieged northern shore of the Dead Sea, recorded in his
diary that he and his comrades had listened on the radio to
David Ben-Gurion reading the Declaration of the Establishment of the State
of Israel (also known as the Declaration of Independence). Later that day, the
soldier wrote, they came across a tome of the British Mandate legislation, and
that evening he and his comrades burned the book.[1]

From the point of view of the people of the Yishuv (the Jewish community in Palestine), the sovereignty they gained that day was not only a matter
of political independence. It was also a restoration of Jewish honor—both
self-respect and the recognition by the other nations of the world that they
were to be respected.[2] Furthermore, the citizens of the new country expected
that their independence would be expressed not only collectively, in the form
of national symbols and ceremonies, but individually as well. They expected
to be recognized by the state as sovereign human beings with a right to freedom and dignity in their everyday lives.[3]

In October 1948, at the height of the war, *Davar*, the widely read daily
newspaper published by the powerful Histadrut, Israel's largest labor organization, which served as a mouthpiece for the ruling socialist-Zionist Mapai
party, published an editorial arguing that individual freedoms needed to be
bolstered. The new country, argued the paper's senior editor, Herzl Berger,
should educate citizens to stand up for their rights. "We must build and for-
tify a spirit of political freedom in our country, the spirit of the free citizen
—the expression of the soul of free human beings, in the name of whom and
for whom the country has been established. . . . Let us not put off concern
for human freedom in our country until our country has been liberated," he

wrote. As he saw it, the state of emergency that had been declared because of the war constituted a clear and present danger to a nation that had not yet established a true democratic tradition and that had not yet tasted freedom. He feared that temporary measures would become permanent ones.[4]

In Israel's Declaration of Independence, which needs to be read in the context of the period in which it was composed, the country's founders committed themselves to establishing a regime based on justice and solidarity. Israeli citizens would be entitled to equality and guaranteed freedom of religion, conscience, speech, education, and culture. The authors of the document envisioned a direct line connecting the universalist exhortations of the Hebrew prophets to the values of the emerging Israeli society.[5] But, as is typical of a newly founded polity, the words inscribed on parchment-like paper and the hopes inscribed in people's hearts were not immediately and automatically put into practice. That required time, national maturity, and many battles for citizens' rights.

This book addresses three such battles that were waged during Israel's first decade. In the first of these, women sought to establish that immigrant children had a right to childhood; in the second, middle-class Israelis demanded the right to travel freely outside the country; and in the third, immigrants demanded the right to be heard. These struggles were motivated by both personal and collective needs. They demonstrated the individual's need to be protected by the state, while at the same time being protected from the state. The stories of these battles are essential parts of the coming of age of Israeli democracy and illustrate the expectations that people of that time had of their government. Most importantly, these struggles demonstrate the strong link between national identity and citizens' rights. They offer a portrait of contemporary Israeli citizenship.[6]

The Jewish people's Zionist revival produced an aspiration to form a new image of the Jewish individual and Jewish nation, as well as narratives about Jewish history. Questions about the nature of the new society were incontrovertibly related to these images and narratives: What should the state of Israel and its regime look like? Which political and social models were worthy of adoption, and which should be rejected? These questions are asked in every new democracy, but in Israel's case they were bound up with Zionism's image of itself and with both positive and negative narratives of Jewish history throughout the ages. Current postnational thinking about democracy views a multicultural society as the best one for treating citizens as individual human beings. But such a concept of democracy was alien to most early Israelis, including members of the country's progressive elite. The attention of the regime and of the Jewish public's core groups[7] was directed at gigantic enterprises such as the ingathering of the Jewish people's exilic communities and the establishment of a new Israeli society that would include a variety of communities differing in dress, language, and culture. The heterogeneous nature of the population made the challenge of shaping Israeli citizenship the society's most important project.

The focal point of national identity for the established elites, whether of the political left or right, was a tight link to the worldwide Jewish community. Yet at the same time that these elites considered the Jewish nation as a whole to be a foundation of Israeli identity, they were also discomfited by the Diaspora. On the one hand, Jews outside Israel gave Israel much-needed influence and funds to further the Zionist project. On the other hand, the Diaspora was seen as a repository of exilic values, the old Jewish way of life that Zionism rejected.

As soon as the new country came into being it was flooded with immigrants. About half the 690,000 newcomers who arrived between 1948 and 1951 came from the Islamic world, while the remainder were survivors of the Holocaust in Europe. They joined the 650,000 Jews already living in Israel, many of whom had been immigrants themselves at an earlier time.[8] In addition, the country was home to about 150,000 Palestinian Arabs, those who had not left or had been expelled during the war.[9] The concepts of citizenship held by these different groups were quite diverse. Some came from areas of colonial rule; others had endured state-sponsored terror. Some were members of the victorious Jewish majority in the new country, while others belonged to the defeated Arab minority.[10]

In addition to establishing the institutions of the new state and laying out its powers, policymakers, led by Prime Minister David Ben-Gurion, devoted a great deal of their attention and resources to the formation of a national identity.[11] A new and modern identity was crafted. Instilled in the public through the civil religion established by the state,[12] it grew and flourished among cultural agents such as writers, poets, thinkers, and educators, who in turn disseminated it more widely.[13] The nation-building process, which began in the late Ottoman period and matured under the British Mandate, thus continued after the establishment of the state, when it fused with the process of molding citizenship.[14]

Because of the tight link between civil identity and Jewish nationalism, Israel's Arabs were not in fact equal partners in the state. The reasons were cultural, not only political. Even though the nation builders were chiefly attentive to the wishes and needs of the Jewish national movement, the Jewish political community in Palestine during the Mandate period did not come of age autonomously. Rather, it was culturally and politically linked to the two other sides of the triangle of that time and place — the Palestinian Arab national community and the British regime.[15] Some aspects of the Yishuv's culture during that time were thus shaped by, and in confrontation with, Palestinian national identity.[16] For this reason, during the fierce war that tore the land apart, and in fear of an invasion by the armies of the Arab states, the authors of Israel's Declaration of Independence devoted only a few words to the Palestinian Arabs who were to become citizens of the new state. They were urged to preserve the peace and to contribute to the building of a state represented by symbols that were not theirs, and they were promised full and equal citizenship.[17]

The formal framework of democracy provided the Arab minority with full political and social rights, but in practice Arabs were discriminated against. For many years most of them lived under a repressive and humiliating military regime that limited their rights. The laws of the land were not implemented uniformly among them.[18] In fact, the Arab minority's lives were shaped by different rules. In retrospect, then, Israel clearly came into being with two types of citizenship — full Jewish citizenship, which included cultural and emotional attachment to the nation, and an incomplete Palestinian Arab citizenship.[19]

Since my subject here is the process by which full Israeli civil identity was developed in the context of nation building, my focus is on Jewish citizens. The Arab minority will thus receive limited treatment. My brief references to the minority will illuminate the state's conduct and the status of the majority, as well as highlight social processes of exclusion and inclusion.

The Challenges of the First Decade

The ceremony at which Israel declared its independence was held just as the armies of Israel's Arab neighbors were about to invade its territory. The first challenge facing the new country was to win the war. There were other challenges as well: to absorb an enormous number of immigrants, to put in place a functioning and prosperous economy, and to establish governing institutions as well as a functioning civil service that would enjoy the public's confidence. Achieving these goals demanded not only human and economic resources but also organizational ability, a willingness to make sacrifices in the present for the sake of the future, and discipline.[20]

Despite the fact that Israel was far smaller than the Arab states facing it in terms of both population and land mass, it was able to field more soldiers, its army was better trained, and its soldiers displayed higher morale than those of its Arab foes. Although at a material disadvantage during the war's first months, Israel was able in time to acquire superior weaponry.[21]

But victory came at a high price in blood. Some 5,800 Israeli soldiers fell in the war, and 1,162 civilians were killed. The war also left thousands of soldiers and civilians with permanent injuries and other impairments. The psychological impact of the casualty rate was severe, as this was a tightly knit society that was also geographically isolated.[22] Victory was due not only to the courage of the country's soldiers, but also to the way the economy and civil society functioned during the war.[23] Money and credit raised in Israel and throughout the Jewish world also played an essential role.[24]

During the state's first year its ministries were established and its army, the Israel Defense Forces, was founded. The court system inherited from the Mandate regime resumed its work, and a Supreme Court was established. Civil servants and policemen were hired. Ambassadors and judges were appointed. A census was conducted. and elections were held to a constituent assembly that later constituted itself as the First Knesset, the new country's parliament.[25] But while the nucleus of the new country's state apparatus was soon up and running, its young agencies and new officials were often stymied in the face of huge needs and cross-cutting demands for funding, attention, and care.[26]

And immigrants were pouring in. They began to arrive while the war still raged, and their numbers surged after it was over. Most of the arrivals were indigent, and many required medical treatment.[27] The economy was rickety, and most of the newcomers were unable to find work. In addition, tens of thousands of discharged soldiers were vying for the few jobs that there were.[28] Living conditions for immigrants were harsh. A severe housing shortage led to large numbers of them being crowded into barracks and tents in abandoned British army camps. Sometimes several families from different countries of origin shared a single tent.[29] On top of these economic and physical hardships, the immigrants faced social difficulties. A common national identity proved insufficient to bridge cultural gaps, especially the gap between the absorbing population and those being taken in.[30]

To ward off hunger in the burgeoning population, the government instituted an austerity program. This was based on the rationing of basic goods, food in particular. The goal of the program was to maintain control over resource utilization and outlays of foreign currency.[31] The program aimed to provide the population with a guaranteed minimum of nourishment. In fact, a huge black market soon emerged, challenging the rule of law.[32]

At the end of 1951 Israel sank deep into economic crisis. It was compelled as a result to revise its immigration and economic policies.[33] The consequence was a sharp drop in the number of new arrivals. The Israeli pound (*lira* in Hebrew) was sharply devalued. As a result of these changes, the economy plunged into recession. The three principal factors that pulled Israel out of the crisis were the Israel Bonds campaign, which sold government bonds to American Jews; economic aid from the United States; and the reparations agreement that Israel signed with Germany, under which Germany paid compensation to the Israeli government to support the absorption and resettlement of Holocaust survivors.[34] The Israeli government's willingness to commence negotiations with Germany over such compensation so soon after the Holocaust led to violent protests in Israel.[35] In 1954, after two years of high unemployment, rising prices, and consequent low public morale,[36] the economy began to recover and the influx of immigrants resumed.[37]

At the end of the war, Israel held areas not assigned to it under the United Nations partition resolution of 1947. Prior to the war these territories had been populated largely by Arabs. To assert its sovereignty over these areas and prevent the return of Arab refugees to their homes, Israel established hundreds of new agricultural settlements. Many of them were populated by new immigrants sent there by the government. Large amounts of capital were invested in founding and supporting these new communities, many of which were in frontier regions. (In fact, the lengthy and convoluted borders that Israel found itself with after the war created a situation in which most of the country's territory was either within a few kilometers of a hostile border or in the southern Negev Desert, with its difficult climate and great distance from the country's commercial and governing center). But the difficulty of making a livelihood in these remote and resource-poor communities led many immigrants to abandon them. The large investments made in equipment and personnel thus ended up being for naught.[38]

Following the war, the security situation stabilized. The menace of war was replaced by the daily tasks of routine defense. Palestinian refugees who had lost their lands, homes, and personal property crossed the borders to return to their homes, harvest their crops, or take possession of their property, a phenomenon that Israelis termed "infiltration." Some Palestinians came with theft or sabotage in mind, and some had murderous intentions, hoping to demoralize the Jews. This Palestinian infiltration constituted both a physical and psychological threat to Israeli security, in particular in immigrant settlements. This, too, prompted many settlers to leave. They preferred to live in the cities along Israel's Mediterranean coast, which were safer from military threat and where it was easier to find employment and make a living.[39]

Israel held the countries from which infiltrators crossed its borders responsible for violating its sovereignty and thus conducted reprisal operations in those countries' territories. In the mid-1950s the areas along the borders became more unstable. Tension increased between Israel and its neighbors. In September 1955 it was revealed that Egypt had signed an arms deal with Czechoslovakia, one large enough to upset the strategic balance of power between Egypt and Israel. Israel's leaders and citizens were alarmed, and tensions increased still further.[40] In 1956, following a secret compact between Israel, France, and Great Britain, Israel invaded the Sinai Peninsula. Following this campaign, Israel's borders became more secure.[41]

Given the military, economic, and social circumstances prevailing in Israel during the country's early years, the government's ability to govern was constrained. The needs were too great and the ability to address them too small.

Rights in Dispute

The Zionist movement and the Yishuv embraced varied democratic traditions, cultural connections, and worldviews that drew on both Western liberal democracies and the ethnocentric nationalism of Central and Eastern Europe. Other influences were Soviet statist authoritarianism, Jewish law, and the Enlightenment values of equality, humanism, and socialism. All these vied in the arena in which the character of the new country was shaped.[42] British influence was especially salient. Despite the hostility that Israelis felt toward the colonial ruler from which they had just freed themselves, the lion's share of Mandate legislation—including its emergency regulations, originating in 1945 and severely criticized by the Yishuv at that time—remained on the books.[43] British democracy, especially as it functioned under Labor governments, served as a reference point and exemplar during Israel's early years.[44]

The British example was also at work in the fateful decision made in July 1950 not to promulgate a constitution for the new state, but to legislate a series of basic laws instead.[45] The historical and political circumstances leading up to this decision have been the subject of many studies. Scholars have pointed to the significant role that Orthodox and ultra-Orthodox legislators played, demanding for instance that the Torah (the Bible) be the only constitution of Israel. But it was David Ben-Gurion's objection that was crucial. Many scholars believe that his rejection of a formal constitution was motivated by political interests; without a constitution (and without judicial review), the parliament and the executive branch, led by Mapai, would possess more power. But there are other compelling explanations that shed a positive light on his decision.[46]

Critics of this decision felt that the country had relinquished an important means of guaranteeing civil rights and building a national identity.[47] Whatever the case, some civil rights struggles took place before this decision was made, and even more occurred afterward. In these battles, individuals, groups, third-sector organizations, legislators, judges, and government ministers sought to mold a social and legal order in which rights and freedoms would be protected and would serve as an expression of national identity. The correct nature of this order, however, was controversial.[48]

Critics of the modern Western concept of law have charged that its purpose is to create harmony and coherence in an industrialized capitalist world that is full of contradictions. In doing so, the law's aim is to reconcile oppression and exploitation of the working class with liberty and freedom of choice. Another claim made by such critics is that the attributes of liberal law, such as the demand for formal equality, are the result of papering over the inequality that is built into a society's economic relations.[49] At least some members of Mapai—the labor Zionist party that was Israel's largest, and thus its ruling party for the country's first three decades—shared this distrustful attitude toward liberal capitalist values. They looked askance at the agents of liberalism, such as judges and lawyers, who in their view were advocating legal equality at the expense of socioeconomic equality.[50] One of the most prominent reasons Ben-Gurion opposed a constitution was that he was leery of judicial review. It could, he feared, allow a reactionary court, such as the US Supreme Court in the early twentieth century, to hold back the other branches of government as they sought to promote the progressive value of distributive justice.[51] In contrast with the neoliberal world we now live in, the debate over freedoms in Israeli society in the late 1940s and early 1950s did not just address negative freedoms, as was the case in the United States. Social rights were considered by many Israelis to be an essential part of the state's commitment to its citizens. They wanted not just the rights of freedom of speech, press, and religion, but also rights to employment, housing, education, and health.[52]

During the state's early years, this struggle between the socialist-Zionist and Western liberal concepts of government and the struggle between conservative religious and secular progressive views of society, were the major forces that shaped the way the Israeli collective and its individual members viewed themselves. These struggles were also fed by the inherent tension and conflict between the needs of the state and society and the needs and desires of the individual. The contest between progressive and secular values and traditional values was intensified by the immigration of large numbers of religious and traditional Jews, many of them from the Islamic world. The events described in this book occurred in the context of these historical circumstances and political-ideological divisions and how they played off against each other.

Scholarship on Rights

Civil rights in Israel in the 1950s have been studied only in part. Certain rights, such as those of freedom of expression and of occupation—that is, the freedom from government interference in an individual's choice of profession or livelihood—have received considerable attention.[53] Freedom of association and assembly, property rights, equality, and educational autonomy have also been the subjects of a number of studies.[54] Yet the connection between these specific struggles and the advancement of rights in general and the relationship of the struggles to the establishment of civil and national identity have not been the focus of historical inquiry. The struggles to protect certain rights have often been presented as having been conducted in isolation from society as a whole — that is, in the separate sphere of the law. In other cases they have been analyzed only in a narrow political context.

Only recently have legal historians begun to make use of theoretical and thematic frameworks that enable them to examine Israeli law in its social and cultural contexts. The interactions of law, society, culture, and identity in Israel are now an area of lively study. Law and jurisprudence are beginning to be seen as concepts of culture production. Along with the study of the ideas that are the foundation of law, scholars have begun to examine the practices, cultural agents, producers, and consumers who together shape it.[55] According to the constitutive approach, law is not a force that operates on society from the outside, but rather is itself the result of social action that finds expression in the daily lives of ordinary citizens.[56] In other words, scholars today pursue the legal norms immanent in mutual relations among citizens in their everyday lives no less than those which find expression in court cases. In texts and in the daily actions of ordinary people, they find reflections of hegemonic social concepts. At the same time, they are attentive to manifestations of resistance to these hegemonies. Such resistance may be clandestine, discernible only to a scholar who can divine them from accounts of events.[57]

In this book I also look at everyday life, along with the actions of decision makers in civil rights struggles, and show how dominant concepts are reflected in society. But unlike other writers, I point to broad, unabashed, and clearly voiced examples of resistance as well as covert ones.

There have been many critical social scientific studies of the Israeli regime in the 1950s. In this rich and varied research field, the young country's democracy has often been depicted as having been limited to its formal dimensions, and the government has been portrayed as being unresponsive, arbitrary, and, especially, intolerant. The encounter between citizens and the state, especially in the case of marginal social groups, has often been portrayed as an aggressive one, in which one side is entirely subordinate to the dictates of the other.[58] This approach may have been useful in blazing a new trail of research and in highlighting the flaws of Israeli democracy. But, in my view, it is not precise in its account of history. In particular, it neglects one of the central players in shaping the country: the public.

Israel's social order was quite fluid in its early years. Israel was exceptional even among other immigrant societies, simply because of the proportion of immigrants in the population. Israel was both a new country and one that absorbed huge numbers of heterogeneous immigrants. While the state apparatus and the elite groups whose members filled positions of authority had no little power, ordinary citizens had much more influence than most students of the period have hitherto recognized. Consequently, the government and the citizens engaged in constant negotiation. Relations between the state and society were clearly dynamic. Citizens imbued concepts and rules dictated to them with their own meanings.[59] Citizens challenged the established order in many ways. Most of all, they demanded a role in shaping that order—that is, they asserted their right to a place in the institutions that formulated the rules, the conventions and the procedures they lived by. The demand by different groups to take part in shaping the general good was tantamount to a refusal to accept things as they were. This refusal represented the first stirrings of an alternative order.[60] The labor movement's ethos was powerful, but it was not the only ethos that shaped the period. Alternative concepts of society, including liberal capitalism, also wielded considerable influence.[61]

Israel was a new country with a bureaucracy that was just taking its baby steps. Despite the state's ability to restrict the rights of certain disempowered groups, the Arab minority in particular, the government was far from being all powerful. It thus chose where and when it would invest money, time, and authority in arranging the daily life of Israelis. As a result, at least at some times it only pretended to control the lives of the citizenry.[62] In practice, the regime toiled to win the hearts and minds of its citizens and to lay the groundwork for constructing their civil consciousness.[63]

Like every other country, Israel was never a single coherent entity devoid of contradictions. It was divided into units that had different and even contradictory interests. A real gap yawned between government initiatives and the society that took form under their influence. This disparity was due in part to the state's weakness and in part to the fact that groups of citizens and state agents had complex mutual interactions. In practice, both shaped society, despite the asymmetry of the power relations between them.[64]

Despite notable constraints, and despite the large discrepancy between the aspirations of leaders and citizens and the actual functioning of the bureaucracy, Israel operated in the main as a democratic state. The regime thus largely depended on cooperation, citizen mobilization, and public support. Furthermore, the state needed not only the cooperation of its own public, but also that of Jews living outside Israel. The Jews of the Diaspora had to be persuaded to immigrate or to support the Jewish state from the outside, including by donating their time and money. Key to the success of such persuasion was a positive image for the state, and especially for its elected government. As a new country, Israel was also subject to international criticism. Needing the aid of other countries, Israel had to act cautiously toward its citizens, especially when injustices it perpetrated were reported outside its borders. This international exposure seems also to have further limited the regime's reach.[65]

A measure of skepticism regarding the actions of the Israeli regime is healthy. But we may and should presume that, in the case of this young nation-state, which aroused such hopes, the battles to shape the character of its government and the image of the country did not touch only on positions of power or on the relations between certain groups and others. Rather, the fundamental assumptions held by the parties fighting for change or preservation, or for restrictions or freedoms, were connected to the way in which they understood the nature of the general good and the identity they desired for the state and society. They struggled not merely to win naked power but also to realize the genuine optimistic expectations that citizens, politicians, judges, and civil servants had about the nature of the state they were so devotedly working to establish.

Three Fights for Rights

Each of this book's three chapters connects a struggle for a certain right with the collective (and at times the personal) identity that citizens, organizations, and policymakers sought to fashion during Israel's first decade. In each chapter I cast light on the needs of a different segment of the population and its quest for equality, freedom, and solidarity. The three struggles touch on that delicate cord that ties the individual to the state.

It should first be noted that in the period under study, the term "right" had two distinct meanings. The first was the accepted and familiar one used today in liberal democratic and social democratic societies, the citizen's inherent right to freedom from government interference. The second meaning was the citizen's right to receive certain services from the state. An example of the former is freedom of expression, and an example of the latter is the right to education.

The second meaning is tied to the republican worldview of the labor movement, according to which rights are awarded to those who devote themselves and their families to the building of the nation. In this view, the term "rights" incorporates obligations to the state and society.[66] In this book, I will address rights in the first sense, but it should be understood that, for many people in the labor movement, the conditioning of rights on obligations to the state and society seemed unexceptionable and indeed necessary during the new country's difficult and perilous early years.

In terming these fundamental rights, I do not have in mind only legally recognized rights, but also contemporary perceptions, whether the right was explicitly guaranteed or implicitly taken for granted. I will address recognized legal rights, such as freedom of movement, but also two rights that do not fall under formal legal categories: the right to a childhood and the right to be heard or to be heeded. The latter right can be subsumed under the more general rubric of the pursuit of recognition.

The book's first chapter discusses the right to childhood as embodied in the Age of Marriage Law of 1950. The law was intended to protect a marginalized and voiceless group, girls of the Mizrahi community—that is, Jews who came to Israel from the Islamic world. It reflects the national society's utopian horizon, according to which Jewish children are the children of the entire society. The fight to raise the marriage age aimed to draw a clear line between childhood and parenthood. It clearly marked those groups and individuals who conducted themselves properly and those who did not. It is also a struggle that clearly marked the boundary between full and deficient citizenship—that is, between Jews and Arabs.

The book's second chapter focuses on the freedom to leave the country. During Israel's first decade, anyone who wanted to leave had to receive the state's approval in the form of an exit permit. Most Israelis who sought to leave the country (aside from emigrants) were members of the middle class, and thus the struggle to end the permit requirement was promoted largely by the bourgeois political parties. It was a struggle that articulated the liberal view that the state should impinge on and constrain the lives of citizens as little as possible. The battle for freedom to leave the country also dealt with borders, both political ones (those drawn on maps) and social boundaries.

At the center of chapter 3 are the new immigrants who arrived just after independence. The accepted foundation for discussing the voice of the citizens of a democracy is freedom of expression. In this chapter I break away from that foundation and discuss the claim that citizens—especially those from weak groups, as the immigrants were when they arrived—need to be able to do more than voice their opinions. They need the active attention of state agents; a shoulder to lean on; and the feeling that the leadership, bureaucracy, and citizens from the sociopolitical mainstream feel a sense of solidarity with them. The right to be heard also involves boundaries separating immigrants from established Israelis. The tracing of such borders is related to the distribution of material resources by the state and by access to power centers, but it also involves how the resource of attention is divided up.[67] The stories of these struggles thus lay out the boundaries between different kinds of citizens and between citizens and decision makers, while also showing the agency displayed by individuals and groups.

A Portrait of Citizenship in Formation

Democracy is not some winged being that descended from heaven. It is a form of government that is constantly developing and changing. During Israel's early period, in addition to attempting to use its powers to regulate its citizens and adopting a strict attitude toward them, the government provided the country's Jewish citizens with protection and shelter. Even if that led to a healthy portion of frustration, those citizens were sympathetic to the national identity that it fostered. Not all Jewish citizens were interested in creating a new Israeli identity and disengaging from their Jewish heritage,[68] but the large majority wanted the country to be strong enough to defend them against repression, subjugation, and annihilation. Whatever the new country's drawbacks, they recognized its positive value: it provided its Jewish citizens not only with defense, but also with identity and existential meaning. With regard to fundamental rights, the new state was enlightened in some areas and dark in others. The struggles portrayed here show both of those aspects.

The picture of Israel painted in this book is thus multifaceted, as is the portrait of its citizens. Their fights for rights reveal a profound demand for change in the status of Jews and a reshaping of their identities in light of the values of mutuality and equality that lay at the foundation of the new country. But they also show how a dynamic system of power relations developed among citizens and groups and between them and their government. The government, in this picture, was a decentralized and not always coherent source of power. Between the law and its juridical interpretation, between the law and its enforcement, and between the law and its social interpretation stood human beings, social and organizational systems, and their varied agendas.

The process of shaping Israeli citizenship was directed by policymakers and public activists to whom the state gave tools to shape it. But that process was also significantly affected by the state's weakness and the cracks that appeared in its governing apparatus. The looseness of the government's efforts and the multiplicity of opinions within it enabled certain groups to behave in ways that were not consistent with the position of the governing majority, while others were able to act even in violation of the letter of the law. The Israeli civil identity that formed as a result of this was not, then, only the outcome of hegemonic discipline. It was also the result of a great deal of self-formulation. The very demand of different groups to take part in shaping the social agenda and their activities in a variety of public sectors shaped their identities and their consciousness of themselves as citizens. In spite of their experiences of frustration and alienation and the feelings of rejection and scorn they complained of, most citizens found ways to build a sense of themselves as citizens of Israel.

CHAPTER ONE

. . . .

The Right to Childhood and the Age of Marriage Law

A few dark-skinned, dark-eyed little girls, new immigrants from Yemen, displayed astounding audacity and courage. Girls who were twelve years of age, ten, even eight, dared to wave their tiny fists against their husbands, firmly announcing that they refuse to be married women and that they fully intended to attend school. . . . Some of the "husbands" (there were cases in which fifty-year-old men had taken a ten-year-old girl for a wife) insisted that the young girls continue to live with them. "I love her," said one of these gentlemen, "and she must be my wife. She is already ten years old, that's old enough. I paid the bride price that was quoted, I am married legally according to Jewish law. Why should I let her go?"[1]

I N NOVEMBER 1949, Ada Maimon, a member of the ruling party Mapai serving in the Knesset, raised the question of child marriage at a meeting of the Knesset's Constitution, Law, and Justice Committee. She demanded that the Criminal Code Ordinance of 1936 be amended to raise the permitted marriage age. Maimon had previously headed the Council of Women Workers, Israel's largest women's organization, which had been established in 1921 as part of the Histadrut. In 1949 she also served as a member of the board of the Women's International Zionist Organization (WIZO), a philanthropic group that represented middle-class women. In a letter she sent to Yosef Lamm, another of Mapai's representatives on the committee, she rehearsed the long history of involvement in this issue by the Yishuv's women's organizations. Proposals to raise the marriage age, she noted, had been tabled from time to time in the National Council (the Yishuv's representative body), and no significant action had been taken. Her demand (and a subsequent bill she submitted) that the issue be addressed was prompted by the arrival of a large wave of immigrants from Yemen that had begun a few months earlier.[2] "It is an urgent matter," she wrote, "because in the Yemenite camps we now see mothers of the age of thirteen–fourteen with babies in their arms."[3]

Maimon's motion to raise the age of marriage to eighteen makes it clear that she viewed allowing children to become mothers as being in utter contradiction to the identity, values, culture, and morals of Israeli society in general and those of its women's organizations in particular. She demanded that her bill be taken up quickly, so as to save as many girls as possible before they were married off.[4]

At the beginning of the wave of mass immigration that began when the Israeli state was founded, the newcomers came primarily from Europe. But in 1949 the balance changed. In that year, nearly half the immigrants came from the Islamic world, and they constituted the great majority of newcomers in the years that followed.[5] While the immigrants included only a few tens of thousands of Yemenites, they attracted unprecedented public attention. From the perspective of old-time Israelis, in their short airplane trip from Yemen to Israel these immigrants seemed to have traversed centuries, coming from the Middle Ages straight into the modern age. On the one hand, they were held up in wonder as examples of authentic Jews unsullied by the ills of modern life, while on the other hand, they were mocked for their ostensibly primitive habits.[6] Child marriages (those in which the bride was under the age of fifteen according to the British Mandate Criminal Code Ordinance 1936) were common among these newcomers, and there were also cases of marriage of prepubertal girls.[7]

The larger Jewish world had undergone changes in this regard, but not the Jews of Yemen. Beginning in the eighteenth century, Jewish women in Central Europe began to marry no earlier than their mid-twenties, and sometimes even later. In the nineteenth century, following the impact of the Haskalah (Jewish Enlightenment), the standard marriage age rose among Eastern European Jews as well. The Haskalah also had a major impact on other aspects of marriage. For example, the tradition of parents arranging matches for their children waned, and more Jews married for love. In 1902, only about a quarter of the Jewish women in czarist Russia married before the age of twenty.[8] Because more and more girls were attending school in Jewish communities throughout the Middle East and North Africa, the age of women at marriage there also rose gradually, beginning at the end of the nineteenth century, although at a more moderate rate. These changes were most pronounced in the cities; in some rural communities girls continued to be married off at the age of twelve or thirteen. In Yemen, however, girls did not attend school and did not learn to read and write.[9]

The Age of Marriage Law in Current Scholarship

A number of scholars have written about the Age of Marriage Law. Shoham Melamed and Yehuda Shenhav claim that the law's purpose was to restrict the fertility of the Mizrahi Jews, which the absorbing population viewed as a demographic threat. Following the lead of Jacqueline Portugese, who has claimed that the law's purpose was to curtail Arab reproduction rates, they also argued that the law was enacted under the influence of neo-Malthusian fears that prevailed in the West after World War II. The law, they say, was part of a structured and deliberate government policy.[10]

Aharon Layish found that the *sharia* courts and Muslim population did not comply with the law and were able to evade it. Nevertheless, the marriage age among Muslims rose during the 1950s and 1960s. In Layish's estimation, however, the law played only a secondary role in this change, and economic and cultural factors had far more influence.[11] Andrew Treitel, who has also examined the interplay of Israeli law with Muslim law and the Muslim religious courts, claims that it was Muslim pressure that led to an amendment to the law in 1960 that granted judges discretion in awarding marriage permits to underage minors.[12]

Melamed and Shenhav's studies contradict Layish's and Treitel's. If the growing size of the Arab (and the Mizrahi) population was perceived as a menace, the state would certainly have enforced the law, and Israeli legislators would not have revised it in 1960 to make underage marriages easier.

The following discussion covering the campaign to amend the criminal code to include a minimum marriage age during the 1920s and 1930s will disprove the claim made by Melamed and Shenhav that the effort to raise the marriage age was inspired by postwar trends. Their second claim, that the law was one part of a comprehensive antinatalist government policy is also open to serious doubt given the contemporary campaign to enlarge Israel's Jewish population — including its Mizrahi population — at that time. In July 1949, the government voted to grant mothers of ten or more children a one-time payment of 100 Israeli lira. In September 1949, as a "first step in the government's action to encourage the birthrate in the country," birth prizes were awarded.[13] That same year a Birth Fund in the Office of the Prime Minister provided financial aid to needy mothers to pay for housekeeping help and baby and maternal products.[14] Most of the women who won the birth prize during the state's early years were from the Mizrahi community. Prizes were also awarded to Arab women.[15] In 1950, the year in which the Age of Marriage Law was debated, and in 1951 huge numbers of immigrants continued to arrive, including tens of thousands from the Islamic world.[16] Furthermore, policymakers frequently gave voice to maternalist ideas, praising mothers as the producers of the nation's children, and this outlook had practical consequences — for example, preventing women's service in combat roles in the Israel Defense Forces.[17] Along the same lines, a provision in the Social Security Law of 1953 mandated that the state pay for the costs of giving birth in a hospital. In addition, new mothers were also given a grant to use for the purchase of basic equipment for the baby. Given the dire living conditions of immigrants at the time, this money undoubtedly helped babies and mothers survive.[18] This provision was motivated by decision makers' alarm at the sharp rise in infant mortality among the immigrants, including among the Mizrahim.[19] In 1959, the Social Security system began paying child allowances to families with four or more children.[20]

Contrary to Melamed's and Shenhav's claims, the Age of Marriage Law was not even a government initiative. It is clear, however, that demographic anxiety was indeed part of the discourse surrounding the law. Moreover, Melamed has persuasively captured the ambiguity that was inherent in the absorption into Israel of the Jews of the Islamic world, who found themselves walking a narrow line between inclusion and exclusion.[21]

Laws are founded on broad and solid conceptual frameworks, as Shenhav, Melamed, and I all agree. We differ, however, in identifying the historical facts that enable the reconstruction of the actual ideational framework on which the Age of Marriage Law was based.

The Right to Childhood

Maimon's bill to raise the age of marriage was a direct continuation of the modern Western society's refashioning of the family. That project had its origin in the reform movement in the field of health (specifically related to sexuality), welfare, and education, as well as the movement to advance the status of children and women, which gained momentum at the beginning of the twentieth century.

In 1900 the Swedish feminist Ellen Key published *The Century of the Child*, laying out what was at the time an innovative theory of education.[22] It was translated into English in 1909, as well as into eight other languages, and quickly became a bestseller. To a large extent, it served as a foundation for the ideas of the Progressive Era in the United States and highly influenced thinking about the status of children in other countries as well.[23] By the beginning of the twentieth century, child welfare projects included a large range of philanthropic programs and legislative initiatives. In the United States, children were viewed as the largest group requiring assistance and intervention. These broad and varied efforts to care for and assist children were not motivated solely by compassion. Children were seen as the key to social control. For future generations to possess the strength of mind, body, and character necessary to fulfill the responsibilities of democratic citizens, children needed to be protected. Children were the hope—or the threat—of the future.[24]

The right to childhood was defined as a child's right to life, education, happiness, and protection. Saving children and guaranteeing their right to childhood became both a moral and a national mission in the United States and other Western countries. But doing so required that the state insert itself into the life of the family.[25]

The nature of the change in the status of children and childhood in the nineteenth century and especially in the early decades of the twentieth is explained most clearly in discussions of the economic value of children. The birth of a child in eighteenth-century rural America was welcomed as the arrival of a future laborer and as security for the parents later in life.[26] By the 1930s, lower-class children had joined their middle-class counterparts in a new nonproductive world of childhood, a world in which the sanctity and emotional value of a child made child labor taboo.[27] Children became economically worthless at the same time that they became emotionally priceless.[28]

The revolution in the lives of children in the West was accomplished in part by women's organizations that sought to improve and celebrate the lives of mothers. The members of these organizations were middle-class women who wanted to remake the status of women in the capitalist-industrial order without challenging the superior position of the father in the family. They viewed advances in women's rights as inextricably bound up with the status of children, and they lauded women's role as mothers.[29]

Founded in the period from the 1870s to the 1930s, these organizations transferred the traditional housekeeping and child-care roles of women into the public and political sphere. In the organizations' rhetoric, women were important to society because they were the primary caretakers of children and thus responsible for society's future. Therefore, society had to do all it could to enable women to be better mothers. These women's organizations were decisive shapers of Western welfare policy and legislation — in particular, of labor laws and legislation addressing the health of children and infants. Scholars have named this movement maternalism.[30]

Yet at the same time, other women's organizations waged a feminist struggle to gain full rights for women outside their role as mothers. The most prominent of their demands in the United States and Europe at the beginning of the twentieth century was the right to vote. The Yishuv was no exception: its women demanded the right to vote in elections to their society's representative institutions and finally won the suffrage battle in 1926.[31] In the Yishuv and Israel, bourgeois women's organizations such as WIZO and the Union of Hebrew Women for Equal Rights, as well as the labor movement's Council of Women Workers, combined maternal and feminist messages, in varying proportions.[32] Since theirs was a society preoccupied with building a nation in the context of a national struggle for self-determination,[33] and because one of a mother's duties was to instill her children with Zionist values,[34] their campaigns were highly maternalist and nationalist in tone. Yet this does not mean that they were entirely devoid of feminist sentiments.[35]

The larger Western discourse influenced the Yishuv and Israel both because the campaigns in other countries served as models for reform, and because many local reformers came to the Yishuv and Israel from countries where issues pertaining to children's and women's rights were of central public concern.[36]

Maimon's bill grew out of a long effort during the Mandate period to enact legal limits on when young people could marry. This campaign, like the later effort to enact and enforce the Age of Marriage Law in Israel, marks an important change: women and their allies began to demand that the state take part in promoting social change, specifically in properly shaping one of the most intimate areas of human life — marriage and sexual relations.

The Campaign for Reform of the Penal Code

After the British conquest of Palestine, which was followed by Great Britain's receiving a mandate from the League of Nations to govern the territory, tensions between modernity and tradition in the region increased. The new political order was viewed by the Yishuv's progressives as the beginning of a new era. The lives of women and children, they believed, were about to change. Some of the women who arrived in Palestine along with the new rulers also believed that one of the British administration's missions was to bring progress to the country. In 1921, Lady Beatrice Samuel, the wife of the new British high commissioner, Lord Herbert Samuel, founded a Women's Council. In 1928, its members began pressing the Mandate administration to raise the marriage age for girls.[37] In their view, it was incumbent on the British colonial administration to further progressive reforms in the family. To this end, they advocated for the appointment of a woman to oversee the welfare of women and children. Margaret Nixon, who arrived in Palestine to take up the post of superintendent of all women convicts, was later appointed the country's welfare inspector. She would play an important role in enacting the marriage age provision of the criminal code ordinance.[38]

The Union of Hebrew Women for Equal Rights, formed in 1919 by middle-class Jewish women in Palestine, became in 1920 the first organization to petition the Mandate administration on the subject of child marriage. It demanded that the marriage age be sixteen for both sexes. In furtherance of its campaign, it asked for and received the support of international organizations and petitioned the League of Nations to assist them and pressure the Mandate government, providing documents and reports in support of its position. For example, a memorandum it sent to the International Women's Suffrage Alliance in 1923 stated:

> Ottoman law forbids the marriage of a man under the age of eighteen and a woman under the age of seventeen, without the consent of parents or guardians. But the parents or guardians themselves are permitted to marry off their children if the man's age is not lower than seventeen and the age of the woman not less than nine! Jewish law has not yet established a minimum age for marriage, but despite this there are no cases of the marriage of non-adults among Jews of European ancestry. In contrast, child marriages are common among Yemenite Jews and among Muslim and Christian Arabs. ... Early marriage, it is well known, hold[s] back the development of women in the East. We hope to receive aid and support from all women in other countries that are subject to conditions similar to those described here.[39]

This memorandum presents several subjects that need to be fleshed out. First, the author presents Ottoman family law as applying to all of Palestine's inhabitants, but in 1919 the British incorporated this law into the Mandate's code only after restricting its application to Muslims.[40] Furthermore, the law, enacted at the tail end of imperial rule, raised the marriage age for boys to eighteen and for girls to seventeen but left a very broad loophole that was inspired by Muslim *sharia* law — a *qadi* (Muslim cleric) could sanction the marriage of a nine-year-old girl (and a twelve-year-old boy) if the child's guardian for matters of marriage (generally a girl's father) agreed and if the girl had reached sexual maturity.[41] Since marriages were arranged in any case by parents, the law constituted no real obstacle to younger marriages. As for the Jews, the Chief Rabbinate announced that it would not permit the marriage of girls under the age of sixteen, but there were exceptions.[42] The letter portrays Mizrahi and Arab women as in need of help and contrasts them with women of European origin, whose conduct is appropriate. In other words, it presents European women as members of an enlightened community seeking to bring succor to the suffering women of the Orient.[43] As a rule, the Zionist Ashkenazi women sought to represent all women, but they also made clear distinctions between different groups of women. They labeled the Mizrahi society as one in which women were hurt and degraded far beyond the humiliations that were the lot of all women according to the law of the land.[44]

The ethnic parsing of the Yishuv into its Ashkenazi and Mizrahi components became prevalent in Zionist public discourse in the 1920s and would later be salient during the state of Israel's early years. The distinction grew out of the fact that Jews of various origins formed separate communities in the Old Yishuv, the Jewish population that predated Zionist immigration and persisted thereafter. Beginning in the nineteenth century, however, this traditional separation was supplemented by an Orientalist approach.[45] European Jews perceived the Mizrahim as primitive, unhygienic, and incapable of caring for their own children. While they were perceived as part of the Jewish collective, they were also seen as in special need of rehabilitation.[46]

In 1928 the Union of Hebrew Women sent a long memorandum to the Mandate administration's chief secretary Harry Charles Luke. The Union demanded that the marriage age be the same as the age of consent, sixteen.[47] It petitioned the administration again in 1930, noting that the marriage law had already been changed in other parts of the British Empire. It offered as an example the enactment of the Child Marriage Restraint Act of 1929 in India and the amendment of the relevant legislation in Egypt in 1926, which raised the marriage age of girls to sixteen.[48]

The reply to the 1930 memorandum, signed by Edwin Samuel, acting chief secretary of the British Mandate administration, was that although the high commissioner was naturally interested in rectifying the injustices caused by child marriage, he had concluded that legislation was not a feasible means of doing so at this time.[49] The imperial context is quite evident, despite the fact that Palestine, as a territory governed through a League of Nations mandate, was not legally part of the British Empire. Nevertheless, revisions of laws in parts of the Empire made an impression in Palestine.[50] In 1927 the marriage age in Transjordan was raised to sixteen. The same happened in Great Britain itself in 1929. The age of marriage was also raised in Iran.[51] Palestine remained a backwater, as legal changes took place throughout the region and the British Empire.[52]

The subject of child marriage was also raised in the League of Nations Permanent Mandates Commission in 1931 and 1932. The commission asked the Mandate administration in Palestine to report to it on the legal situation.[53] In 1932, the Union of Hebrew Women for Equal Rights again petitioned the Mandate government. This time it gave an account of its contacts with the League of Nations. The Union further claimed that the administration was promulgating laws to defend working children, but that it had issued no law to defend girls who were purchased to serve as brides, sometimes to men much older than they. This practice, the Union wrote, was indistinguishable from slavery.[54]

It requested, and received, an opportunity to present its arguments to the high commissioner. He expressed his concern about overly hasty progress far in advance of public opinion but promised to take up the subject.[55] Following the meeting and a consultation with the colonial secretary, the high commissioner sent a letter to leaders of Palestine's religious communities notifying them that the government was weighing the possibility of setting a minimum marriage age and soliciting their reaction.[56] The responses most at odds with the proposal were those of 'Agudat Yisrael, an organization that represented most Haredi (ultra-Orthodox) Jews, and the Supreme Muslim Council. They asked explicitly, even bluntly, that the government defend the prerogatives of the religious courts.[57] Following this correspondence, the Supreme Muslim Council issued several regulations meant to assist in the enforcement of the existing law. The regulations were in fact an acknowledgment that the existing law was not being enforced.[58]

Nixon's report to the Mandate government on her fieldwork in the Hebron district was consistent with the information it had received in letters from some of the respondents who had opposed current practice. In dry, clinical language, Nixon wrote of the plight of the girls in the Hebron region who were married at a tender age, tied up so that they would not run away. She informed the government of suffering endured by girls who sought refuge from their husbands in police stations and of the beatings and marks found on the body of a ten-year-old girl. Another girl, she wrote, had tried to kill herself. Her report substantiated the claim that the Ottoman family law was a dead letter in the Hebron district, and in many other rural areas of Palestine as well.[59] With its heart-rending stories, the document seems to have been instrumental in moving the Mandate's legislative process forward —just as later reports would be after independence.

The superintendent of the census took the opposite position. He claimed that child marriage was a negligible problem in numerical terms and that it affected only a marginal population. He confessed, however, that he had no information about marriage age in the Bedouin community and that "in many cases marriage among Bedouin can be described as child-marriage." He also maintained—despite the fact that it is not clear what expertise he had in the subject—that "a girl of fifteen years of age in Palestine is not only more mature than a girl of sixteen years of age in England, but is far more precocious in sex matters, of which she has had knowledge from her earliest years."[60] While the superintendent advocated a marriage age of fifteen for girls, the tenor of his report was that it would be best for the Mandate government not to get involved in the subject at all.[61]

The Union of Hebrew Women for Equal Rights again petitioned the high commissioner on July 6, 1934, to set the marriage age for girls at sixteen. It noted that there had been advances in legislation. An amendment to the criminal code, promulgated in December 1926, had set the age of consent at sixteen, and legislation on child labor had set sixteen as the age at which childhood ended. Under these laws, "boys and girls below this age were termed children."[62] The Union thus highlighted legislation as one of the major arenas through which the concept of childhood could be constituted and its boundaries established.

But the British administration took its time. The documentary evidence indicates that the major cause of its slow pace was the opposition of the Supreme Muslim Council, which refused to accept any limitations on its exclusive power over the marriage of Muslims.[63]

In 1936 an amendment to the Palestine criminal code ordinance set the marriage age in Palestine at fifteen, but the law enabled religious courts to marry younger girls if their parents or legal guardians consented, and if a doctor certified that the marriage would not cause harm to the girl. This solution would later be termed a "legal contradiction in terms."[64] Nonetheless, it was an important achievement for Nixon, the Union of Hebrew Women for Equal Rights, and the international organizations that supported it. In 1933 the campaign also gained the support of the Social Service Association, a private organization of Christian, Moslem, and Jewish women.[65] But the law was full of holes and did not eliminate child marriage. At most, it offered an optional cultural norm.

The Status of Women in the New State

The Jewish reformers who lobbied to raise the marriage age in Mandate and later Israeli law wanted the Zionist revolution to be a comprehensive one that would not only remake the Jewish male as a productive laborer (as opposed to the Diaspora stereotypes of Jewish men as merchants and scholars), but also establish a new and modern model of the Jewish woman, the Jewish child, and the very nature of childhood.[66]

Both before and immediately following independence, the question of the status of women and their role as citizens of the new country was intensively discussed in various public forums, including during the postindependence elections to the Constituent Assembly (which transformed itself into the First Knesset), in the Knesset, and in the press.[67]

The Union of Hebrew Women for Equal Rights demanded that women be named to the legal commission set up by the Yishuv leadership to prepare for the establishment of the Israeli state. The Union argued that women's interests had to be represented in the commission's deliberations on issues such as marriage and the family, inheritance, labor legislation, social insurance, citizenship, and criminal law.[68] The Council of Women's Organizations, founded during the Mandate as an umbrella organization for all Zionist women's groups, sought to bridge the gap between the wide-ranging activities of Zionist women and their low level of political representation.[69] The two most prominent women's organizations in the council were WIZO and the Council of Women Workers. The latter was the Yishuv's largest women's association. During the 1948 war these organizations, operating independently and as part of the council, supported the war effort: they fed soldiers and provided them with clothing, and they assisted civilian war victims and newly arrived immigrants. They also helped soldiers' families. Yet they never ceased to demand equal rights for women and equal representation in governing bodies.[70] In the elections to the Constituent Assembly, which were held on January 25, 1949, WIZO fielded a slate of candidates and won a single seat in the 120-member body. Members of the Council of Women Workers were included in the slates of the parties of the left. The country's major women's organizations had gained access to the legislature and would use their presence there to further the passage of legislation on women's, children's, and family issues.[71]

In a radio broadcast six days after the election, in which Mapai, as expected, emerged as the largest party by far but fell short of an absolute majority, David Ben-Gurion presented the principles on which he would base his governing coalition. One of these was full and equal rights for all women — Jewish, Muslim, and Christian.[72] We may doubt whether Ben-Gurion was genuinely interested in gender equality in Israel's Arab minority.[73] However, in stressing the importance of gender equality, he demonstrated that it was a value with support beyond that of the women's organizations. The country's leaders were eager to have Israel seen by the world as a bastion of democratic rights and practice, and in their view domestic equality for women was essential for the image Israel needed to project internationally.[74]

The women's organizations wasted no time. In February the Union of Hebrew Women for Equal Rights wrote to the prime minister, demanding that the minimum marriage age be raised to eighteen.[75]

Fighting Child Marriage on the Ground

Public organizations had begun fighting child marriage and seeking to dissolve or terminate such unions well before independence.[76] The legislative battle that will be described below was only part of the story. The campaign to end child marriage required these organizations to work closely with the Chief Rabbinate as well. The Chief Rabbinate was a government agency established in 1921 under British rule to serve as the central Jewish religious authority in Palestine. Under Mandate law, which continued in force after the establishment of the Israeli state, the Chief Rabbinate, with its network of municipal and local rabbis, was responsible not just for ritual matters but also for personal and family matters, such as marriage, divorce, and burial. Thus, when — during the Mandate era — the Union of Hebrew Women for Equal Rights opened a network of legal aid bureaus to provide individual assistance to women in distress, these bureaus worked closely with the religious authorities, soliciting their assistance in preventing specific cases of child marriage and in enforcing the minimum age of marriage.[77] Other important actors in this field during the Mandate and thereafter were the Zionist Executive; the Jewish Agency, the Jewish self-governing authority in Palestine that, after the founding of the state, remained responsible for immigrant absorption and the establishment of new settlements; and (before statehood only) the National Council, the executive branch of the Assembly of Representatives, the Yishuv's elected legislature under the Mandate. All these bodies worked with the Mandate administration and Chief Rabbinate to protect the rights of children in general and to prevent child marriage in particular.[78] Along with the Union, Hadassah: the Women's Zionist Organization of America helped inculcate among Yemenite immigrants the value of education for girls and the importance of not marrying them off early.[79]

During the state's early years, both public and private organizations invested considerable resources and many work hours in instilling "good parenting" principles in the population.[80] The Union's legal aid bureaus continued to operate after the founding of the state.[81] The Council of Women Workers and its sister organization for stay-at-home women, the Organization of Working Mothers, also continued to instill progressive values.[82] Another organization working in this field was Youth Aliyah, founded in 1933 to aid German Jewish teenagers who arrived in the country without their families. After independence it provided board, education, and vocational training to thousands of immigrant teenagers. Youth Aliyah took under its wing girls who had been married against their will or who wished to leave their husbands. There was a financial side to these problems—husbands refused to grant divorces to their wives unless they repaid the bride prices the husbands had paid for them in Yemen. The Jewish Agency Executive had difficulty finding money to finance such divorces. A controversy raged over whether married girls who wanted to leave their husbands should be permitted to reside in Youth Aliyah facilities; the Chief Rabbinate opposed allowing this unless the girl was divorced.[83]

The Battle over the Marriage Age: The Chief Rabbinate and State Agencies

The Yemenite community posed a unique challenge to the Chief Rabbinate. Child marriage was not the only problem; polygamy was also practiced by these newcomers. The practice had been forbidden to the Ashkenazi Jews by an eleventh-century edict, but this did not apply to the Mizrahim. Another ban by the same authority had ended the practice of *yibum* (levirate marriage), under which a woman whose husband died before they had children was expected to marry her dead spouse's brother.[84]

Ada Maimon's bill spurred government agencies into action even before it was passed. In December 1949 the Ministry of Religions asked the Chief Rabbinate's Rabbinic Council to issue regulations to govern how problems relating to such marriage practices should be addressed, among them "the sale of a young girl of the age of twelve-thirteen for marriage."[85] In response, the Rabbinic Council reaffirmed the decision it had reached during the Mandate period, setting the minimum marriage age for girls at sixteen (and for boys at eighteen), "since a girl of a younger age than this is at risk during pregnancy and there is a danger of death for the mother and the fetus." It also forbade all marriages not registered with the Chief Rabbinate and explicitly prohibited fathers from marrying off their daughters at an age younger than the legal minimum, thus attempting to close the loophole that the Mandate legislation had left open.[86] The decision was preceded by a discussion of Halakhah (Jewish law) during which the Ashkenazi Chief Rabbi Yizhak HaLevi Herzog gave voice to his doubts in the form of a response to a previous response by his colleague, the Sephardi Chief Rabbi Ben-Zion Meir Hai Uziel. Herzog's inclination seems to have been to set the minimum marriage age for girls at seventeen. But for a variety of reasons, one of which no doubt was his reluctance to hand down a ruling that the public might disregard, he suggested that the age be set at sixteen. Herzog displayed great sensitivity to the plight of young wives and to that of children born out of such marriages. The Rabbinic Council's final decision was a balancing act between two clashing needs. On the one hand, to maintain its own political and moral authority and that of the Halakhah, it had to raise the marriage age in accordance with what was seen as enlightened contemporary standards. On the other hand, it could not tolerate a situation in which marriages performed according to Jewish law — even if they were illegal according to secular law — were not recognized by the state. Likewise, it could not institute changes that would not be accepted by religious Jewish immigrants, because if it did, it would lose its standing among them.[87]

But the Chief Rabbinate's major efforts were directed at shoring up its authority over marriage and divorce in the face of what it viewed as an effort by the newly formed state to give precedence to civil over religious law in this area.[88] The Knesset's members also sensed growing tension between the two authorities. In February 1950, at a session of the legislature's Constitution, Law, and Justice Committee, David Bar-Rav-Hai, a member of Ben-Gurion's Mapai party, protested that the Rabbinic Council had moved too fast in setting the minimum age at sixteen. In doing so, he said, the Rabbinate was seeking to bolster its authority at the expense of the nation's government.[89]

When the marriage age issue was taken up by the Knesset and the press in December 1949, state and other agencies began addressing this problem in the immigrant camps. They sought to recruit the Chief Rabbinate, which was adamant that whatever solution was found for the problem of child marriage would have to accord with Halakhah, to their efforts. So, for example, the Chief Rabbinate was not satisfied when it learned in December 1949 from a newspaper article that the director of the immigrant camp in Netanya had reached a financial arrangement with a thirty-five-year-old man according to which he would agree to release the eleven-year-old girl he had married. The Chief Rabbinate told the local rabbinate to find the girl and her husband and end the marriage legally and officially through a religious divorce.[90]

In January 1950, prior to the enactment of the law by the Knesset, the Ministry of Welfare sought to address the issue. Its legal advisor wrote to the Rabbinic Court of Appeals asking for assistance in finding a comprehensive solution to a problem that had arisen as a result of the wave of Yemenite immigration: "Young girls have arrived, of bat-mitzvah age [twelve, the age at which, under Jewish law, a girl becomes responsible for religious observances], whose fathers have married them off to aged husbands whose relations with their young wives are by nature cruel." The advisor also informed the court that welfare offices all over the country were reporting that such girls were running away from their husbands' homes and taking refuge with their parents or other relatives. "There is no power in the world," he wrote, "that can compel them to return to their husbands." He added that he had received requests from social workers that a solution be found that would free "these girls from the yoke of these unnatural marriages and return to them the freedom to be educated and to grow up that they have not yet experienced, and without which they cannot become citizens useful to society." The legal advisor noted that standard sanctions, such as a separation order issued by a District Court or the appointment of a legal guardian, had no effect on these husbands. He asked the rabbis to find a way to address the suffering of these girls and to guarantee their natural rights.[91] The Chief Rabbinate responded that each such girl had to apply to a rabbinic court and request a divorce, according to normal procedures. There was no other way to dissolve the marriages, it said.[92]

Bat-Zion Eraqi Klorman explains that for a child bride to flee her husband's home was a familiar phenomenon in Yemen. The families they fled back to accepted and understood them. Usually the husband would ask for his wife back several weeks or months later, sometimes offering to pay compensation to the girl's family.[93] What seems to have been a familiar problem of adjustment in Yemen, and one that was usually resolved, was viewed by Israeli social workers, women's organizations, and the rest of the established population, as a shocking and intolerable instance of social pathology.[94]

One example among many appeared in *Haboker*, the newspaper of the middle-class center-right General Zionist Party. The item's headline read: "A Shocking Incident Regarding the Marriage of an 11-Year-Old Girl to a 40-Year-Old Yeminite Immigrant." The article offered an account of a hearing before a rabbinic court over a petition to end the marriage:

> The girl was very upset and refused to enter the rabbinate office out of fear that she would encounter her husband there. She had to be brought into the hearing room forcibly. When she had calmed down a bit, she told the story of her marriage: when she was ten years old, her father sold her to Salam Tzoref for the sum of twenty pennies. She had absolutely refused to go under the marriage canopy but her father beat her and forced her to do so. Her husband lived in Yemen among Arabs and for this reason she was unable to run away from him, out of fear of the Arabs. In despair, she tried to kill herself by jumping off the roof of her house. Her husband forced her to live with him and on more than one occasion bound her hands and legs. Immediately after her immigration to Israel she fled to her uncle, who resides in a transit camp in Netanya. . . . When she finished her story, she added: "In Israel I am considered a little girl and go to school."[95]

In the matter of the distress experienced by the girls themselves, the cultural gap between the two cultures could not be greater. It was later highlighted by Avraham Taviv, a member of Mapai serving in the Knesset and a member of the Yemenite community, when the marriage age law had its first reading. He acknowledged that in his country of origin girls had been married at the age of ten or twelve, but he claimed that nothing bad had happened to them as a result.[96] Implicit in his position was the claim that the Western concept of childhood as a distinct and integral stage in life, with the accompanying sovereign rights of each girl to her own body and mind — the view that served as the moral and legal basis for the policies pursued and promoted by the Israeli state's legal system, women's organizations, medical experts, and social workers — differed entirely from those of the Yemenites.

The Welfare Ministry's legal advisor also contacted the State Attorney's Office. At the beginning of May 1950, the state attorney wrote to the secretary of the Chief Rabbinate, Rabbi Shmuel 'Aharon Shazuri (formerly known as

Weber) and invited him to take part in a series of visits to immigrant camps. The visits were meant to look into reports that the state attorney had received about illegal marriages of underage girls. The information that the girls involved were in distress seems to have come from social workers as well as the report of a commission of inquiry, the Frumkin Commission, that had studied the unrelated issue of education in the immigrant camps. Its report described several cases of child marriage. In one case, recounted by a social worker, a girl had been married to a man twice her age. She "was nauseated by him, outraged, reaching a state of hysteria each time she faced another encounter with him."[97]

The first invitation sent to Rabbi Shazuri by the state attorney was accompanied by a personal letter from the Ministry of Welfare's legal advisor explaining why the visits were needed and that the visitors would include representatives of the Jewish Agency's Absorption Department and the Investigations Branch of the Israel Police, and a physician acting on behalf of the Ministry of Justice.[98] The legal advisor's office conveyed to the Chief Rabbinate, apparently to demonstrate the nature of the problem, a letter it had received from the social work office in the Ein Shemer Bet immigrant camp. The letter offered a dry, clinical account of a difficult case of child marriage. The girl was eight years old and an orphan. She had been married to a fifteen-year old boy. The couple immigrated to Israel with the boy's parents. The social worker handling the case reported that from the start the boy had refused to grant the girl a divorce. The social worker recommended placing the girl in a Youth Aliyah camp in Netanya, a camp in which large resources had been invested and that took in only adolescents. The husband had been offered payment in exchange for a divorce but refused. According to the social worker, "The husband himself and his parents . . . , 65 years old and . . . 38 years old, abuse [their daughter-in-law] brutally, impose hard labor on her, and beat her. As a result of their reign of terror the girl is afraid to have contact with me. All her opposition has been repressed and her will to disengage from her hostile surroundings has been taken from her." The social worker requested assistance in freeing "this innocent girl from enslavement and degeneration."[99]

The visits to the immigrant camps at Ein Shemer, Beit Lid, Atlit, Beer Shev'a, Netanya, and Rosh Ha'ayin and the work village 'Eshtaol took place in May and June. Despite the escalating tension between the Knesset and the Chief Rabbinate, the two sides seem to have cooperated at first. In mid-May, 'Al Hamishmar reported that a large meeting had been held at the Beit Lid camp with the participation of representatives from the State Attorney's Office, the Chief Rabbinate, the Jewish Agency, and the police. These officials informed the Yemenite immigrants at the camp about the Age of Marriage Law that was about to be enacted.[100]

But within a month Rabbi Shazuri changed his tune, responding to further invitations with the message that the chief rabbis saw no point in taking part in a propaganda campaign meant to promote the new law.[101] The reversal of the Chief Rabbinate's attitude had been prompted by the legislative battle over whether the law should set the minimum age at sixteen, as the Rabbinic Council had ruled, or seventeen, which was the cabinet's proposal. The struggle between the Chief Rabbinate and the Knesset was over who should have the power to establish social norms and the capacity to enforce them.

Despite its lack of cooperation with the State Attorney's Office, the Chief Rabbinate sought to enforce its authority over immigrants and to prevent marriages of girls under the age of sixteen. In May, the Netanya rabbinate heard the case mentioned above of the forty-year-old man married to an eleven-year-old girl. After strenuous efforts were made to persuade him to grant his wife a divorce, the man finally agreed.[102] A month later, the Netanya rabbinate dissolved the marriages of several minors who were under the age of fifteen (the age of marriage specified by the Criminal Code Ordinance of 1936). This was done after the intervention by social workers and in their presence, and under the aegis of the legal counsel to the Ministry of Welfare. The marriages thus ended involved a fifteen-year-old boy married to an eleven-year-old girl; a fifty-year-old man married to an eleven-year-old girl; a man of twenty-two married to a girl of nine; and a boy of fifteen married to a girl of eight. In all these cases the girls had been the victims of violence at the hands of their families or their husbands. Following the divorce procedures, the girls were placed in Youth Aliya boarding institutions.[103]

The different ages of marriage (sixteen or seventeen) stipulated by the two authorities represented more than just a political rivalry or a struggle for power. They chiefly represented differing views about the nature of childhood, the role and status of the individual, and gender roles and gender equality; they indicate a different cultural repertoire and *Weltanschauung*.

Enacting the Age of Marriage Law

Despite the urgency with which Maimon spoke when she presented her bill to the Constitution, Law, and Justice Committee, two months passed before it was first brought for preliminary debate in the plenum. On January 24, 1950, Maimon presented her bill in the Knesset. First, there was a procedural discussion of the agenda for the session. "This bill is intended to prevent child marriage, which has become quite common in Israel," she declared. Maimon protested the fact that the bill had not been brought up for deliberation and called on her colleagues "to debate it this very evening."[104] A procedural debate ensued that, while it did not address the substance of the proposed legislation, offers an indication of the attitudes of the Knesset's members. Maimon's brief remarks urging her colleagues to take up the bill give the clear impression that she was offended by the Knesset's indifference to the issue. Why, she asked, had consideration of her bill been postponed for so long? She also reminded her colleagues that it was only after she submitted her private member's bill that the Ministry of Justice had rushed to submit one of its own.[105] In the end, she was successful. The plenum voted to bring up both Maimon's and the government's bills that same evening.

Like the Mandate authorities, the Israeli government was forced to deal with the question because it had no other choice once Maimon had introduced her bill and once the women's organizations began to push for its passage. Mapai was the Knesset's largest party and the center of the ruling coalition. Its largest coalition partner was the United Religious Front, which represented Orthodox and ultra-Orthodox Jews. At the time the two coalition partners were already at loggerheads over the issue of whether secular or religious education should be provided to the immigrant children in the camps. Understandably, Mapai was reluctant to open a new front against its coalition partner. It was the education controversy that led to the appointment of the commission of inquiry known as the Frumkin Commission just as Maimon introduced her bill.[106]

Despite Maimon's position of weakness, the news that the subject was to be brought before the Knesset was reported by the press even before the initial plenum debate in January. The newspapers continued to follow the legislative process as it dragged out over the following months, and this publicity spurred eventual passage of the law.[107]

Before considering the differences between Maimon's and the government's versions of the Age of Marriage Law, it is necessary to consider Maimon's claim that child marriages had become common in Israel. Since no data are available on the extent of the phenomenon at that time, there is no way of proving or disproving her claim. Figures on age at marriage only began to be included in the government's statistical yearbooks in the mid-1950s.

Furthermore, the numbers of child marriages are suspected of being biased toward the low end, given the many means used to hide the true age of girls who were married in circumvention of the law, as will be discussed below.[108]

The first section of Maimon's bill set the marriage age for both sexes at eighteen, with marriage a year earlier permissible with the consent of the child's parents or legal guardian. Section two contained a proviso empowering the minister of justice to grant a marriage license to a person who did not meet the law's criteria for marriage when preventing the marriage would endanger the petitioner's health or his or her physical or mental well-being. Maimon also proposed that any marriage entered into by a girl of sixteen years of age or younger be automatically voided by law.[109] In addition to Maimon's bill, the Ministerial Legislation Committee received two different drafts of a proposed government bill, setting the minimum marriage age for girls only at sixteen and seventeen, respectively. These drafts also proposed eliminating the provisions contained in the Mandate's law, under which marriages under the age set by law could be allowed if parents or guardians granted their consent and if a physician ascertained that the marriage would not result in physical injury to the girl. Penalties for violating the law were also increased.[110]

Right after Maimon submitted her bill but before it came up for discussion in the Knesset plenum, the managing director of the Ministry of Justice contacted a Dr. Ostern, chief of the Health Ministry's Social Medicine Branch, and asked for an expert opinion on whether "the enactment of such a law is desirable from a social and hygienic point of view."[111] Ostern recommended raising the marriage age:

The maturity of the head of a family and his wife are a condition for the normal development of its children, both physically and mentally. It is unthinkable that a girl of seventeen or even less possesses the bodily and psychological vigor necessary to care for and raise children. . . . As for mental hygiene, there is sufficient basis for the presumption that marriage at less than seventeen or eighteen is liable to hinder the mental, psychological, and social-professional development of the marriage partners. Hence the danger of growing numbers of people who, as a result of marriage at a young age, will become "handicapped" in the psychological and social sense, and who will thus become a heavy burden on themselves, their children, and society as a whole. Furthermore, we cannot expect that such marriages will be based on an appropriate choice [of partner].[112]

The Mandate law had been aimed primarily at protecting the bodies of girls and women. By 1950 the medical establishment felt responsible for defending the psychological well-being of women and the welfare of their children. Note that Ostern was not addressing the case of a particular girl forced into a marriage, but rather the price that society would pay by tolerating the general practice of marriage at a young age. Like American physicians, Israeli experts acted in line with the zeitgeist, conceiving of the family as a fundamental unit of the nation and worrying about its proper functioning.[113] Women and children were perceived as an integral part of the national fabric, and the nation required a strong foundation. Ostern's expert opinion was thus given as part of the discourse of the mental hygiene movement.[114]

This position was adopted by Minister of Justice Pinhas Rosen, who used it to legitimize the government's bill during the Knesset debate.[115]

THE KNESSET DEBATE

Rosen opened the debate by citing the marriage of girls ages 12–14 as a severe social problem, "one of the most negative phenomena in our national life." He suggested that all members of the Knesset would agree with him about the need for a law that would provide recourse for girls who had not yet reached even sexual maturity, much less social maturity. Nearly every one of the world's countries set a minimum marriage age by law, he noted. In an apologetic tone, Rosen added that the government did not propose, as Maimon's bill did, that underage marriages should be voided. The cabinet proposed to amend criminal, not religious, law, just as the Mandate administration had done. But whereas the Mandate law had defined the legal age of marriage on the basis of sexual maturity, Rosen argued that Israeli law should attend in particular to the bride's "mental, psychological . . . and social maturity." The important question, he said, was "not just whether the woman is sexually capable of conjugal relations, but rather whether she is competent to head a family, to educate children, and to serve as one of the pillars on which the family is built." The problem of child marriage, he concluded, could not be solved only by legal sanctions. The country, he said, needed the help of the women's organizations in inculcating new values in the population through education and "psychological and mental" influence.[116]

Rosen's speech was a practical one. It recognized the limits of state power and of the criminal code in bringing about change in the intimate lives of Israeli citizens. The same approach was evident in the deliberations of the Knesset's Constitution, Law, and Justice Committee.[117] But the speech also had a symbolic nature: Ostern referred to any man as the head of the family and to his wife as a secondary entity, but Rosen referred to women as heads of the family.[118] It is hard to tell whether Rosen was the sole author of his speech, as senior figures in his office often wrote speeches that he delivered,[119] but we can assume this was an intentional reference, not an accidental one.

Maimon spoke after Rosen and set off a storm. While there is no recording of Maimon's speech, the written transcript reveals her anger and frustration. She may have been upset about the long delay in bringing her bill up for discussion, but she seems to have been particularly incensed by the government's dawdling approach to underage marriage. At the time, Maimon was devoting the greater part of her time to Ayanot, a school with a large number of immigrant students. She was thus closely acquainted with Yemenite children. Barely controlling her anger as she spoke, she seems to have exaggerated the extent of child marriage when she said that "in our country, a large part of the population maintains its custom of marrying off girls at the age of twelve to thirteen." And she claimed that this problem was becoming more severe with the arrival of large numbers of immigrants from the Orient. Her most controversial sentence was: "A prognosticator has run the numbers and found that in just a few decades we will all be Mizrahim — that is, our children after us — so we are all interested in enacting an appropriate law."[120] Melamed and Shenhav have made much of this statement and the way it was interpreted by subsequent speakers. It serves as the foundation of their claim that the law was aimed at restricting the Mizrahi and Arab birthrate, in response to Asheknazi demographic concerns.[121] In fact, however, it was no more than an expression of pain at the bitter plight of Yemenite girls, a sharp critique of the status of women in Israeli society in general and among the Mizrahim in particular, and an expression of frustration at the magnitude of the change that this population would have to undergo, as Maimon explained a week later.[122] Furthermore, she feared that past progress would be undone and that she would be incapable of advancing the status of Israeli women in the future. She seems to have wanted to serve as a voice for the thirteen- and fourteen-year-old girls married to much older men. In her speech, Maimon spoke of mothers of ten children who were themselves only twenty-five years old, prematurely aged because they had lost some of the children they had borne. Maimon revealed great compassion: "Such a girl-woman lives in constant fear that her husband will leave her alone with her little ones. These husbands do not need to wait until their wives pass their prime to send her [sic] away — they may do [so] whenever they wish, at any time, and buy another, younger woman. This is how these unfortunate women live, degenerating in servitude and slavery and remaining illiterate. As we know, these girl-mothers have not even been taught to read and write." [123]

Maimon conveyed a sense of urgency and anger in the Knesset. She repeated her performance before the Constitution, Law, and Justice Committee and a few months later, again in the Knesset plenum, during the deliberations over the bill's second parliamentary reading. Once more she demanded that work on the bill be expedited. [124] She clearly felt it to be her personal responsibility, as a representative of women's organizations with large memberships, to uproot this social ill and save girls from a horrible fate. During one committee session she argued with Zerach Warhaftig, a member of Hapo'el Hamizrahi party (then a part of the United Religious Front): "I see the situation prevailing in this country as negligence, if *not* to call it by its proper name," she said." "I want to ask Warhaftig: if there are cases — and don't think that we are talking about a single case — in which a forty-five-year-old man has married an eleven-year-old girl, can we make do with the fact that this can be a ground for asking for a divorce? Do we not need to demand that such a marriage be invalid?" [125]

Maimon here leveled an implicit and harsh accusation at older men who marry girls. In her view, such men were pedophiles. "Negligence" for her was simply a polite way of saying that, which her audience would have understood. [126] Her emotional language was a product of her long, exhausting, Sisyphean labors to advance the status of women. [127] The sentiments she expressed were not hers alone — they are evident in the words of other members of the Knesset who supported the bill, such as Nahum Nir-Rafalkes of Mapam and Rachel Cohen-Kagan, the WIZO representative, as well as her Mapai colleagues Hasya Drori and Eliyahu (Lulu) Hacarmeli, Beba Idelson, and Yitzhak Ben-Zvi. [128]

Maimon focused on the plight of girls as individuals. In her view of the problem, there was no theoretical issue. She saw faces and knew names. She and several of her colleagues believed that, beyond the individual suffering of these girls, the damage caused by child marriage continued into the child brides' adult years, and that the practice was detrimental to their children and to the character of the Israeli nation. The question of how Israel ought to look was a constant concern of the supporters of the bill. Unsurprisingly, the battle lines were drawn between the religious and nonreligious camps — in other words, between the traditionalists and the revolutionaries. Religious and traditional Jews wanted Israeli society to be another link in the chain of generations, a society that adhered to its past, including religious law as it stood. The secularists and revolutionaries wanted to create a new and progressive society that blazed a modern trail for the Jewish people. They wanted Israeli society to be as progressive as the most advanced countries of the world — if not even more progressive. In this latter group, certain differences of approach were evident between right and left, in particular differences in their views of women's proper roles in society.

The most intractable problem the members of the Knesset grappled with was the status of religious law in Israel and the monopoly over marriage and divorce law that the British Mandate had granted to the religious courts. In the country's early years, that law remained in force — Israel's Marriage and Divorce Law would be enacted only in 1953. The greater part of the Constitution, Law, and Justice Committee's discussion of the age of marriage bills was devoted to this issue. It was clear, however, from an early stage of the deliberations that the inclination of the majority was to leave marriage and divorce in the hands of the different religious communities and not to allow civil marriages. While the committee focused largely on the Chief Rabbinate, it also heard and discussed the positions of the religious courts of other confessions. In the deliberations, Warhaftig, who represented the Chief Rabbinate's position on the committee and in the Knesset, expressed agreement with his Arab colleague Amin-Salim Jarjora (of the Democratic Front of Nazareth, a satellite party of Mapai), who represented the positions of both the Muslims and Christians. Both men sought to protect and preserve the prerogatives of the religious court systems, just as the Supreme Muslim Council had sought to do during the Mandate period.[129]

The battle lines were drawn in meetings of the coalition. David-Zvi Pinkas and Zerach Warhaftig of the United Religious Front pressed the members of Mapai to allow marriage at the age of sixteen, but the latter refused, agreeing only to a compromise that would set the age at seventeen. Behind the scenes, at a meeting members of the Mapai faction held with their party's secretariat in mid-May 1950, an effort was made to avoid damaging the delicate fabric of relations with the religious parties (forming the United Religious Front), while at the same time living up to Mapai's moral imperative to defend young girls and advance the status of women. David Bar-Rav-Hai, a member of the Knesset, criticized the Chief Rabbinate's decision to permit marriage at the age of sixteen, as well as the compromise to set the age at seventeen, while permitting girls to marry at sixteen with the consent of their parents or guardians. He pointed out that the parents and guardians were the ones marrying off these girls in any case, so that the provisions of the compromise "made hash of the whole thing."[130] He proposed setting the age at seventeen without exceptions, or permitting younger marriages only with the approval of a welfare officer. Bar-Rav-Hai took this opportunity to criticize Warhaftig for having made common religious and legal cause with Jarjora. Beba Idelson explained to her colleagues, who asked about this, what the role of welfare officers was. She reported a case in which a twelve-year-old girl who had been married to a forty-eight-year-old man was taken away from him and sent to a series of institutions. In the end, both the girl and the social worker responsible for her case went into hiding to prevent the husband from kidnapping his underage wife. Lamm depicted the pro-Soviet Kibbutz-led socialist-Zionist Mapam party as hypocritical and too willing to compromise because it had agreed to a marriage age of sixteen. Another member of the Knesset, Ziama Aharonowitz (who later Hebraicized his name to Zalman Aran) said that the issue should not be treated politically. He and his colleagues, he maintained, should consider "the body and soul of the girl, not as a part of intrigues. . . . How will we look to Israeli society if we give our seal of approval to marriage at the age of sixteen? If we do not oppose it, it means that we are for it."[131] This discussion demonstrates the very different conceptual meanings attached to the ages sixteen and seventeen. Aharonowitz's words in particular reveal the association made between age sixteen and a backward patriarchal society that objectifies girls and women.

When the law came up for its second Knesset reading in June 1950, it was clear that the question of the status of religious law would be separated from the discussion of the age of marriage law. Another controversy was over the Knesset's sovereignty, since in the end it decided to set the minimum marriage age at seventeen, in contradiction to the Chief Rabbinate's position. Despite the demand of the Orthodox and ultra-Orthodox parties, the clauses of the criminal code concerning the age of consent for sexual relations were not modified—it remained sixteen. This was outrageous as far as the religious community was concerned, as it left intact a period in which young people were allowed to have sexual relations but not allowed to marry.[132]

But this was only a display of power, pushing the boundaries without breaking through them. The majority of Knesset members simply wanted to demonstrate that the legislature was sovereign. Nevertheless, it refrained, for example, from decreeing that child marriages would automatically become annulled, because it feared the wrath of the religious courts of all communities.[133] The precedent of the British Mandate made it easier for the Knesset to pass the Age of Marriage Law. The debate over the standing of religious courts held back the law's passage but, in the end, did not stop it.[134] The solution was a compromise—a two-year increase in the minimum marriage age. Furthermore, the Knesset revoked the defenses that had been in Section 183 of the Criminal Code Ordinance, which permitted marriages at an age under the minimum with the consent of the child's parents and medical approval.

During the debate at the first reading of the Age of Marriage Law, religious and Haredi members of the Knesset had opposed the imposition of civil law requirements on religious law. In addition to seeking to protect the base of religious power and authority, they claimed that their aim was to protect young girls. Better, they said, for a girl who was married to remain in her marriage than to be divorced.[135] In support of this presumption, they cited "biological" facts—by which they meant the loss of the girl's virginity. Yosef Burg of the United Religious Front argued that setting the minimum marriage age at seventeen was tantamount to a demand for equality where there was no equality, "neither in personal development nor in physical development." There was, he said, a psychological disparity between Mizrahi and Ashkenazi women —the former, he said, matured more rapidly. Other speakers took the same position.[136] This claim was supported by medical opinion. In March 1950, Dr. Miriam Aharonova published an article in *Davar* asserting that living in a hot climate causes girls to mature earlier. Nevertheless, she warned against early marriages because of the physical harm they cause to both the girl bride and her children and because of the detrimental consequences for society.[137]

Still others who did not see raising the marriage age as a pressing issue cited examples of mothers and grandmothers in their own families who had married young and given birth to large numbers of children and who nevertheless enjoyed good health and long lives.[138] In other words, a number of members of the Knesset subscribed to an Orientalist view of the bodies of Mizrahi women and an essentialist approach to women in general, much like that of the superintendent of the census under the Mandate. Burg offered a further reason for setting the minimum marriage age for girls at sixteen. Putting off marriage, he said, placed an economic burden on parents who had to feed many children. Nor were there sufficient social frameworks to support girls ages 14–18, he argued. In economically secure urban Israeli families, he said, girls attended high school, but that option was not available to many Mizrahi girls. The response of Esther Raziel Naor of the right-wing Herut party was to demand that mandatory education be extended to ten years, instead of eight—that is, to the age of sixteen.[139] Burg's argument was, in fact, fairly weak. At the time, many teenage girls worked and provided their families with income.

Supporters of the law also cited the fact that girls who were compelled to marry young were marked for life, even if the marriages were terminated. No longer virgins, they had difficulty finding husbands. Early marriage also caused them to age prematurely. Israel Rokach of the General Zionists, who seconded Maimon's claims across the board, said that twenty-year-old Yemenite girls looked as if they were forty. He added that "Yemenite boys" also suffered from health problems because they were the product of child marriages.[140] In this, he echoed the expert opinion offered by Ostern.

. . . .

The demographic issue on which Melamed and Shenhav focus was certainly not absent from the discussion, but they vastly exaggerate its importance. In fact, it figured in only a minor way. Eliyahu Eliashar, of the Sephardim and Oriental Communities faction, accused Maimon of seeking to control Mizrahi fecundity. She feared, he said, the demographic growth of his community. In his faction's periodical, *Hed Hamizrah*, he wrote: "When I recently visited America and Europe I heard from Jewish intellectuals, and from the Zionist cohorts—it's been written about everywhere . . . these dangerous words: a black menace hangs over us, the danger of the Mizrahi communities. Recently there is a tendency in well-known circles to adopt in the field a position of 'let us deal shrewdly with them, lest they multiply' [Ex. 1:10]. I declare that, at least in this house [the Knesset], there should not be such an approach, certainly not on the part of MK [member of the Knesset] Maimon."[141]

Others argued that the marriage age should remain low to keep the Israeli birthrate high. Avraham-Haim Shag of the United Religious Front wondered why the government was awarding prizes to the mothers of large families, while at the same time promoting a law that would lower the birthrate.[142] Avraham Taviv of Mapai saw women simply as machines for producing sons. The womb, he argued, had to be harnessed in the service of the nation:

We need an army of our own, of the scions of our land, raised solely in Hebrew, properly disciplined. . . . We need such an army of youths. . . . Have we not seen how few of these we had in the War of Independence, in which they enlisted at the age of fifteen and sixteen, those lion cubs who leapt into every place of danger. . . . We are situated in the midst of seven hostile countries populated by natural increase. . . . And we are sitting here passing laws to prevent natural increase. . . . Natural increase should be encouraged, procreation for the purpose of raising sons . . . because only there lies our salvation, with God's help.[143]

Rokach harshly disparaged the direction of the Knesset debate: "First of all, I'd like us to stop repeating so mercilessly that a woman is no more than a machine for producing children. No few here have spoken in that tone. The Knesset should be the populace's intellectual leadership and it should know that a woman is not born only in order to multiply the number of children, and only to give birth. The time has passed to think of women as tools; women have their roles in the country and in our nation's social life."[144]

In other words, the idea that Mizrahi or Arab fertility should be repressed, while certainly voiced in the debate, was not the motivation for the passage of the law in 1950. On the contrary, precisely because the Arabs were viewed as external to the national collective — not citizens in the full sense of the word — participants in the May 1950 meeting of the members of Mapai faction with their party's secretariat proposed that a way be found not to enforce the new law on Arabs and to apply different rules to them. As I will show below, the law enforcement authorities were not concerned with protecting the childhoods of Arab girls, nor were they concerned about the demographic consequences of this population's birthrate.[145] In the case of the Mizrahim, the women's organizations had fought against that community's patriarchal practices since the Mandate period. Notwithstanding any demographic anxiety, Israel continued to take in immigrants from the Islamic world throughout its first decade, and the period immediately following the enactment of the new law was no different. True, the selection criteria instituted in 1951 caused the immigration rate to plummet in 1952–53 and significantly curtailed immigration from North Africa, yet immigration from that region resumed in 1954.[146] Even at the beginning of the 1960s, despite the alarm at the riots that broke out in Wadi Salib in 1959, with their manifestly ethnic character, Israel continued to promote North African immigration (see Table 3.2).[147]

THE RIGHT TO CHILDHOOD AND THE AUTONOMY OF WOMEN

Minister of Justice Rosen presented the Age of Marriage Law to the Knesset as a way of providing girls with a period of personal development that would enable them to become better mothers. Maimon's argument was more complex. She argued that the victims of child marriage were first and foremost the girls involved, not the nation. Girl mothers could not attend school; were subject to threats and abuse by their husbands; and quickly deteriorated, physically and mentally, under a regime of subjection and servitude.[148] Speaking before the Knesset's Constitution, Law, and Justice Committee, she declared: "I proposed eighteen [as the minimum marriage age] because it is written [in the Mishnah] 'eighteen for marriage.' I did not want to propose a high age, but self-aware women make an effort to marry only at a higher age, so that they have a position in life."[149] Maimon focused on the individual instead of the wife, the mother, and her contribution to the nation. In other words, Maimon presumed that the nation had an obligation to protect the rights of all of its children, and that this obligation was unconditional and not predicated on what a girl might or might not do for her country. Maimon clearly indicated that she would like to provide all Israeli women with self-awareness and social standing as part of their transition from traditionalism to modernity. Hasya Drori, of Mapai, made this point even more clearly in a speech on the Knesset floor: "Following the mandatory education law, this law has come to protect the elementary right to childhood, the most human right that a person should enjoy, the right to learn, develop, and grow up. If we deny the child the elementary right to physical and mental development, if a girl cannot enjoy the happy day when she says 'my heart's choice' to a person she herself has chosen — we rob her of everything."[150] Here Drori expressed a wish for a transition from a traditional to a progressive society, in which romantic love would replace arranged marriage.

Maimon and Drori did not make a connection between the girl and the mother she would become, or one between defending her in the present and her future contribution to society. In their view, both parents and husbands acting in the context of a patriarchal order, as well as patronizing medical experts, sought to control and supervise the bodies of girls and women. The positions of Maimon and Drori were, in contrast, based on a profound concept of rights. By this I do not mean a discourse of rights based on the libertarian concept that the principal role of civil liberties is to defend the individual against state tyranny. Rather, I propose a positive concept that advocates rights to childhood and personal development, a woman's control over her life and body, and her freedom not to be subjugated to the needs of others. In the view of Maimon, Drori, and other supporters of the Age of Marriage Law, protections of the right to childhood were on the same footing as Zionist values such as returning to the homeland or shaping a new model of Jewish manhood. In their view, the right to childhood, like these other principles, were essential to the complete redemption of the Jewish people — the entire Jewish people, including Jewish women. This concept is not only universal; it also has a local and Zionist aspect. Granting the right to childhood, according to the law's advocates, was part and parcel of becoming a free and sovereign nation.

All advocates of the law — Maimon, Drori, Rosen, and others — sought to curb the view voiced by Taviv, according to which women were mobilized to give birth to sons who would be mobilized for military service. The advocates insisted that childhood needed to be a protected zone. All children, not just those born to established Israeli families, should be given time for personal development and growth. They demanded individual rights and personal autonomy. They viewed adolescence as a period of development, maturation, and relative freedom. Army service, marriage, and parenthood were seen — by both the Ashkenazim and the Mizrahim — as a heavy burden requiring considerable self-sacrifice. For precisely this reason, the law's advocates argued, people needed, a brief period of childhood in which they could play, enjoy themselves, and be free from responsibility.[151]

The disparity between Taviv's views and those of Maimon and Drori can be attributed to differing fundamental cultural assumptions. Taviv had a conception of society in which an unmarried person had inferior status and in which marriage and childbearing were religious and social obligations, not a means of achieving personal happiness and existential meaning. Maimon and Drori, in contrast, shared the assumptions of feminism, viewing women as autonomous individuals who could choose to marry and have children — or not. Such autonomy, they believed, was a precondition for women's ability to contribute to the nation, so women needed first to live in a progressive society that guaranteed their personal independence.[152] Maimon's and Drori's successors in the Fourth Knesset, which passed the amendment in 1960 that made it easier for girls under the age of seventeen to receive special court approval to marry, also held this view. Rachel Tsabari of Mapai opposed the amendment on the ground that the situation that made passage of the 1950 law necessary still existed. The amendment would weaken the law, she claimed. The principal reason for the passage of the original law, accepted by a majority of the Knesset, she said, was "the human need to protect the right of girls to live their childhoods and adolescence" — in other words, a right of the individual person. The collective reason came second:

"Our national-social need was stressed, to prevent the creation of families in which the mother of children is still a girl unready mentally, psychologically, and physically, unable still to bear the responsibility of raising children and educating a generation healthy in body and mind."[153] Jenia Tversky, also of Mapai, supported the amendment, saying that it would help resolve special problems and exceptional cases. But in the Knesset debate she dismissed a proposal to lower the marriage age for girls to sixteen across the board. "Marrying off sixteen-year-old girls robs them of their youth," she declared. "In the case of social legislation, it seems to me that a person should measure what he proposes by standards that apply to him. Do the members of the house [the Knesset] who say that the marriage of sixteen-year-old girls should be allowed really think that this is an appropriate age for marriage? I presume that they would not want to see their daughters marry at this age. If that is the case, they should not be proposing it for Israel as a whole."[154]

The Age of Marriage Law passed the Knesset on August 1, 1950. It set the minimum marriage age for girls at seventeen, but it allowed state (secular) courts to grant marriage permits to younger girls if they were pregnant or had already given birth. The law imposed a maximum sentence of two years in prison or a fine of 600 Israeli lira, or both, on all parties to the act — the husband of the underage bride, her parents or guardian, and those who registered and performed the marriage.[155]

The Morning After

The passage of the Age of Marriage Law was a milestone, yet it did not change the country overnight. Some communities resisted and circumvented the law, and Orthodox legislators almost immediately began to seek to lower the marriage age once again. Enforcement proved difficult.

Implementing the law in the Arab sector presented special problems. The public discussion of the marriage age, as well as the Knesset debate over the law, had focused primarily on Jewish girls.[156] Most members of the Knesset were more concerned with the image of the Jewish majority than with the fate of young Arab girls. During the floor debate at the law's first reading, Jarjora spoke in favor of the law, but later his major concern became the independence of the Christian and Moslem religious courts rather than saving girls from early marriage.[157] Andrew Treitel has noted that the ideas about the rights of women and girls that were voiced on Knesset floor went almost unheard in Arab villages.[158]

The question of how best to manage enforcement of the marriage age among the country's Arabs was disputed by officials and decision makers.[159] Correspondence between various branches of government, among them the State Attorney's Office, the police, and the Ministry of Religions, provides evidence of the factors these bodies took into account. At the beginning of February 1952, the ministry decided that, for the time being, the letter of the law should not be enforced in the Muslim community. Among the extenuating factors enumerated by the inspector of Shari'a Courts was "the situation of the Muslims in the country, and especially current circumstances such as their location in areas under military rule." Another such factor was that the Knesset's law contradicted Muslim religious law; still another was the fact that illiteracy was so common in this community.[160] This decision delayed investigations and indictments of violators. The police force was unsure whether "to act in accordance with the provisions of the Age of Marriage Law, which is meant to apply equally to all the country's citizens." At first the police refrained from investigating cases of underage marriage and closed cases that had already been opened.[161] In November 1952, however, State Attorney Erwin S. Shimron protested this policy. In a letter he sent to the chief of the Investigations Division of the police force's National Headquarters, Shimron asked why police units had been ordered not to file criminal charges in cases of underage marriage among Muslims. Furthermore, he noted that the Ministry of Religions and the prime minister's advisor on Arab affairs maintained that such violators were to meet with the full force of the law.[162] In response, the chief of the Investigations Division argued that he had issued no sweeping order to refrain from criminal investigations and the submission of cases to the State Attorney's Office. Rather, his order had related only to certain special cases. He argued, however, that the authorities need to "view the problem among the minorities in a different light than in the Jewish community."[163]

Disregarding the objections of the officials and officers who had daily contacts with the Arab population, the State Attorney's Office ordered categorically that the law was to be fully enforced, even if this required "the indictment of clergymen . . . without regard to their religious affiliation."[164]

Despite the insistence of the State Attorney's Office in 1952, and despite the fact that many criminal cases were opened that year,[165] until the amendment of the law in 1960 a number of reservations were raised regarding the wisdom of enforcing the law in the Arab sector. One consideration against bringing to trial those who performed the ceremonies, especially among officers of the different Christian churches, was the fear that doing so would cause diplomatic incidents.[166] In the period 1950–63, only four Christian clergymen were brought to trial for violations of the Age of Marriage Law.[167] In a similar case, the attorney general voiced his uneasiness about a criminal investigation against a Muslim sheikh. Most of Israel's Arab population lived under a humiliating military regime that accorded them little respect, but when it came to religious customs and religious leaders, Israel's law enforcement authorities displayed considerable ambivalence about impinging on the community's autonomy.[168]

Nevertheless, the Arab community's leaders were incensed by state interference in their internal community affairs. In fact, during the decade that followed the passage of the law, Muslim religious courts ignored it and married underage girls.[169] The desire to evade the law's provisions — and the fact that religious leaders cooperated in doing so, often with the tacit acquiescence of the authorities — ensured that marriages of underage Muslim girls continued to be common.[170] This development was no coincidence, as in practice it gave a minority group a certain measure of independence in a country ruled by a majority community and in the milieu of a deeply divided society.[171]

How Was the Law Circumvented?

Before we look at the variety of ways in which the law was circumvented, some background is needed. In theory, all citizens were legally required to update the national population registry of any change in their personal status. In practice, however, the government did not enforce this requirement. The police and State Attorney's Office conducted investigations and sought indictments only when a violation of the law was brought to their attention.[172] For example, in one case the Chief Rabbinate reported to the police that it had received a request from a couple to register their marriage, which had been performed by an unauthorized person.[173]

One common way of getting around the law was simply to lie about the bride's age. *Haaretz* reported that "the Muslim community's resentment of the Age of Marriage Law, which forbids the marriage of girls under the age of seventeen, has led to a plethora of forged identity cards for girls in minority areas." This could be accomplished, the article explained, by bribing officials in the Ministry of Minorities, which issued identity cards to members of the Arab population, or by claiming to have lost a girl's identity card and having a new one issued that displayed the desired age. *Haaretz* reported that religious officials authorized to perform marriages in the Muslim community were aware of the forgeries. The article was based on an anonymous letter that had been sent to the Interior Ministry's Acre district officer. It alleged that at least one and possibly more officials responsible for issuing identity cards to the Arab population were suspected of taking bribes.[174]

The mayor of Nazareth, Yousef Ali al-Fahum, offered another explanation for why the ages of girls were being changed in the population registry. In a letter he sent to the Ministry of Welfare, he claimed that "when Arab girls were recorded in the population registry [after the country was founded], many parents lied about their ages [recording them as being younger than they really were], out of fear that they would be drafted into the army. Consequently, when it came time for them to marry the age listed on their identity cards was lower than their actual age." The mayor proposed that the ages of Arab girls listed in the population registry could be changed with the certification of a physician or on the basis of a sworn statement by the girl's father, with the approval of a Shari'a Court judge.[175]

The mayor's claim seems logical because the same phenomenon was evident among Jewish immigrants as well. Seeking to keep their daughters out of the army for religious and social reasons — a girl who was removed from her family's supervision and sent off to a permissive environment like the army would, parents feared, have trouble finding a husband or, worse, adopt a modern lifestyle. Then, when it came time for the girl to marry, parents sought to restore her registered age to her ostensibly real one.[176] Faced with such requests, the authorities had to draft regulations to cover when and how the age listed on a girl's identity card could be revised. A new procedure was put in place after the Age of Marriage Law was passed, under which girls could apply to the court of the religious community to which they belonged and request that the court determine their age. In such cases the religious court sometimes requested that a government physician certify the petitioner's age. Apparently, however, during the first year that the regulation was in force, the religious courts did not regularly consult with doctors.[177] At the beginning of 1951 Maimon submitted a parliamentary question, stating that despite the enactment of the law, girls younger than seventeen continued to be married.[178] At the end of 1951 the attorney general ruled that religious courts had no standing with regard to the population registry. A medical examination was made a precondition for any change in the registration of a girl's age. A sworn statement by the girl's guardian or her father before a judge was also made mandatory.[179]

Yet enforcement was not easy because religious functionaries and courts were not always careful to observe the letter of the law. The careless ones include some of those who were permitted by law to conduct marriage ceremonies in Muslim courts — which in any case sometimes failed to register the girl's age at marriage.[180] Jewish wedding ceremonies were sometimes conducted by unlicensed men and were still considered lawful by the Chief Rabbinate because they met the conditions laid down by Jewish law. For example, *Ha'olam Hazeh*, a popular radical and sensational weekly, reported that a divorce suit had been filed by a girl whose wedding ceremony was conducted by a seventy-two-year-old kosher butcher (who had proclaimed himself a rabbi) while she was fifteen and a half. Less than a year later she bore a daughter. The butcher was given a suspended three-month prison sentence and fined 100 Israeli lira.[181] Since these actions were illegal and thus often went unreported, there is no way of knowing for certain how often the law was violated and to what extent the penalties prescribed by the law served as a deterrent.

Another common practice was the registration of marriages by Muslims in Shari'a Courts only after the fact, once the girl reached legal age or even later.[182] Some Jews did the same. A correspondent for *Haboker* who visited the immigrant village 'Eshtaol reported that a local Yemenite resident he interviewed explained to him how his neighbors circumvented the law. He related the case of a man who wanted to marry a fourteen-year-old girl. The Chief Rabbinate refused to conduct the ceremony without a physician's certification. The man asked a doctor to certify that the girl was physically mature, but the doctor refused. The couple were then married in an underground ceremony. The girl became pregnant, and shortly before she was to give birth the couple submitted a court petition asking for permission to marry.[183] *Ha'olam Hazeh* told its readers about a rabbi at a transit camp who had, with the collusion of a physician, helped get a thirteen-year-old girl registered as being seventeen.[184] Newspapers ran stories about trials of people charged with violating the Age of Marriage Law and about requests for exceptions, in which they gave prominent play to the very young age of the prospective bride. *Ma'ariv*, an independent evening newspaper, told its readers about a nineteen-year-old boy who asked the court to be allowed to marry a thirteen-year-old girl who was in her third month of pregnancy by him.[185] There were also many reports of cases in which Rabbinical Courts sought to arrange divorces for girl brides. In general, the articles were highly critical of the loopholes in the law and the laxness of the courts.[186]

The Position of the Courts

Only a few court decisions on violations of the Age of Marriage Law were published in the 1950s. But press reports provide another source for the position taken by the courts. In many cases newspapers published detailed accounts of trials. Such documents make it possible to reconstruct something of the family story of the bride and groom in such cases, to understand the conditions under which the marriages were performed, and also to learn how the parties — generally the families of the bride and groom — sought to avoid being brought to trial. This evidence indicates that the child-centered message of the law and the new norm that it sought to instill did not put down roots in the Jewish population.

In seeking to enforce the law, the State Attorney's Office and the courts had to navigate between the obstacles put in their way by the public's considerable ability to evade the law. In one typical case, a man was accused of having had sexual relations with a girl of fourteen and a half. The act took place after a marriage ceremony that did not include standing, as tradition demands, under a marriage canopy. Since the wedding ceremony was not a proper one, the man could not technically be charged under the Age of Marriage Law. Instead, he was charged, in accordance with section 152c of the Criminal Code Ordinance, of engaging in sexual relations with a girl under the age of sixteen. In his decision, the judge found that the marriage ceremony took place in the home of the girl's parents and before a large crowd of friends and relatives. On the one hand, he wrote, "this was without a doubt not a marriage ceremony, as there was no canopy." On the other hand, the defendant placed a ring on the girl's finger and recited the legal formula "you are consecrated to me" before witnesses. The judge thus convicted him of violating section 2 of the Age of Marriage Law (for having married a girl under the age of seventeen). But the judge acquitted him of the crime of having had sexual relations with the girl, on the grounds that according to personal status law (that is, Jewish religious law), having sexual relations after marriage, even with an underage girl, was permissible.[187] While the law set the punishment for this crime at up to two years in prison, the judge sentenced the man to only six months. To the man's discredit, the judge cited the fact that he had previously been convicted of desertion from the army and theft. Although the judge had not given the maximum sentence possible, he felt it necessary to explain the severity of the punishment, which he justified on the ground that it was meant to deter other potential offenders. The convicted man appealed to the Supreme Court, which let the sentence stand.[188] Notably, only the groom was charged of any crime, even though the Age of Marriage Law stated explicitly that anyone involved in or officiating at such a marriage was culpable — including relatives who were present at the ceremony and, presumably, had made the arrangements.[189]

Ha'olam Hazeh published the complete testimonies and judgment in another case. In this instance the defendant was also a groom, Yosef Za'arur, but the bride, Dizi Marima, testified that her parents had pressured her to marry, sometimes using force. Za'arur married Marima with her family's consent and after he agreed to pay a bride price of 200 Israeli lira. The magazine also described the bloody rags that were displayed after the wedding as proof that Marima had come to her marriage bed a virgin. According to the story, when Za'arur failed to pay the sum agreed on, Marima's family took her back from him. In the end the court took a lenient view of the community's customs: "There can be no doubt that the defendant's intention (like that of Dizi's parents) was to circumvent the Age of Marriage Law, and that this was the only reason that they chose to act as they did, nor do I have any doubt regarding the defendant's malicious intentions. . . . The entire affair puts on display customs and concepts that are not to our country's credit, but they must be understood in the context of the experience and against the background of the new groups of immigrants."[190] The judge acquitted Za'rur of having had sexual relations with a minor but convicted him of violating section 2 of the Age of Marriage Law. In handing down his judgment, the judge wrote:

> In this matter, the court must assume not only the role of meter out of punishment but also that of educator, and it must see to it that strata [of society] that see as foreign cultural concepts that we consider elementary become accustomed to these concepts. Thus, on the one hand, the punishment cannot be lenient, but on the other hand I do not think that the defendant should be sent to prison without giving him the possibility of showing that he is able to accommodate himself to social life in accordance with the concepts held by a majority of the population.[191]

The judge imposed a suspended sentence of three months and a fine of 100 Israeli lira (half the bride price). While Marima had been given the opportunity to tell her story to the court, no one involved was concerned with her right to a childhood and to determine the course of her own life — not her family, who had married her off by force; not her husband; not the judge who presided over the trial; and not even *Ha'olam Hazeh*, which seemed more interested in painting a demeaning picture of the new immigrants than in helping her or saving any other girl from a similar fate.[192] Other accounts of underage marriage in the press also seemed more intent on defamiliarizing the immigrants, especially the men, than on mobilizing assistance for the girls involved.[193]

In contrast with the revolutionary view of the law's drafter and supporters, the courts appear to have sought to maintain social order and the community fabric, allowing change to take place gradually. They understood that the law imposed a foreign system of values on some of the immigrants, one opposed to the traditional norms of their communities. One judge, Yosef Lamm (who belonged to Mapai and had been a member of the Knesset), went so far as to call on the legislature to revise the law:

> I myself brought it about that this law was passed as it was in the First Knesset, when I was a member. But from my experience as a judge I see that I made a mistake then when I voted to pass the law in the form in which it was passed. In the hundreds of cases I have heard on the matter of [marriage] age, I have become convinced that, taking into account the situation in Israel, it would be right to place the limit on the marriage age at no more than sixteen, and I hope that the country's legislative body will give consideration to what I have said here.[194]

Immigration to Israel caused a crisis of authority in many families. Policymakers in the welfare and legal fields were not unaware of this. Many young people found themselves suspended between two normative systems that conveyed opposing messages. The courts were consequently more concerned with keeping families strong and preventing the erosion of parental authority than with promoting the revolution hoped for by the law's supporters.[195] Judges seem to have viewed this as the least bad option.

One of the greatest concerns raised by the crisis of immigration — one shared by the immigrants and those absorbing them — was that girls would descend into what was then called "sexual delinquency." The welfare system was far more fearful that girls would end up on the street than it was confident in its ability to educate them and inculcate in them a sense of personal responsibility and autonomy.[196]

This began to change in the 1970s and 1980s. As this later period lies outside the bounds of the current study, I will refer to it in passing just as a way of demonstrating how unique the 1950s were. The transformation in the attitude of the courts is best shown by two versions of the same case of underage marriage, one from the early 1960s and one from the end of the 1970s.

In 1961, Judge David Reifen of the Juvenile Court recounted the case of Miriam, a sixteen-year-old girl whose hand was promised by her father to a man she did not want to marry. The judge explained the conflict the girl faced as a result of her acquaintance with two prevalent but contradictory social norms. On the one hand, she was told to accept her father's authority and marry the man to whom she had been promised. On the other hand, she thought that things were better "among you Ashkenazim" — that is, in that part of Israeli society where it was taken as given that a girl should not marry at the age of sixteen and that she should choose her own husband. In this account of the story, Reifen largely passed over the welfare system's involvement in the girl's life and stressed the importance of preserving the family framework. But in an account of the same case that he wrote nearly two decades later, he cited the father's admission that he preferred to marry off his daughter because he was incapable of coping with her behavior as an adolescent. Reifen recounted that he had decided to place the girl under the care of a probation officer. This later version of the old case stressed the importance of the welfare system and stated that the well-being of the girl required that marriage be put off.[197]

Further evidence of the wholesale change in the attitude of the courts can be found in a decision rendered by Justice Aharon Barak of the Israeli Supreme Court in 1981. The case was an appeal by the attorney general of a District Court ruling that had permitted an underage marriage on the ground of the ethnic affiliation of the couple and their families and the overcrowded conditions in which they lived.[198] Barak's decision, cited as a precedent over and over again in subsequent judgments, displays an inclination toward change, in dialogue with the new tone taken by Reifen in his later account of the trial he presided over.[199] The case involved two young members of the Jewish community from the Georgian Soviet Republic. The two were betrothed, which, according to the community's customs, meant that they were permitted to meet freely. However, Barak noted, "unfortunately, danger was attached to this freedom." The parents of the plaintiff—the girl—voiced their concern that their daughter would become pregnant. If that were to happen, her father declared, "the customs of our community are most severe. I and my wife will be required to condemn my daughter and banish her from the house, and this will, God forbid, be a catastrophe for both her and us." Barak ruled that the legislative branch had not established precise tests for defining the cases in which there was cause to grant an underage girl permission to marry, and thus "we will try to formulate, via judicial interpretation, such precise tests." He proceeded to overrule the decision of the lower court, asserting that the law's purpose was to protect the girl. Her consent to the marriage was a necessary condition for carrying out a wedding, he ruled, but not a sufficient condition. "As we have seen," he wrote, "the law's purpose is to defend the girl against her own consent." Neither was the consent of her parents sufficient cause to grant authorization for a marriage. Barak stressed that "the law's purpose, at times, is to protect the girl from her own parents, who for reasons of their own seek to marry off their daughter before she has reached the age of seventeen."[200] He wrote:

> The customs of the community to which the couple belongs, according to which it is acceptable to conduct a marriage ceremony for the girl before she reaches the age of seventeen, are not in and of themselves a sufficient reason for sanctioning the marriage. As we have seen, the law's purpose is precisely to uproot such customs.... I am not prepared to view the community's customs, which may respond harshly to a girl who engages in sexual relations outside of marriage [as a justification for granting the marriage permit]. Otherwise, one sacrifices the girl to the community's customs. It was this that the legislative branch sought to prevent.... The legislature assigned responsibility on this matter to the judicial branch, which must take into account but not surrender to the conditions and customs surrounding it.[201]

In his concurring opinion, Justice Yitzhak Shilo used an even sharper tone to refer to the character of the Georgian family, the justification given by the plaintiff for her request for a marriage permit. If the plaintiff feared the Georgian community's custom of not permitting sexual relations before marriage, then it was up to her to respect those customs and refrain from such relations. With regard to Israeli society, he wrote:

> For better or worse, patriarchy is not a characteristic of family relations in the country as a whole. For better or worse a certain permissiveness between people, including young people, of the two sexes, is customary among us. It is reasonable for anyone who belongs to a community with a worldview that rejects such permissiveness, and who values the customs of the community, while fearing the imposition of the authority of the head of the family ... will avoid behavior that violates those customs. Especially behavior in matters between men and women, which is looked on askance by the community he belongs to.[202]

It seems to have taken three decades after the passage of the Age of Marriage Law before girls became subjects, rather than merely objects — at least in practice.[203] Only then did their welfare and sovereignty over their actions and lives, rather than social and community order and parental authority, become the most important consideration for the courts.[204] Justice Shilo portrayed the girl in the 1981 appeal as an independent actor capable of acting in accordance with her community's standards and refraining from sexual relations if she were to decide to do so. Moreover, the girl had a choice — she could be part of the permissive majority culture or maintain her ties to the minority community in which her family lived. Barak's ruling was a watershed inasmuch as it stated explicitly that a minority community's values cannot override those of the majority. Clearly, by this time the justices of the Supreme Court believed that a majority community had come into being in Israel. The permissive mores of this community reflected the collective national identity, and the justices were no longer concerned that practices like those of the Georgian community would sully Israel's image — either of itself or as it was seen by the rest of the world. The law, born as a means of constituting common norms, no longer served this need. Originally, at a time of optimism about bringing the immigrants into the Israeli collective, the law was perceived as a means of guidance and of instilling proper values in communities that did not yet hold them. That time was over. By the time Barak and Shilo wrote, these traditions had become more or less stable options that a girl could choose to accept or reject. They were no longer ways of life that were expected to surrender and adhere to the standards of the majority.[205]

The Orthodox and Ultra-Orthodox Communities Respond to the Law

No sooner had the Age of Marriage Law been passed than the political parties representing the Orthodox and Haredi communities began to challenge its validity and seek to amend it. *Hakol*, the newspaper published by the Haredi Po'alei 'Agudat Yisrael party (part of the United Religious Front), published a sharp attack on the conduct of social workers who were seeking to implement the law. These women, the newspaper said, were hostile to the sanctity of marriage and intervened in cases where their interference was not needed. The issue of child marriage, it declared, should be handled by Yemenite rabbis.[206] *Hatsofe*, the daily newspaper of the religious Zionists, claimed that "any Knesset law remains valid only if the public is capable of

living accordingly" and that "a divine law [cannot] be changed by a law leg-
islated by human beings."[207] In 1953, during the term of the Second Knesset,
an amendment to the law was submitted by the minister of welfare. A professional committee comprised of representatives of the Ministries of Justice,
Health, Religions, and Welfare was set up to discuss two alternatives. The
first stipulated that courts would be authorized "to permit the marriage of a
girl between the ages of fifteen and seventeen not only 'if the girl has given
birth to a man's child or if she is pregnant by him' . . . but also in other cases,
so long as the court believes that the girl's welfare requires this and that not
granting a permit is likely to cause her an injustice." The second alternative
proposed to set the minimum marriage age for girls at sixteen and to authorize the courts to permit marriages of fifteen-year-olds in special cases.[208] The
second initiative came from the Ministry of Religions and the Ministry of
Welfare (both portfolios were held by a single minister, Haim-Moshe Shapira of Hapo'el Hamizrahi, a religious Zionist party). The reason the change
was needed, according to the ministries, was that the Welfare Ministry had
reported many cases of girls engaging in sexual relations outside wedlock.
Those girls wished to marry but were prevented from doing so by the law.
Under the law as it stood, wrote Uri Yadin of the Ministry of Justice to the
secretary of the cabinet, there was a perverse incentive for such girls to get
pregnant so they could get a marriage permit. At the same time, so long as
their relationships were not sanctified by marriage, "the tie is likely to become undone before they reach the age of seventeen, with all the adverse
results that can be expected in such a case."[209] Social workers reported cases
in which religious marriage ceremonies were conducted without the marriage being registered with the Chief Rabbinate and the Interior Ministry
(which was in charge of population registry), while in other cases a religious
betrothal ceremony was conducted, after which the couple was permitted to
have sexual relations while waiting for the girl to reach the age of seventeen
so that the actual marriage ceremony could take place.

The initiative to amend the law was backed by an expert committee
appointed by the Ministry of Health. The committee, whose members included gynecologists and pediatricians, said in its report that there was no
evidence that lowering the marriage age to sixteen would be detrimental
to the physical health of mothers and children. While it would be best, the
committee suggested, for marriage to be delayed to the age of seventeen,
when girls would be more psychologically mature and prepared for motherhood, it acknowledged that the public, in particular immigrants, did not

abide by cutoff at age seventeen specified in the current law. The committee recommended, however, that parental consent should be reinstated as a requirement for marriages of girls at the age of sixteen, and that the law be changed for only a set period of time, until the new immigrants absorbed the mores of the established population.[210] The fact that the committee sought to bring parents back into the picture shows that its members were more cognizant of the fact that girls were being married without the consent of their parents than they were of the root problem — that of parents marrying off their children at a young age. It could well be that the committee's members believed that parental authority and family support were more important, at least at that time, than girls' right to sovereignty over their bodies and futures. Clearly, the committee, like government officials and religious members of the Knesset, viewed sexual relations outside marriage as undesirable.

Despite these recommendations, the law was not quickly revised. At the beginning of 1956, Minister of Religions Shapira once again submitted to the cabinet a proposal to amend the law. The draft, first taken up by the Ministerial Committee on Interior Affairs and Services, proposed to lower the marriage age to sixteen and to authorize judges to grant marriage permits to girls under this age if they found that circumstances made doing so advisable. Such permits were not conditional on the girl's being pregnant or having given birth. The draft also proposed empowering the religious courts of each confession to grant marriage permits in such cases. In the explanatory material attached to the bill, Yitzhak Glasner, legal counsel to the Ministry of Religions, wrote that the Age of Marriage Law had not succeeded in preventing underage marriages. The law imposed, he said, a stricture that the public could not abide by.[211] In June the proposed amendment was revised to make parental consent a condition for the granting of a permit.[212] In August the amendment was brought before the full cabinet. Foreign Minister Golda Meir categorically opposed lowering the marriage age to sixteen. Prime Minister Ben-Gurion suggested that the age limit remain at seventeen but the law be amended so that the state courts (rather than religious courts) would be authorized to grant an applicant a marriage permit not only when a girl was pregnant or already a mother, but in other cases that the court thought justified, in light of the circumstances. The cabinet sent the bill to the Ministerial Committee on Legislation.[213] That committee referred it back to the full cabinet a year and a half later, in May 1958. In a cabinet discussion of the bill, Minister of Religions Shapira asserted that "the situation among the Mizrahim in particular, and among the Muslims as well, is that they cannot live with this restriction." Minister of Justice Rosen opposed lowering the marriage age, stressing that he was not alone in opposing the change to the law. Ben-Gurion said (apparently directing his words at Shapira) that "were you to add to this law a requirement that each family has to have at least four children, I would vote in favor. The Jewish community's birthrate is steadily declining, among the Mizrahim as well, and that is a matter for great concern." He then asked Rosen what doctors had to say about the issue. Rosen responded that "doctors for the most part, as well as women, oppose it." "For health reasons?" Ben-Gurion asked. "Yes," Rosen replied, disregarding the recommendations of the expert committee. He added that Meir "vociferously opposed lowering the marriage age, and there are women who propose raising it to eighteen."[214] Presenting the position of the Ministerial Committee on Legislation, Rosen said that District Courts should be authorized to grant marriage permits to girls from the age of sixteen, if special circumstances require it, which need not be limited to being pregnant or having given birth. Rosen consented only to this mild change to the law. The cabinet resolved, in opposition to Shapira's memorandum, not to grant Rabbinic Courts powers in this area because, as Ben-Gurion noted, they "proclaim outright that they do not recognize the law of the land."[215] The Mapam and 'Ahdut Ha'avodah ministers also opposed lowering the marriage age and allowing the religious courts to sanction underage marriages.[216]

When the proposed amendment was submitted for debate on the floor of the Knesset in 1959, the religious Knesset members continued to fight the distinction between the age of consent and the minimum marriage age.[217] Warhaftig (who now, following the dissolution of the United Religious Front, represented the Orthodox-Zionist National Religious Party) again demanded that the two be equated. The two Haredi parties demanded that the law be repealed entirely. Still representing the position of the Chief Rabbinate, Warhaftig also proposed that consideration of exceptions to the marriage law be transferred from the state District Courts to the religious courts.[218] The amendment finally passed in 1960. Under its terms, judges were granted greater discretion in deciding when to grant marriage permits to underage girls. According to the new provisions, a sixteen-year-old girl would be permitted to marry if extenuating circumstances justified it. But the statutory minimum age for girls to marry remained seventeen, and the only agency with power to grant exceptions remained the District Courts.[219]

Cultural Disparities in the Conception
of Youth and the Individual

In October 1954, Yemenite rabbis and leaders from all over the country submitted a petition to the Chief Rabbinate demanding that the Age of Marriage Law be amended. The text of their petition demonstrates the cultural gap between those who wanted to forbid child marriage and those who wanted to permit it:

> We the undersigned, rabbis and leaders of the Yemenite community . . . hereby address . . . our firm protest against the unfortunate regulation . . . prohibiting the marriage of a Jewish girl under the age of seventeen, calling this child marriage. Consider, sirs, what the results of this miserable regulation have had for the ramparts of Judaism. Instead of marriage according to the laws of Moses and the Jews, we have lawlessness. Jewish boys and girls are more wanton because of this regulation and say, if the girl becomes pregnant then it will be permitted [for her] to marry. *Will Jewish girls be as prostitutes?* Woe to the ears that hear and woe to the eyes that see. Do we want to imitate the [other] nations? Is their image ours? The gentiles have no prohibitions against harlotry, but the Jewish people do. Our Holy Torah has forbidden harlotry, and the new law has forbidden marriage. The result is that we grasp the rope on both sides, and what can boys and girls do if the natural heat and the fire of their natural urges burn within them? . . . We petition [you] . . . to stand in the breach and revoke this law or amend it to allow the younger generation to cohabit according to Jewish law to the extent possible. Because to our great sorrow, the generation is already wanton as it is.[220]

The petition clearly voiced a strong protest. It shows how far the logic of the law was from the petitioners' worldviews, or what Robert Cover called their *nomos*, their "normative universe."[221] Their anxiety concerned the proper channeling of young people's physical urges. Their view of the individual, especially the female individual, and of the individual's connection with the society in which she lived, was far distant from the individualist or modern view that sought to create sovereign persons, including by establishing a distinct realm of childhood and adolescence. The widespread view among both liberal and socialist thinkers was that this time of life played a decisive role in shaping the adult citizen.

Hagit Rigger, the author of a study examining the acculturation of Yemenite youth published in 1952, noted the discrepancy between the way the immigrants and established Israelis viewed childhood. She may have been unaware of the cultural revolution that had raised childhood to its current status in the West, although she did recognize the differences among communities. Communal identity among Yemenite Jews, she argued, was built on Jewish tradition, which granted legitimacy to social institutions. Therefore, she wrote, "the sacred past of the people's tradition is a kind of 'magnet' of life." Yemenite society, she found, discounted childhood, while elders and sages enjoyed social prestige. This was diametrically opposed to established Israeli society, which was focused on the present and future, and which thus ascribed special importance to young people. Married Yemenite adolescents were no different from other adults in the community. She argued that even if people married at older ages — as was starting to happen — the lives of adolescent Yemenite immigrants would remain unlike those of their established Israeli peers. The latter experienced adolescence as a "dynamic age, a period of passion for ideals, a period of intensive learning and intensive interest in social life." But immigrant Yemenite teenagers "lack the 'natural' conditions that grant discrete content to the experience [of this life period] and which underline its distinctness from adulthood."[222] She recommended pursuing a policy of instilling the special nature of adolescence in Yemenite teenagers, maintaining that no experience of youth could develop without direction from outside. She also reported a high incidence of weeping and depression among young girls under pressure from their parents to marry.[223]

Since immigrants living in camps and communal villages (*moshavim*) were subject to professional supervision by established Israelis, child brides were easier to locate among the Mizrahim than in the Arab population, and underage marriages could more easily be prevented or terminated among the former than among the latter.[224] Yet, as shown above, even Jews disregarded the Age of Marriage Law in many cases.[225] The law did not immediately change the lives of Yemenite girls. It was not easy to prevent early marriages, but it was even more difficult to instill in the new immigrants the concept on which the law was based — that the periods of girlhood and adolescence were important for girls' physical and emotional development and that those benefits would accrue only to girls who were free of the responsibilities of marriage and motherhood.[226]

Inculcating the Law's Values into Daily Life

In the main, the campaign against child marriage was not pursued under the aegis of the criminal code. Minister of Justice Rosen declared at the opening of the Knesset debate in 1950 that most of the work would have to be done by the women's organizations, in the form of education and social interventions. The primary purpose of the law was thus expressive — that is, it was not chiefly meant to deter offenders or to mete out punishment, but rather to instill a complete moral system and to facilitate a public discourse aimed at educating the immigrants, with the purpose of eventually creating a national citizenry sharing the same norms. Women leading this reform were deeply invested in this piece of legislation because they wanted "to capture the state's *expressive* power."[227] While some state authorities had difficulty implementing the law or thought it inappropriate for parts of the population, the law was a powerful instrument supporting women involved in combating underage marriages. And in fact volunteers, teachers, child-care workers, and social workers active in immigrant communities, sometimes organized as special intervention teams, did everything in their power to prevent such marriages.[228] The law was an effective tool for advancing the effort to allow girls to remain in school and served as a cornerstone of the women's struggle to empower immigrant women.[229]

Shoshana Basin, from the established *moshav* Kfar Yehezkel, worked as a counselor with immigrants and herself came from a Yemenite family that had arrived in Israel before independence. She reported that married girls approached her to ask for help. "On more than one occasion," she wrote, "one of these children would come to me and reveal a secret: 'Shoshana, you should know that X is not my father, he's my husband, and I don't want to have a child by him.' In such cases I used all available means to get the older man to give a divorce to his girl-wife." Basin also reported that she received money from an anonymous female donor to pay men to get them to grant divorces. When the number of cases multiplied and the donor was unable to provide sufficient funds, Basin asked for contributions from neighboring kibbutzim and moshavim. "I viewed ending these forced underage marriages as a humanitarian mission of the first order, and I did not rest until I had freed each girl from the bonds of early marriage," she reported. Basin was not alone. Most counselors believed that immigrant women needed to be helped in advancing their social status, and that the values of the Age of Marriage

Law and other progressive legislation should be inculcated among the immigrants. This same view was at times adopted by the mothers of the girl brides and by the girls themselves.[230] Yemenite immigrant women and girls used the new legal, social, and economic conditions to postpone their marriages, raise their social and economic status, and acquire some control over their lives.[231]

In December 1949, Tehila Matmon, editor of *Haisha Bamdina*, a periodical put out by the Union of Hebrew Women for Equal Rights, included an article on a number of thirteen- and fourteen-year-old Yemenite girls who had run away from their husbands and from the Ein Shemer immigrant camp. The girls had asked the Union to help them end their marriages.[232] The fact that immigration had changed the way girls and women viewed their status was reflected also in the way the men of their communities spoke. At a public assembly in May 1950 a number of Yemenite men complained before representatives of the State Attorney's Office, the Jewish Agency, and the Chief Rabbinate that their wives, after arriving in Israel, "felt that here they had excessive rights and they were 'rebelling.' . . . [The men] demanded that sanctions be enforced against the rebellious women and suggested that their food cards [which entitled them to receive meals in the dining halls of immigrant camps] be taken away from them."[233]

We can hear the voices of the girls themselves only at second hand, through the reports of women involved in interventions, through newspaper reporters and judges, and in the report of the Frumkin Commission. One married girl filed suit for a divorce from her husband, whom she had married at the age of eleven in Yemen. She told a rabbinic court that she was requesting a divorce because she wanted her freedom.[234] Other girls related that they had run away from home to avoid being forced into marriage, because they wanted to go to school to learn how to read and write.[235] An article in the Communist Party daily *Kol Ha'am* quoted a number of such girls. "'He woke me up at night,' one girl related, 'and threatened me that he would go to Israel and leave me alone in Yemen with the Arabs, if I refuse[d] to get married. He's my brother and I don't have parents. I was very frightened and I did as he told me.' She must still be frightened, because while she spoke she cast her eyes at the social worker as if asking for deliverance. . . . 'My father and mother forced me,' another girl said. 'They beat me until I agreed. But I don't want to stay with him, I want to go to school.'"[236]

When asked by a religious court rabbi why she wanted a divorce, an eleven-year-old girl who had been married to a twenty-six-year-old man replied, according to *Davar*: "I still like to play."[237] These girls offered confirmation of the cultural assumption that prevailed among the established population — that immigrant girls also had a right to childhood.[238]

At least some of the women involved in interventions were aware of the cost of the necessary cultural shift. An article in the Progressive Party daily *Zmanim* cautioned:

> We must not . . . ignore the tragedy that we have imposed on the soul of the Mizrahi immigrant woman, whom we have made a sacrifice to our reality. We must acknowledge that we are partly to blame for the great bitterness that has become her fate and that of her husband, the foundations of whose tranquil world have also been shaken, his fundamental faith in his wife. . . . [A]nd it is only the gratefulness that the next generation of Mizrahi women will feel that we can [use to] justify the revolution that has taken place in the world of the Mizrahi woman.[239]

In the 1960s it would become evident that the normative gap between the two societies actually exacerbated the plight of girls, who could no longer acquiesce in the expectations of their parents and communities. A sixteen-year-old girl named Shoshana who tried to kill herself by drinking rat poison said: "My parents treat me as they were accustomed to treating a girl in their old country: at the age of fourteen they wanted to marry me to a man twenty-five years older than me, and they still don't leave me alone, they want me to get married, bring me matchmakers and marriage proposals, my aunts and older brother are involved and make my life miserable."[240]

. . . .

In 1932 the Union of Hebrew Women for Equal Rights sent a letter to the Chief Rabbinate. "What was appropriate for Jewish communities among the Oriental nations is not appropriate for the Mizrahi communities in the Land of Israel. The Yishuv, including the members of all Jewish communities that returned to the Land to build and plow it, must be a single unit that lives according to a single law," the letter declared.[241] This was a common view among the Yishuv's activist women, one that was later prevalent in the new state as well.

Maimon, Drori, Idelson, Cohen-Kagan, Tsabari, and Tversky all wanted their country to be an enlightened state that worked to remedy social injustices. Members of women's organizations felt obligated to contribute to Israeli society by facilitating the absorption of the newly arrived immigrants.

Professional women who worked with immigrants would later testify that their period of labors on behalf of their new nation was their finest hour.[242] In their view, it was their duty as established Israelis and women to do all they could to secure the rights of their country's children and women, no matter what their background and socioeconomic position. They took it as given that girls' ability to take charge of their own lives was being seriously impaired and that, as child brides, they were likely to become victims of violence and exploitation. Maimon, along with social workers and journalists, stressed the connection between the two phenomena.[243]

Liberal and socialist ministers and members of the Knesset, like professionals in the health and welfare fields, were also keen supporters of raising the marriage age. Some derived their positions from feminist principles, while others took a maternalist view. Still others—at least the physicians among them—drew on the principles of mental hygiene. While aiming to secure girls' autonomy through social and legal intervention, the discourse was suffused with paternalist and Orientalist attitudes.[244]

Yet this local Orientalism was not identical to colonial civilizing rhetoric, in which, to paraphrase Gayatri Chakravorty Spivak, white men and women were charged with saving women and children of color from men of color.[245] There was a considerable discrepancy between rhetoric and practice, and rescue activities were the product of heterogeneous coalitions that took on different guises.[246] The Orientalist approach that established Israelis took to the immigrants from the Islamic world was tempered by an Israeli nationalism that sought to use its images, rituals, symbols, and actions to integrate the immigrants into Israeli society. In the process, the most injurious manifestations of Orientalism were avoided or mitigated.[247]

Interventions of women's organizations in communities of recently arrived Mizrahim were intensive.[248] From the point of view of the absorbers, molding immigrant society and defending its children were ways of shaping the entire collective. In other words, it was a way of fashioning the Israeli self.[249] As I have showed, the construction of a seamless national fabric out of numerous cultural communities was not an undemanding emotional process of simply identifying oneself with the other, but rather a difficult process rife with ambivalence. This feeling of ambivalence led to disagreements about the proper way to act (and whether to act at all) to bridge the cultural gap. Some of the supporters of the Age of Marriage Law did not think that the need for change was urgent. For others, the law was more a declaration of intentions, a way of representing the identity of the established progressive elites rather than a standard meant to articulate the identities of all parts of Israeli society — at least not for the time being.[250]

When the Knesset held its third vote on the final version of the amendment, in July 1960, the house did not divide between the governing coalition and the opposition. Dan Horowitz, political correspondent for the pro-government *Davar*, wrote an incisive article in which he lashed out at the women in the Knesset who remained adamant about preventing underage marriages. They displayed emotional allegiance to abstract values and devotion to outward manifestations of progress.

> But a girl from those social strata and the cultural background in which the problem generally arises is not destined to live her life in the society of members of the Knesset who were educated in the best ideals of the equality of women and the rights of children. [If she opposes her community's standards and refuses to marry young or demands that her underage marriage be ended], what awaits her is suffering, difficulty earning a livelihood, banishment, and social pressure from her "natural" social environment, whose concepts do not change as a result of the progressive approach contained in one or another law passed by the Knesset.[251]

Horowitz demanded that Israeli society accommodate the different culture of the immigrants and allow it to endure, if only as a necessary evil. This, he maintained, was preferable to aggressively imposing change. Social change should not be rushed. In other words, he believed that the immediate social environment in which these girls lived was their fate and that there was no way to extricate them from it. Furthermore, the needs of Mizrahi girls were not identical with the needs of girls who lived in the same circles as the women in the Knesset. Clearly, he did not think that these cultural and socioeconomic disparities would be eliminated any time soon.

One of the areas in which a considerable educational and social effort was made in Israel's early years was the establishment of a direct republican connection between Jewish citizens and their representative government, one not mediated by institutions such as family, religious community, or political party. This principle, termed *mamlahtiyut*, was accepted, in its various right-wing and left-wing guises, by most political actors, and one of its important principles was a uniform approach to all Jewish citizens.[252] Nevertheless, not all Jewish citizens were perceived as equal subjects for protection and civil education. Girls married off by their families were close to the bottom of the ladder. Despite opposition in principle to underage marriage, in practice the citizenship of men, who were the focal point of the political order, was seen as more important.[253] But the women who worked to intervene in immigrant society saw these girls as having both voice and agency and refused to give up on them as future adult citizens.[254]

The efforts of some policymakers to reduce or even prevent intervention in the patriarchal culture of the immigrants and to ease the state's burden of law enforcement were thus seen by these women as tantamount to excluding immigrant girls from Israeli society. This was unacceptable to the activists. The bottom line, they maintained, was that these girls were part of the nation, and to abandon them to their fate was to make Israel ugly. Their activity displayed one of the contradictions characteristic of Israeli politics at the time. True, Maimon felt that her efforts to advance her bill against underage marriage were treated dismissively. But in fact, women in leadership positions and women's organizations wielded no little political power. No one else could have done what they did to care for infants, children, youth, and women. This power was evident in cabinet debates over the Age of Marriage Law.

During their campaign and in their work among the immigrants, these women sought to empower other women and girls. In doing so, they fashioned a model of active female citizenship that some immigrant women eventually joined.[255]

CHAPTER TWO

· ·

The Right to Travel Abroad

IN OCTOBER 1950, Mrs. Dora W.[1] of Haifa requested an exit permit from Israel. On her application form she declared that she intended to take a two-month trip to Switzerland and the United States. She also informed the authorities that she had spent time in Britain and France earlier that year.

At this time, Mrs. W was appealing a previous denial of her request. Concerned that her appeal might be rejected as well, she hired a well-known lawyer, Yaacov Shimshon Shapira, who had just left his post as Israel's first attorney general. Given the stature of her counsel, the Interior Ministry officials who handled the application were understandably careful in their response. The Interior Ministry asked Elazar Leib Globus, legal counsel for the Ministry of Immigration, to comment on the appeal. In his response to the Interior Ministry, he laid out in detail why the application should be denied. "One might speculate that the applicant has requested . . . a period of only two months due to the [typically] optimistic Jewish [assumption] that later, when she reaches the United States, she can apply for additional time, as most do. . . . The applicant has already spent time abroad this year in England and France. . . . It looks as if the applicant has fallen ill with the notorious Jewish illness known as 'travelitis.'"[2]

Israeli Exit Policy 1948–1961

Between 1948 and 1961, Israeli citizens seeking to travel abroad needed to obtain an exit permit in addition to a passport or, before 1952, a *laissez-passer* (a limited travel document). The exit permit approved their departure from Israel to specified destinations for a limited time. During the early years of statehood, it was relatively difficult to obtain an exit permit. Worried about Israel's international reputation and anxious to maintain a certain level of control over individual citizens even beyond the state's borders, officials made it their business to know the whereabouts and plans of every Israeli.[3]

This chapter examines the limitations on foreign travel during the period from the establishment of the State of Israel in 1948 through 1961, when the general requirement that all Israeli citizens obtain an exit permit as a condition for being allowed to leave Israel was abolished. As opposed to the previous chapter, in which I considered a positive right, in this chapter, I focus on a negative right — that is, a right to freedom from state interference.

I will not discuss the case of Palestinian Israeli citizens, who lived in the main under martial law during this time and endured severe travel restrictions even within the boundaries of the state. Additionally, the travel patterns of Palestinian Israelis and the nature of their relationship with the state differed greatly from those of their Jewish compatriots.

One might presume, given Israel's geopolitical situation during its first decade, that shifts in its policy governing trips outside the country would largely reflect security considerations. But in fact the picture is much more complex. At least some of the variations in the regulations impinging on the right to leave the country had to do with political developments and needs rather than the country's defense. Furthermore, functional explanations seem to be only part of the story. Other components of the national discourse were involved, from the shaping of the nation to the identity of the New Jew and how to inculcate good citizenship. Globus's concern about Mrs. W's "travel-itis" gestures toward these matters.

When crafting the exit policy, policymakers had three models in mind: the Soviet, British, and American. The Soviet example was a negative one, while both the British and the American travel policies served as points of reference. Like the reformist women of the first chapter of this book, Israeli policymakers, judges, and citizens measured Israel according to the standards of other Western nations and thus had expectations about how their new state could and should act and the image it should project.

As nation-states emerged during the nineteenth and twentieth centuries, they defined who qualified as a citizen. This practice institutionalized citizenship and made it the determinant of who could cross a nation-state's borders. Passports were first used during World War I, when they served as a means of controlling the movements of populations and of restricting freedom of travel.[4] Currently, states use passports to impose near-absolute control over their citizens' ability to move about globally. It is understood that a state is permitted to restrict its citizens' right to travel abroad in cases when the citizens in question are criminals, litigants, minors, or those seeking to shirk their civic responsibilities.[5] In the 1950s, several democratic countries, Israel among them, also barred foreign travel by their citizens for other reasons.

After World War II and with the inception of the Cold War, the Soviet government (but not the governments of all its Eastern bloc allies) imposed draconian restrictions and conditions on travel outside the country. The major impetus for this approach was the peculiar nature of Soviet Marxism, specifically a fear of foreign influence and a sense that the rest of the world was hostile.[6]

The United States also responded to the Cold War by limiting the right of its citizens to travel overseas, first on the basis of an existing law dating from 1926, and then supplementing that with further legislation in 1950 and 1952. Communists were barred from obtaining a passport. Moreover, the State Department refused to issue passports to Americans suspected of harboring communist sympathies or whose political opinions and anticipated activities abroad were defined as contrary to the best interests of the US government. The policy was criticized by civil libertarians and brought before the US Supreme Court.[7] It was not until 1958, however, that the Court ruled that the laws from 1926 and 1952 did not afford due process.[8] Furthermore, the Court declared that the right to travel abroad was a fundamental liberty and was thus protected by the Fifth Amendment. In a case in 1964, the Court ruled that the State Department's denial of a passport to a prominent communist was illegal and invalidated the section of the 1950 law that had prohibited the granting of passports to communists, as well as prohibiting communists from applying for passports or using ones already issued to them.[9] US restrictions on the freedom to travel abroad were only one aspect of a much larger anticommunist witch hunt that made its mark on the fields of entertainment, communications, and education.

In theory, Britain permitted its citizens to travel freely abroad even during the Cold War.[10] However, such travel was difficult because, due to the country's pressing need for foreign reserves during World War II and the postwar reconstruction period, the purchase of foreign currency for overseas travel and the amount of such currency that a traveler could take out of the country was severely curtailed. The most stringent travel restrictions — a ban on obtaining foreign currency for travel to any region — went into force in September 1947. From April 1948 through June 1957, Britons traveling abroad were allowed to take out of the country the equivalent of only £20–25, and they could take this amount only to nondollar regions. In ensuing years these restrictions were gradually eased.[11]

In Israel, communists and Arabs were the victims of official discrimination, but they were not the only people whose overseas travel was constrained (although they endured more strictures than others).[12] The government sought to reduce foreign travel by all citizens.

Legally, in Israel, as in Britain and the United States, the state could prohibit any of its inhabitants from leaving the country simply by refusing to issue a new passport or by not renewing or revoking an existing one.[13] As noted above, in Israel, in addition to requiring a passport (or a laissez-passer) citizens who wished to travel abroad also needed an exit permit. This requirement was in force until 1961. On top of this, during the early years in which this policy was enforced, nearly all Israelis traveling abroad were barred from exchanging Israeli currency for foreign money. Like Britain, but even more acutely, Israel suffered from economic woes and a perennial shortage of foreign reserves. Moreover, travelers had to pay an array of fees and taxes.

Foreign currency grew increasingly scarce in Israel after February 1948, when the Palestine pound was untied from the pound sterling, even prior to the end of British rule. From this point on, the Palestine pound, replaced in August 1948 by the Israeli lira issued by the Anglo-Palestine Bank, had for all intents and purposes no value outside Israel's borders and could not be exchanged overseas for other currencies. For a small, new, and undeveloped country like Israel, foreign currency was a lifeline both during and after the 1948 war. Without it, Israel's government could not purchase anything from other countries—not arms, food, raw materials, or industrial equipment, all of which were vital to withstand the war, feed the burgeoning population, and fuel the local economy. Israel had few exports at the time, and thus little foreign currency was entering the country. Under these circumstances, the government had to ration its reserves with care.[14]

The Israeli debate over the freedom to travel abroad took place in three arenas: first, government policy, legislation, and bureaucratic procedure; second, public opinion and the press; and third, the public campaign to change the policy and the stance of the courts to which the disputes were addressed. My objective here is not merely to offer an account of the public debate over the right to travel abroad, but also to explain the motivations of those who advocated restrictions and those who imposed them.

Facts and Figures

The vast majority of Israelis who flew or sailed abroad in the period 1949–60 were Jewish (see Table 2.1). In contrast, the great majority of non-Jews who traveled abroad did so overland, crossing the cease-fire lines into neighboring countries.[15] Compared to their share of the country's population and in contrast to the level of Jewish travel, the number of non-Jews who traveled via sea and air was negligible.

The Jewish population nearly doubled during this period, primarily as a result of the government's immigration policies.[16] However, immigration was not steady throughout this period. Few newcomers arrived in 1952 and 1953 (see Table 3.2), while emigration from Israel increased (see Table 2.2). At the end of 1951, the rate of immigration was curbed pursuant to government policy. In 1952 the government instituted a new economic policy aimed mainly at lowering national outlays while significantly devaluing Israel's currency, which led to a substantial rise in unemployment. This explains the increase in emigration (Table 2.2). The trend reached its climax in 1953, when departures exceeded the number of arrivals.[17]

Throughout this period the rate of Israeli Jews making short-term trips abroad was very low, ranging from 1.68 percent in 1949 to 3.28 percent in 1960 (Table 2.1). Nevertheless, the figures show that it rose steadily, at a moderate rate, with intermittent fluctuations. Jewish travelers increased dramatically in 1950, plummeted in 1951 and 1952, rose again in 1953, and dropped in 1954. From 1955 on, it rose moderately until 1960, when there was a significant rise in the rate of Jews exiting the country.

Most Jews traveled for pleasure, to visit relatives, for business, on assignment from commercial concerns, for medical reasons, for studies, and to liquidate property or receive inheritances — all activities associated with the middle class (Table 2.3). Only members of the middle class had the means to take trips overseas for these purposes. The vast majority of the immigrants who had entered the country were indigent refugees. Some were Holocaust survivors, others had come from behind the Iron Curtain, and still others came from the Islamic world. Whatever their origin, in most cases any property or money they might have had in their countries of origin had been taken from them when they emigrated. This being the case, the middle class was largely made up of Jews who had been living in what was now Israel prior to the establishment of the state.

TABLE 2.1 · Population of Israel and Number of Inhabitants Traveling Abroad

Year	Total population*	Jews*	Non-Jews*	Sea and air travel			Overland travel, non-Jews**	Percent of Jewish population traveling
				Total travelers	Jews	Non-Jews		
1949	1,173.9	1,013.9	160.0	17,461	17,017	444	—***	1.68
1950	1,370.1	1,203.0	167.1	30,018	29,183	835	3,208	2.43
1951	1,577.8	1,404.4	173.4	26,676	25,886	790	5,213	1.84
1952	1,629.5	1,450.2	179.3	29,404	28,563	841	6,647	1.97
1953	1,669.4	1,483.6	185.8	34,745	33,828	917	5,856	2.28
1954	1,717.8	1,526.0	188.8	30,897	29,988	909	3,767	1.97
1955	1,789.1	1,590.5	198.6	34,321	33,484	837	4,107	2.11
1956	1,872.4	1,667.5	204.9	41,950	41,091	859	2,964	2.46
1957	1,976.0	1,762.7	213.3	48,255	47,544	711	2,616	2.70
1958	2,031.7	1,810.1	221.6	52,050	51,463	587	4,024	2.84
1959	2,088.7	1,858.8	229.9	54,951	54,393	558	5,283	2.93
1960	2,150.4	1,911.2	239.2	63,305	62,606	699	5,558	3.28

Source: Adapted from *Hashnaton Hastatisti Leyisrael* [Israel Statistical Yearbook.] 13:31 and 95 (Jerusalem 1962), and 10:59–60 (Jerusalem, 1959)

*Estimated, in thousands.

**Non-Jews traveling by land, mostly through the Mandelbaum checkpoint to Jordan with special permits.

***Data not available.

TABLE 2.2 · Emigrants from Israel, by Population Group and Year of Emigration

Year of emigration	Total emigrants*	Jews	Non-Jews	Emigrating Jews per 1,000 Israeli Jews*	Persons declaring emigration
May 15– December 31, 1948	1,154	1,040	114	1.5	—**
1949	7,407	7,207	200	8.0	3,259
1950	9,966	9,463	503	8.6	4,313
1951	10,476	10,057	419	7.2	7,646
1952	13,500	13,000	500	9.1	11,128
1953	13,000	12,500	500	8.5	8,644
1954	7,500	7,000	500	4.7	5,774
1955	6,400	6,000	400	3.9	3,922
1956	11,400	11,000	400	6.8	6,245
1957	11,400	11,000	400	6.4	6,411
1958	11,700	11,500	200	6.4	7,724
1959	9,750	9,500	250	5.2	7,095
1960	8,800	8,500	300	4.5	7,206

Source: Adapted from Hashnaton Hastatisti Leyisrael [Israel Statistical Yearbook.] 13:11 (Jerusalem, 1962) and 8:44 (Jerusalem, 1957).
*Estimated.
**Not available.

Even though in absolute numbers very few Israelis were traveling, members of the cabinet, government officials, the Jewish Agency, the Knesset, the media, and the courts were clearly troubled by the phenomenon. Since most travelers came from the country's upper socioeconomic echelons, their activities and demands were very much in the public eye. Furthermore, many emigrants preferred to conceal their intentions: throughout the period, the number of those explicitly stating their intention to leave Israel for good was much lower than the number of those who actually did so (Tables 2.2 and 2.3). Emigration profoundly disturbed the authorities and was a major factor in the policy fluctuations that affected the granting or refusal of exit permits. Israelis who sought to emigrate were seldom prevented from doing so, but at times administrative measures were imposed that made it very difficult.[18]

There was a discrepancy between the numbers of applicants for exit permits and the numbers of people who traveled abroad. While the data

TABLE 2.3 · Travelers Leaving Israel, by Year and Stated Purpose

Purpose	1951	1952	1954	1955	1956	Total residents 1957	Jews 1957	Total residents 1958	Jews 1958	1959	1960
Total	26,676	29,404	30,897	34,321	41,950	48,255	47,544	52,059	51,463	54,951	63,305
Pleasure, family visits, and other personal reasons	6,441	7,899	14,128	17,083	20,236	26,659	26,482	31,332	31,022	33,640	36,534
Medical treatment	598	542	306	309	480	340	338	250	249	316	328
Business	2,648	1,352	1,703	1,805	2,234	1,801	1,796	920	920	893	1,486
Liquidation of property, inheritance	1,164	957	287	281	418	343	343	90	88	19	65
On assignment from commercial concerns	—*	808	1,131	1,175	906	981	980	1,225	1,224	1,485	2,302
Temporary employment	295	610	1,214	1,567	2,108	2,247	2,246	2,242	2,239	1,477	2,692
Crews (sea and air)	2,399	2,398	2,673	3,660	4,325	4,608	4,604	4,261	4,259	4,188	5,116
Arts and sports	220	238	340	519	495	331	327	147	146	558	838

Purpose	1951	1952	1954	1955	1956	Total residents 1957	Jews 1957	Total residents 1958	Jews 1958	1959	1960
Science, education, culture, and journalism	218	237	233	302	392	258	258	343	341	553	1,142
Pilgrims and others	62	94	98	167	214	200	120	182	136	—*	—*
Study	1,461	1,226	1,361	1,501	1,547	1,335	1,315	1,564	1,537	1,571	1,945
Diplomatic missions	***	681	509	742	948	561	560	264	264	1,260	2,088
Missions for institutions and organizations	1,981	1,032	783	914	919	1,484	1,447	723	723	750	560
Emigration	7,651	11,128	5,774	3,922	6,245	6,411	7,411	7,724	7,541	7,095	7,206
Not stated	1,538	204	297	374	483	696	689	783	774	1,146	1,003

Source: Adapted from *Hashnaton Hastatisti Leyisrael* [Israel Statistical Yearbook.] 9:73 (Jerusalem, 1958), 10:59 (Jerusalem, 1959), and 13:109 (Jerusalem 1962).

*Data not available.

***In 1951, "diplomatic missions" and "missions for institutions and organizations" were combined.

available from this period are incomplete, they are sufficient to illuminate government policy. During the country's early years, there was a large gap between the number of applicants for an exit permit and the number of actual travelers. From September 1, 1948, through June 30, 1951, approximately 120,000 applications were filed. A total of 64,425 exit permits were granted, but only 62,166 were used.[19] In comparison, in 1960, nearly all applications were granted—40,476 from January through the end of November. Only 50 were turned down, following a court order prohibiting these citizens from leaving Israel.[20]

In comparison with numbers from the Mandate period, the number of travelers after 1948 was lower, both in absolute terms and relative to the total population. In 1946, for example, 89,197 residents left, accounting for 4.9 percent of Palestine's population of 1,820,661.[21] The differences reflect the closing of the country's land borders to Jews after independence, changes in the composition of the population, and restrictions on the freedom to travel abroad during the period after the establishment of the state—both those restrictions applying to the Jewish population and those restrictions, not examined here, that applied to the Arab population.

Shifting Government Policies

In March 1948, prior to the establishment of the State of Israel, the Jewish Agency Executive issued a special order prohibiting anyone who had not received an exit permit from its Central Command for Conscription from leaving the country. This order was copied from regulations that the British Mandate administration had imposed immediately following the outbreak of World War II in 1939.[22] Five months later, in August, the government officially promulgated the State of Emergency Regulations (Exit from the Country), which stipulated that travel overseas required an exit permit. The Ministry of Immigration was given the responsibility of processing applications for these permits.[23] The emergency regulations provided the minister with absolute discretion to grant or deny an exit permit from Israel. Under the detailed directives issued by the minister for implementing the regulations, those applying to leave the country were required to file a personal application form, to which they were to attach a passport or laissez-passer; a document from the Finance Ministry certifying that they did not owe taxes or other money to the state; a similar document from the local authority in which they lived; a document from the Ministry of Labor and Construction specifying that they were not required to perform labor service or had been exempted from such service; a document from the Defense Ministry attesting that they were not subject to the draft; and, where relevant, a document from an authorized medical office declaring that the medical care they were seeking overseas could not be provided in Israel. In the case where a patient seeking treatment was also subject to the draft, the medical certificate also had to be endorsed by the draft office's medical board. The exit permit application with these documents attached had to be submitted to one of the district immigration offices (there was one each in Tel Aviv, Jerusalem, and Haifa) at least two weeks prior to the planned voyage.[24]

Ministry officials operated according to the principle that, for the duration of hostilities, exit permits were not to be issued even for those who were not fighting, unless travel was deemed essential.[25] The 1948 conflict was a total war on Israel's side. All fit men between eighteen and thirty-five were called up for combat duty, as were all women between eighteen and twenty-five who were unmarried or married but without children. Citizens unfit to fight were mobilized for labor service in vital sectors and for the building of fortifications.[26] The restriction on foreign travel was aimed at preventing both the departure of those seeking to evade military or civilian service and the transfer of information to the enemy.[27] Evasion of military service was not a negligible phenomenon, and there was good reason to fear that people eligible for military service would flee overseas. By April 1948, only 80 percent of Jewish men of military age had reported for service, and not a few of those who failed to report had left the country. Once the state was established enforcement measures were put in place, but even then draft evasion remained common. By November 1948 an induction police force established in June had located and arrested 3,579 draft evaders and 616 deserters.[28] While these were the functional justifications for the restriction on foreign travel, it seems to have had another dimension as well: it enforced national solidarity, which leaving the country was seen to violate.[29]

On November 19, 1948, the emergency regulations were extended so that they would remain in force until the end of the state of emergency declared by the National Council, the provisional parliament. This state of emergency has, in fact, never been revoked and remains in force to this day.[30] Some changes were made to the language of the regulations—for example, the absolute authority over whether or not to grant a permit that had been vested in the minister of immigration was removed.[31] This opened the way for the Supreme Court to hear cases relating to the law. In 1951, in *Es-Said v.*

Minister of Immigration, the court ruled that, as a consequence of the revision of the regulations—specifically, the removal of the phrase "sole discretion" with reference to the minister of immigration—the minister's authority and decision-making power had been significantly reduced. His discretion was now subject to judicial review, and the court was empowered to rule on whether the minister had exceeded his authority. In this specific case, the court compelled the minister to grant an exit permit to the plaintiff and imposed court costs on the state.[32] In contrast, US citizens had to wait until 1958 before their Supreme Court intervened in any significant way in this area.

After the 1948 war, restrictions were somewhat eased and the number of travelers increased (Table 2.1).[33] Gershon Agron, who headed the Government Information Office in the years 1948–51 (and who had previously founded the English-language daily *Palestine Post*, which after independence became the *Jerusalem Post*), declared that most Israelis understood the need to maintain the restrictions, but more and more dissent began to be heard. Walter Eytan, director general of the Ministry of Foreign Affairs, wrote to Foreign Minister Moshe Sharett that "a feeling of resentment toward the state and the government [is spreading], giving rise to a psychological mindset that the country's citizens are imprisoned within their borders."[34]

In July 1949, the attorney general proposed establishing an appeals procedure for those refused permission to exit the country. "The exit permit laws without a doubt impinge upon human rights," he wrote.[35] His position was accepted by the government, and an appeals board was established under the Ministry of Justice.[36] In the United States at this time, in comparison, citizens who had been denied passports had to go to court, and eventually to the Supreme Court, to gain the right to an appeals hearing.[37]

In August 1949, the Ministry of Immigration distributed to its local branches a list of categories of people for whom they could issue exit permits. The head office was to handle the more unusual or difficult cases. The list constitutes a bureaucratic attempt to catalogue a complex array of human needs and desires. Local offices could issue exit permits to representatives of institutions of higher education; students seeking to continue their studies abroad; businessmen, including importers, exporters, and manufacturers; athletes; individuals seeking to salvage property or take possession of an inheritance; official delegations sent by government or other public and political agencies; wives and children seeking to join a male head of family overseas; and individuals wishing to attend international conferences. Such permits were not issued automatically—in each case, applicants had to submit ample proof that their trips were indeed necessary and that they intended to travel for this purpose only and then return. Furthermore, in most cases, a letter of recommendation from a relevant government ministry was also required. So as not to discourage immigration from the West, recent immigrants from North America and Western Europe were permitted to travel abroad even if they did not meet these requirements.

I will not consider here the requests submitted by those Israelis whose goal was to emigrate rather than simply travel. Certain categories of citizens received permission to emigrate without difficulty. These were people who were not considered vital assets for the new state — those on the bottom of the socioeconomic ladder, those age sixty or older, and immigrants who did not adjust well to life in Israel.[38] My main interest is in those who sought to travel abroad with the full intention of returning to Israel. They were the people who had the greatest difficulty in obtaining an exit permit. I will consider emigration only briefly.

As a result of public pressure, some cabinet ministers felt uncomfortable with the policy of restricting Israelis' freedom to travel abroad. They were cognizant of the fact that Britain had lifted its direct bars to foreign travel after the end of World War II.[39] A cabinet committee in September 1949 considered a proposal to end the need for an exit permit altogether, or at least to make the process of getting one much less onerous. A tax on travel tickets was also discussed.[40] Minister of Immigration Haim-Moshe Shapira and Justice Minister Pinhas Rosen advocated repealing the exit permit requirement.[41] But Prime Minister and Defense Minister David Ben-Gurion and Police Minister Bechor-Shalom Sheetrit were strongly opposed, so the policy remained in place.[42] It should be kept in mind that such policies were neither unprecedented nor unparalleled, and that decision makers in Israel justified their policies by referring to the precedent of the Mandate administration's requiring exit permits. There were other precedents and parallels as well. Many European countries had imposed or were imposing strictures on the purchase of foreign currency and regulated exchange rates. The United States levied a travel tax, in the form of a surtax on transport tickets, on its citizens who went abroad.[43]

The growing number of Israelis leaving the country, particularly during the first half of 1950, impelled the government to review the right to travel abroad, taking into account not only the country's security but also its economy.[44] As I related in the introduction, the government imposed an austerity regime in April 1949. Food and other commodities were rationed and their prices controlled. By the beginning of 1950, Israel had absorbed approximately 350,000 new immigrants, who imposed a huge financial burden. The country was running out of foreign currency. Food reserves dwindled and rations were cut.[45]

Despite these dire straits, several ministers voiced reservations about abridging freedom of travel when the cabinet discussed the issue that April. Both Rosen and Sharett opposed an extension of the restrictions. Ben-Gurion, who took a hard line on the issue, retorted to Sharett that the country remained in a state of emergency. Sharett fired back: "Is there a law that a state of emergency remains in force?" "There certainly is," Ben-Gurion answered. Sharett then asked: "And what is the justification for maintaining that law?" Ben-Gurion replied: "That there isn't peace."[46]

Following this exchange, the cabinet resolved to make the application process for an exit permit easier. It also imposed a tax on foreign travel, citing the travel tax imposed by the United States as a precedent.[47] This pattern of pairing regulatory relief with the imposition of taxes designed to discourage travel was repeated in the future. In time, the state came to depend on the revenues derived from exit permit and passport application fees and the travel surtax on air and sea tickets.[48] The method enabled the government to claim that its policy on travel was a liberal one that did not infringe on basic rights, while still discouraging overseas travel by making it punitively expensive.[49]

As foreign currency reserves dwindled, fewer exit permits were issued, creating a situation in which the Ministry of Finance in effect imposed a quota on the number of people leaving the country by demanding that the Ministry of Immigration grant fewer permits.[50] From August 1950 until the spring of 1953, the primary motivation for restricting travel abroad was economic, and the Interior Ministry (entrusted since 1951 with implementing the exit policy) did not authorize travel by persons whose trips its officials deemed were not essential.[51] Mrs. W.'s case, with which this chapter began, should be viewed in this context. Travelers during this period were permitted to purchase and take only $5–$10 of foreign currency out of the country. The only exceptions were for people traveling for what were deemed worthy purposes, such as government emissaries or students. Travelers in most categories were even required to pay for their tickets in foreign currency sent from abroad.[52]

In response to the economic crisis, in the summer of 1950 Minister of Finance Eliezer Kaplan directed travel agencies not to sell tickets even to those who had already received exit permits. Shapira, who held both the interior and immigration portfolios, was outraged. In a clamorous cabinet meeting in July 1950, he accused Kaplan of overreaching his authority and, in violation of the law, infringing on the powers of his (Shapira's) ministry. He demanded that those who already held exit permits be permitted to travel.[53] Kaplan maintained that the majority of Israelis traveling abroad were engaged in profiteering, resulting in the devaluation of Israel's currency.[54] He explained that bourgeois strongholds like the Israel Medical Association and the Israel Bar Association had applied to send large groups abroad, and that he was determined to stifle such "travelitis."[55]

At the same meeting, Minister of Supply and Rationing Dov Yosef charged that the Finance Ministry's demands regarding travel policy were inequitable because people with money were able to travel abroad, whereas those without money were unable to leave the country.[56] Rosen and Minister of Education Zalman Shazar demanded that citizens be able to travel abroad to visit relatives as well as study. "It is common sense to grant permission to travel under such circumstances and not to create panic as if we are erecting an iron curtain between our country and the outside world," Shazar told the cabinet.[57] At this time, Israel had recently managed, after difficult negotiations, to reach an agreement allowing tens of thousands of Jews to leave countries of the Eastern Bloc. Under the agreement, Israel paid Bulgaria, Poland, and Romania for each Jew allowed to leave.[58]

Rosen mentioned the resentment the public felt as a result of the policy. Echoing this, Minister of Transportation David Remez declared that "even in a bad situation, and I would say all the more so in a bad and tight situation, we should certainly be careful about creating a sense of oppression."[59]

The cabinet heard that the obstacles to travel had produced three unintended consequences. First, the limitations on the number of Israelis permitted to leave the country had caused air and shipping lines to reduce the number of flights and sailings connecting Israel with the world. Second, the news that foreign travel was restricted in Israel had made it difficult to persuade Western Jews to move to the country. The impression being made was that anyone who settled in Israel would never be able to get out again.[60] Third, the policy discouraged foreign investors, who feared that if they visited the country, they might have difficulty leaving. Even tourists from abroad at times found themselves targeted.[61]

In 1951, Rosen's Progressive Party, one of two that represented the bourgeoisie, proposed an amendment to the emergency regulations to limit the grounds on which an exit permit could be denied.[62] The amendment was not passed, but the Progressives continued to demand easing of the travel restrictions, and they eventually prevailed.

Nevertheless, the government persisted in reducing the number of permits.[63] In June 1952, Yizhar Harari, a Progressive serving in the Knesset, demanded that this trend be reversed, and that travel be restricted only for security reasons. Harari asserted that, perversely people seeking to leave the country permanently easily received permits, while those who wished only to make a trip — most of them established Israelis, since few new immigrants had the financial means to travel — were prevented from doing so.[64]

At the end of 1952, the General Zionists — a free-market party that represented mostly the bourgeoisie — joined the coalition to form Israel's fourth government. The coalition agreement stipulated that exit permits would be denied only for security reasons. The party's Knesset members, and particularly Minister of the Interior Israel Rokach, worked hard to ease the restrictions.[65] The Supreme Court also intervened. In a ruling issued on June 9, 1953, Justice Moshe Silberg preferred a creative rather than a dry, formalistic reading of the law. He asserted unequivocally that "a citizen's freedom of movement from his country to outside it is a natural right, obvious to every country ruled by democracy — and our country is one of these."[66] He ruled that it was not the grant, but the denial, of an exit permit that required sufficient reason and justification.

Perhaps ironically, the Supreme Court made this groundbreaking assertion of principle at the same time that it upheld the ministry's denial of an exit permit to the plaintiff in the case. Haya Kaufman's application for a permit had been denied on the grounds that her trip would be deleterious to Israel's security, but the ministry did not disclose to her what the specific suspicion against her was or on what evidence it was based. Kaufman, who had been invited to serve as a delegate to a women's conference in Copenhagen, belonged to a radical political faction, the New Socialist Left, which had close ties to the Communist Party. However, at the same time that her application for an exit permit was denied, the application of a Communist Party member who had also been invited to the conference was approved. According to the court, the reason for the denial was not the applicant's political affiliation but rather other suspicions against her.

In comparison, the US Federal Court of Appeals for the District of Colombia recognized the right to travel abroad as a natural right only in 1955.[67] In contrast to the United States, in Israel, citizens with leftist political leanings were not prohibited from leaving the country.[68]

The Israeli court's recognition of a natural right to travel came at a convenient time for the government. Just two months earlier, the government, acceding to demands of the General Zionists, had approved measures to make foreign travel much easier. In a reversal of the previous situation, the default now was granting a permit rather than refusing it. It was decided that an exit permit would be granted to any applicant unless a government agency had specifically forbidden that person to travel. Applications were sent for review to relevant ministries, offices, and local authorities — any agency that might have reason to believe that the applicant was seeking to abscond without having paid his or her debts or seeking to avoid a legal or official proceeding. The Interior Ministry estimated that 30–50 percent of applications were held up because of these agency reviews.[69] Nongovernmental bodies such as the Jewish Agency, the Histadrut, and some immigrant organizations were also allowed to review applications. Some of these had an interest in collecting debts, while others sought to provide aid that would prevent citizens from leaving the country for good.

Concurrently, the process of applying for an exit permit was significantly simplified, and the grounds for barring a citizen from travel abroad were formally limited to criminal activity (past or anticipated) and state security reasons, with all exit permit applications submitted for review by the Shin Bet, Israel's internal security agency.[70] Simultaneously, a requirement was imposed on new immigrants who wished to emigrate — before leaving the country, they had to return all the furnishings and belongings they had received from the state or the Jewish Agency.[71] Furthermore, the travel tax was raised significantly.[72]

On the other hand, a system of exemptions and discounts from these onerous taxes were established for those without means, people who were sick, emissaries, students, and trainees.[73] The relative liberalization of travel policy thus had the effect of enabling most people who wished to travel outside the country to do so.

As a consequence, the number of travelers grew in 1953. In that year more people moved out of the country than into it, leading to calls for restrictions on emigration. But no changes were made in the exit permit policy.[74]

In 1955, two divergent changes occurred. In June, at the initiative of Yizhar Harari, the wording of the emergency regulations was amended.[75] The powers of the minister of the interior were statutorily curtailed and limited to denying an exit permit only under circumstances where there were grounds to suspect that travel by the applicant was liable to breach state security, or pursuant to a court order. Regulations were also revised to reduce the time allotted for processing applications from 3–4 weeks to 10–14 days.

Citizens subject to military conscription and those who served in the reserves were required to attach a consent form from the army or the Ministry of Defense to their application. These provisions went into force on June 16, a little more than a month before national elections.[76]

It thus seems likely that this relief was offered as part of the election campaign. The coalition parties, especially the General Zionists and even more so Mapai, were apprehensive about how they would fare. Ironically, the General Zionists were worried because the economy had improved considerably, compared to where it had been at the time of the previous elections, in 1951. Then, thanks to the austerity regime, they had enjoyed a steep rise in support.[77] The Kasztner affair, in which a high figure in Mapai had been accused of collaboration with the Nazis, was in the news, and the restrained military policy pursued by Prime Minister Sharett, which coincided with an ongoing worsening of the security situation, was unpopular.[78] These parties thus sought the votes of Israelis able to afford overseas fares—that is, well-established Israelis, both members of the bourgeoisie who voted for the General Zionists and members of the labor camp who had, after the arrival of the immigrants, moved up the economic ladder. The numbers support this presumption: In June 1954, 3,785 exit permits were issued; during the same month a year later, 4,635 were granted. In July 1954, the number of exit permits issued was 3,805; in July, the month of the 1955 elections, 5,293 were granted.[79]

But the tone changed once the elections were over. Early in August, Yoel Marcus, a columnist for the Histadrut labor federation's daily newspaper *Davar*, decried the increase in foreign travel and termed the new travel policy "a luxury for a nation struggling for its economic independence."[80] Two days later, *Davar* reported that 15,000 Israeli tourists had already left the country since the beginning of the year. The Finance Ministry, the newspaper declared, was being much too liberal, and it asked: "Have we not gone too far beyond the bounds of the permissible?" Nevertheless, the editors did not recommend taking administrative measures to reduce overseas travel.[81]

Another change of direction followed the appointment of Israel Bar-Yehuda of the hawkish socialist party 'Ahdut Ha'avodah as minister of interior in the new government. During the winter of 1955 he conducted a campaign to tighten the exit permit policy yet again. Bar-Yehuda was motivated by ideological convictions, but these were reinforced by the existence of what most policymakers and ordinary Israelis felt to be the country's increasingly precarious security situation. At the end of September, Israel learned that Egypt had concluded an enormous weapons deal with Czecho-slovakia, which had the potential to upset the strategic balance in the entire region. At the same time, incursions into Israel by Palestinian guerrillas were on the rise. Fear swept the country, and citizens spontaneously showed up at the gate to the Defense Ministry in Tel Aviv, offering cash and jewelry so that the country could buy weapons.[82]

In mid-December, Bar-Yehuda asked the cabinet to reconsider the travel policy, submitting to cabinet a draft that proposed "to carry out a public campaign to explain the issue and other means to halt the torrent of over-seas travel."[83] At a cabinet meeting on December 18, the finance minister reported that he had instructed that the amount of foreign currency travelers could take out of the country be halved.[84]

On January 23, 1956, the Knesset deliberated the first reading of a bill in-tended, for the first time, to transfer from the interior minister to the minis-ter of defense the authority to grant or deny exit permits to soldiers serving in the reserves. The reason for the new legislation was to correct a loophole in the law. In October 1955, some two weeks before the new government was formed, Interior Ministry officials and the military prosecutor's office concluded that there was no legal basis for demanding an exit permit from reservists who wished to travel abroad.[85] Bar-Yehuda supported the change, telling the Knesset that the law as it stood was inadequate to respond to Is-rael's defense needs.[86] The increasingly tense situation on the borders led even the General Zionists, who were now part of the opposition, to support the bill, although they voiced concerns that the defense minister might abuse his new powers.[87]

The Progressives, however, remained cool to the idea. Speaking against the bill, Harari decried the attempt to revoke the liberal changes made prior to the elections. The proposed bill, he observed, would create a situation in which men and women subject to conscription and those serving in the re-serves — that is, the lion's share of male Israelis between adolescence through middle age — were presumptively forbidden to leave the country. He asked if the country existed for the sake of its citizens, or if citizens existed solely for the convenience of the government.[88]

Bar-Yehuda responded to criticism from both coalition and opposition legislators with the claim that the fact that Harari's liberalizing amendment had been passed proved that what was at issue was not a battle between those who wanted to allow Israelis to travel and those who wanted to keep them from doing so. Policy had to change in response to circumstances, he argued.[89]

Nevertheless, Bar-Yehuda's collectivistic views, triggered in part by the deteriorating security situation, seem to have been a key factor in his decision to seek a revision of the law. The public, in contrast, responded not as the collective Bar-Yehuda envisioned, but as a collection of individuals worried that their newfound freedom to travel would soon be coming to an end. During the two-month period between the new legislation's referral to committee, following its first reading, and March 22, when the Knesset voted it into law, Israelis lined up at the Ministry of the Interior to obtain exit permits.[90]

Members of the Knesset continued their attack on the bill during the debate that preceded the final vote. Haim Landau of the opposition Herut party termed the coalition's approach "pseudo-patriotism" and demanded that citizens who served as army reservists and whose applications for exit permits were refused be permitted to appeal.[91] He declared that he had no faith in the government's integrity on this issue and suggested that it had a hidden agenda. Yaakov Riftin of Mapam, chairman of the Knesset's Internal Affairs Committee, confirmed these suspicions. While acknowledging that the security situation was grave, he said that he could not understand why, in the current circumstances, citizens should not be entirely barred from leaving the country unless absolutely necessary.[92]

But the new law hardly forbade Israelis from traveling outside their country. Electoral considerations seem to have prevented Mapai, the ruling party, from imposing drastic restrictions. It had not done well in the 1955 elections, from which it emerged with 40 seats in the 120-seat Knesset, 5 fewer seats than before. The new restrictions were relatively moderate, considering the fact that Bar-Yehuda demanded that a "test of the vital need to travel" be reinstated.[93] In July, for example, the term of exit permits was reduced from six to three months. This made it much more difficult for Israelis to travel, as sometimes a permit would expire before they could arrange visas from foreign countries.[94] A month later, in August, when war seemed to be on the horizon, the minister of the interior ordered that the processing period for exit permit applications be extended from 10–14 days to three weeks. The purpose was twofold: to save foreign currency and to ensure that Israel's citizens remained in the country to provide material and moral support for any impending war effort.[95] Complaints about delays in issuing exit permits and passports increased substantially during the months that followed.

After the emergency regulations were amended in March, the preferred method was to impose relatively minor restrictions through administrative means and not through legislation.[96] It is hard to avoid the impression that the interior minister's orders, and the apparently inefficient operation of his ministry, were aimed at reducing the number of Israelis leaving the country. Each overseas traveler, the minister believed, compromised the country's military readiness and lowered public morale. As opposed to Bar-Yehuda of the socialist 'Ahdut Ha'avodah party, Mapai was seeking to retain the support of those of its voters who had moved into the middle class, which made up the bulk of travelers. At the same time, it was skirmishing with members of the professions over their salary demands, preferring the interests of lower-level employees over those of the middle class.[97] Mapai thus chose its battles carefully. It was politically expedient for the party to refrain from further legislation on the matter while allowing Bar-Yehuda to pursue administrative measures to reduce overseas travel. The blame could thus be placed on the interior minister and his party, saving Mapai face, while achieving some of its goals.[98]

In November, immediately after the Sinai Campaign broke out, Bar-Yehuda cancelled all exit permits issued to reservists who had not yet left the country.[99] He gave verbal instructions to ministry officials (verbal because they contravened the law) to severely reduce the rate at which exit permits were issued, even to ordinary citizens, and to limit them to urgent cases. This directive was rescinded shortly thereafter, following the end of the war.[100] Yet the administrative measures imposed by Bar-Yehuda did not succeed in undoing the liberalization of travel policy that had resulted from the significant changes to the law approved during the summer of 1955. More Israelis traveled abroad in 1956 than in any year previously.

In June 1957 the processing time for an exit permit application was reduced somewhat, and the term of the permits was extended once more to six months.[101] In August the Finance Ministry proposed that the exit permit application fee be raised from 10 liras to 150 liras to fund the costs of housing for new immigrants. A memorandum sent by an Interior Ministry official to his director general in response to this proposal is worthy of note. The ministry, the official asserted, was a service provider, and taxes were customarily imposed on property and income, not on services. Furthermore, he added, granting an exit permit to a citizen was not even providing a service. Exit permits were required for security reasons, he argued, and should thus be granted without a fee, as indeed was the case in other countries. Such fees certainly should not be used as a way of raising money for other purposes.[102] A public outcry squelched the initiative.

Once again, elections effected a change in Israeli policy. With Israelis set to go to the polls, the exit permit requirement was lifted in 1961. The legislation mandating this change was submitted as a private members' bill sponsored by Zvi Zimmerman of the General Zionists. In fact, the only significant opposition to the move in the cabinet came from Minister of Finance Levi Eshkol, who demanded that the income lost from application fees be replaced by income from another source. Cabinet discussions of the bill show that the ministers were aware that the proposal was highly popular. This prompted them to curry popular favor by submitting a similar government bill.[103] In the end, the law was not entirely rescinded. The minister of the interior retained the authority to bar an individual from leaving the country on the ground of endangering state security. Furthermore, until the end of the 1980s reserve soldiers continued to be required to obtain an exit permit from the minister of defense or from the Israel Defense Forces.[104]

Israel and the Right to Travel

Current Israeli law permits restricting the right of a citizen to leave the country on three grounds: if the person's travel is deemed to impinge on national security, public order, or the rights of others.[105] While Israel's travel policy has changed dramatically over the country's history, these justifications for keeping a person from leaving have remained constant. If travel today is much freer, and if Israelis are seldom restricted from leaving the country, the change is thus not in these categories but in the way they are interpreted and applied.

The opinions regarding the freedom to leave the country voiced by decision makers and citizens during Israel's first decade serve to map out a spectrum of conflicting interests and principles based on a range of cultural and ideological perspectives. At one end of the spectrum are the individual freedoms and human rights that serve as the basis of Western democracy, while at the other end is the supremacy of the public interest and the individual citizen's duty to subordinate his or her freedom to the collective's needs, especially in matters of state security and economic survival. Due to acute security and economic circumstances during the country's initial period, policymakers based their decisions primarily on their views of the public interest. The individual's interests and liberties were secondary.

THE ECONOMY

The dire shortage of funds and, in particular, foreign currency in Israel's initial years gave the government a legitimate interest in reducing travel abroad. Nonetheless, it is clear that imposing a needs test for such travel substantially infringed upon the rights of Israelis. After restrictions were eased in 1953, the means test was replaced with economic disincentives to travel. The percentage of travelers rose only moderately during that year, which may indicate that these measures were effective. While in legal terms this was a liberalization of policy, the interior minister at the time, Israel Rokach, argued that its significance was highly overstated. He noted that the number of travelers declined in 1954.[106] Furthermore, the measures were counterproductive inasmuch the difficulty and expense of travel under this regime made it alluring and a status symbol. Although such economic restrictions may have been an effective way to maintain the country's foreign currency reserves, they were detrimental to the desired social climate that the decision makers, on both the political left and right, sought to achieve. Even Rokach, who championed the right to travel and who led a party that represented the bourgeoisie, derided Israelis who insisted that they had to go abroad to recover from illness. When he got sick, he told the Knesset, he did not go abroad to recover but instead found an appropriate place near Jerusalem. Enthusiasm for foreign travel was, he said, alien to the proper values of Israeli society.[107]

SECURITY

When security conditions deteriorated, the country's defense needs were once more invoked as a justification for limiting foreign travel. But in fact, as some members of the Knesset at the time charged, tension on Israel's borders was used as an excuse to impose long-term restrictions on certain citizens: reserve soldiers. Israelis generally viewed this as a legitimate limitation on their rights. This is evidenced by the fact that, despite the huge political, economic, and cultural changes that Israel underwent during its first four decades, the requirement that reserve soldiers obtain exit permits was not rescinded until the late 1980s. It is difficult to determine whether this occurred as a result of long-standing education on the part of the policymakers or as a result of social developments that gave the security issue a unique standing. However, since the change in policy was mainly due to public pressure, it appears that the second view is more likely.

CONTROL AND SOVEREIGNTY

The psychological motives of policymakers must also be taken into account. Decision makers in all countries—especially in a new one—seek to assert and reinforce their power. In Israel's case, the long and convoluted cease-fire lines that became its de facto borders were at first unfenced and nearly impossible to monitor. Infiltrators—initially hungry and desperate Palestinian refugees and later organized hostile fedayeen guerrillas who attacked and killed civilians—crossed into Israel almost daily.[108] Even the country's sovereignty over its territory was under constant challenge in the international arena. On the military level, Israel asserted and displayed its resolve to control its borders and sought to deter its foes by staging retaliatory strikes in enemy territory. Its travel policy arguably served similar functional and symbolic aims. A country with porous frontiers feels more strongly than other countries the need to control its official border crossings, which are potent symbols of sovereignty. This explains the reply made by Interior Minister Bar-Yehuda to a question about travel policy put to him by a Progressive member of the Knesset, Gershom Schoken, in 1956. Bar-Yehuda declared that "freedom of movement is assured . . . to every honest citizen . . . freedom—but not anarchy."[109] Bar-Yehuda's use of the term "anarchy" clearly indicated his feeling that it was imperative for the state to impose its authority over its borders.

EMIGRATION FROM ISRAEL

For the entire period during which Israeli citizens were required to obtain exit permits, the frequent amendments in policy were closely scrutinized by the press.[110] The issue was a crucial one not only for those seeking an exit permit, but for Israeli society as a whole. A certain proportion of those applying for permits never intended to return to Israel. And in this young state, built on an ideology of national solidarity, nearly everyone perceived emigration as a social ill.[111] In fact, mass immigration meant that Israel's rate of emigration never came close to representing a threat to the Zionist enterprise in the same way that, for example, it threatened the East German state.[112] Yet the vast majority of Israelis had left their former homes to escape persecution and adversity. Emigration from Israel was thus seen as an accusation that the Israeli state had failed to offer them an adequate haven. Consequently, it was execrated and seen as an assault on Jewish and Israeli identity. The negative view of emigration was related to the intensity of the nation-building project that Israeli society was undergoing, which at that time was at its height.

In a comparative study, Alan Dowty noted: "As national loyalty came to be perceived as the cement of society, emigration was increasingly regarded as deviant behavior. This became especially true as international differences sharpened along ethnic or ideological lines, making emigration seem almost traitorous."[113]

It was frequently alleged that easing exit permit restrictions would encourage emigration.[114] This view was shared by Jewish organizations seeking to stanch Jewish remigration to Europe. They too pressured the Israeli government to prevent emigration.[115] The Israeli police, like their counterparts in other countries, tracked travel agencies, which, it was believed, promoted not just travel but emigration as well.[116]

Nonetheless, other than during periods of hostilities, Israel did not stop emigrants from leaving, provided that they were not subject to military conscription, had returned or refunded the value of any material benefits received from the government, did not owe taxes, and—later on—provided proof that they had been granted an appropriate entry visa to their intended country of emigration.[117] This declared policy seems to have been implemented in practice, with only a few exceptions.[118] While the conditions it imposed discouraged emigration, leaving the country for good was not barred outright. Israel's concern about emigration is understandable, but it is difficult to explain why this should have affected Israelis who intended to leave the country only temporarily.

As noted above, there was considerable discrepancy between the number of Israelis who declared their intention to emigrate and those who actually did so. Many people who sought to leave the country preferred to declare on their application forms for exit permits that they were going on a trip and planned to return.[119] While avoiding the censure of their peers was certainly one motivation, there were others as well. By concealing their plans to leave the country for good, people could continue to enjoy the material aid that the state provided to immigrants and evade the requirement that they refund such assistance, as emigrants were required to do.

This in and of itself gave the state good reason to be suspicious of applicants for exit permits and to seek to discern their real intentions. Another reason was that emigrants often left behind relatives they had supported, and who after their departure would become wards of the state. The government thus had a manifest financial interest in regulating travel.[120]

Nevertheless, the government did not wish to prohibit emigration or impose overly onerous sanctions on those who sought to leave the country.

Such a policy would discourage immigration, especially from the West. Furthermore, many leaders believed that it would exacerbate the social unrest that had manifested itself as riots in immigrant neighborhoods. Such a policy would also harm Israel's relations with the Western democracies that were its most important allies, not to mention tarnishing the new country's image of itself as a democracy that guaranteed the individual freedom of its citizens. Travel and emigration restrictions were a trademark of Soviet communism, a label most Israeli leaders sought to avoid — as Minister of Education Shazar's use of the term "iron curtain" during a cabinet meeting in 1950 clearly indicated.[121]

POLITICS

Policymakers' privileging of the public interest over individual freedoms was in part a product of the socialist ideologies of Mapai and its sometime allies from the left, Mapam and 'Ahdut Ha'avodah. But this factor should not be overstated. Mapai was a "big tent" party that included people of many different outlooks. Furthermore, the positions the party took at any given time were considerably influenced by contemporary circumstances and political calculations. Mapai's platforms had to be responsive to a multitude of needs: those of the state, the public (even if these were psychological and not physical needs), the party, the coalition, and specific cabinet ministers. Mapai attempted to find a balance among conflicting interests. The fluctuations in travel policy reflected its constant attempts to balance its differing goals and personalities over time. Nonetheless, three things remained constant. First, the government — both elected officials and members of the civil service — recognized, in principle, that citizens had a fundamental right to travel abroad. Second, citizens pressured the government to be allowed to travel. Third, Mapai had to face the voters periodically, and political expedience dictated a more liberal regime.

The campaign for freedom of travel abroad was joined by politicians from nearly all political parties. But it was the Progressive Yizhar Harari who led the charge and made this his signature issue. Much of the time — though not always, and not always with the same fervor that he demonstrated — he enjoyed the support of the other bourgeoisie party, the General Zionists. Harari maintained that the state existed for the benefit of its citizens, not vice versa. His focus on the individual[122] was diametrically opposed to the authoritarian collectivist perspective voiced for the most part by figures on the socialist side of the political spectrum, such as Israel Bar-Yehuda, who held the interior portfolio for a time; Prime Minister and Defense Minister David Ben-Gurion, with his assertion that the country remained in a state of emergency that justified the suspension of some freedoms; Yitzhak Ben-Aharon, 'Ahdut Ha'avodah's leader;[123] and Shlomo Lavi of Mapai.[124]

IDEOLOGY AS MOTIVE

The Pioneering Spirit · Cabinet ministers and members of the Knesset, particularly those on the left, sought to maintain the ethos of frugality that had prevailed among the Jewish elite during the British Mandate. But the new State of Israel was rapidly evolving into an urban, industrialized, and technological society that viewed the old mores as anachronistic. The new generation sought to protect, flaunt, and enjoy their economic and symbolic capital. As most Israeli travelers were middle class, the assertion of the right to travel abroad must be understood against the backdrop of this socioeconomic conflict.[125] Minister of Rationing Dov Yosef objected to the government's policy and maintained that it prevented people with few means from traveling abroad. Mapai's goal was to keep divisions between social strata as small as possible. To balance the government's needs for taxes and levies from the public with the principle of equality, criteria were established to identify those with few means and those who needed to leave the country for health reasons, so as to enable them to travel. Nevertheless, the bulk of travelers continued to be people with means.

Harari and his bourgeois allies also demanded equality, although of a different type. He objected that emigrants found it easier than travelers to leave the country. Attempts to establish an equitable travel policy were unsuccessful. Nonetheless, the imposition of a hefty tax, and the fact that even in 1960 the number of travelers was less than those who traveled in 1946, testifies to an attempt to reach a compromise under which, while only a small minority of citizens traveled abroad, other Israelis benefited, at least in principle, from the taxes this minority paid.[126]

The New Jew · Unlike Britain and the United States, Israel was a new country in the process of nation building. National fervor over its collective narrative was at its height.[127] Policymakers, especially those who wished to restrict travel abroad, felt it was their duty to educate citizens to become loyal to the new state, even if it was necessary to use coercion.[128] This derived from both the needs of the state[129] and Zionist ideology, which aimed to create a society of New Jews in Israel, ones who had shed all identifying marks of their exile.

In my opinion, two images or contexts from European Zionist discourse were involved here. One came from general European medical discourse, which Zionist physicians adopted. The second was the Wandering Jew of Christian tradition. The use of the term "travelitis" as a term designating a typical Jewish malady derives from a widespread discourse that developed during the nineteenth century, largely in Germany, about the fundamental physical and mental nature of the Jew. This discourse depicted the Jews of Europe as being particularly susceptible to nervous ailments.[130] One of the most notable testimonies to the endurance of the negative image of the Wandering Jew is the use that modern Hebrew of the 1950s made of the word for "root." Jews who arrived in Israel from the Diaspora and transformed themselves into workers of the land were "rooted." The rooted Jew was the Zionist counter to the Wandering Jew. This language was especially prevalent in the labor movement.[131] "Travelitis," the disease or plague[132] of Israelis who wished to leave the country, was its polar opposite.[133]

In Zionist parlance, entry into and exit from Israel are not merely the prosaic acts of a person traveling to one country from another. In modern Hebrew, and especially the Hebrew of Israel's first decade, unique words designated the act of coming to and leaving Israel, emotionally charged terms with biblical resonances. Entering Israel is an "ascent" to the bosom of the motherland, whereas leaving or emigrating from Israel constitutes a "descent" from the greatest heights to the lowest depths. Absorption and acclimatization in the Land of Israel are seen, in Zionist ideology, concurrently as guaranteeing the Jewish people a safe refuge and ending their wanderings, and as a way of healing and regenerating the Jewish body and soul.[134] Thus "travelitis" was dangerous because the New Jew of Israel was supposed to be self-confident and self-sufficient. He (Zionist ideology focused on the Jewish male) should thus feel no need to travel. He did not need the culture and ambience of other countries because he was satisfied with and rooted in his own. A need to travel was seen as an expression of fear, a manifestation of low morale during periods of economic hardship or military challenges. The debate over leaving the country thus contained the image of the Wandering Jew, which offered another reason to restrict travel. "Travelitis" was dangerous because it called the image of the New Jew into doubt. The New Jew was meant to be fearless and self-confident. But in fact he was sometimes driven by an abandonment anxiety, fear that the Zionist project might fail because of poor morale in bad times, and a negative self-image deriving from the image of the old Jew he saw in the mirror. "Travelitis" was a disease attributed to the travelers, but it also expressed a fear of contagion. It was thus subversive on the functional level, but even more so on the symbolic level.

Just as the designers of the revolutionary calendar of 1793 sought to utterly revolutionize the concept of time in French culture and identity, so the Zionists sought to revolutionize the concept of Jewish place (as well as time). In this light, the requirement that citizens obtain not just a passport but also an exit permit to travel abroad can be seen on the one hand as an expression of a specific political approach and regime, and on the other hand as a kind of modern rite of initiation, a ritual that amplified the experience of leaving Israel for what Israelis today still refer to as simply *hutz la'aretz* (literally, "outside the land" — that is, the rest of the world outside Israel).[135] The ritual contains the ideological demand to remain in the country and adhere to its Israeli identity.[136] Part of this was an ideological imperative to maintain a separation from the Diaspora and its Jews, a subject I will take up below.

As the previous chapter showed, Israel's legal code was shaped in part by cultural and ideological views. These addressed the individual, the nation as a whole, and the regime that governed it. In my treatment of the Age of Marriage Law I recounted how women campaigned to get the law passed and instill in Israeli society the values it represented. They were motivated both by their desire to shape Israeli society and by their fear that, in the absence of an ongoing struggle against religious conservatism and political apathy, Israeli society would backtrack from the social progress that had been achieved under the British Mandate. Allowing underage girls to marry would not only hurt the girls but would also be a stain on the reformers.

In a similar way, "travelitis" was a threat not only to citizens but also to decision makers and to the Jewish Israeli collective as a whole. It was a contagious disease. It was thus subversive and destructive, on the symbolic as well as the functional level, because it was seen as undoing prior achievements and calling the entire Zionist revolution into question.

However, individual citizens who wished to travel abroad and had been denied an exit permit had naturally other concerns in mind.

Negotiating the Right to Travel

I am engaged to an Englishman who worked for the Jewish cause and who had to go home because his mother died and his father is very old and sick. I had five years ago a spinal operation which need a special treatment and a rupture operation which was a complete failure and must be done once more after I had for eight months an open wound. Ten weeks ago I applied for the permit to leave, and two days ago I got the answer "No Exit." What am I to do? . . . I am since 1944 engaged to an Englishman who can't come to Israel for private reasons. Besides I do need an operation which had been done here without success. Where is freedom and democracy which the Government had promised for the citizens of this country, if they won't let me go and marry to whom I belong and to give me the possibility to get healthy again. Which use am I to this country sick and unhappy?[137]

This impassioned letter to the editor from a woman named Edith L. was sent to the *Palestine Post* in June 1949. Rather than print it, the newspaper's editor, Gershon Agron—who also served as head of the government's Information Agency—forwarded it to Prime Minister David Ben-Gurion. Agron believed that it encapsulated much of the pain, anger, and frustration many Israelis felt at not being allowed to leave their newly born state. Edith L.'s letter shows that policymakers were well aware of the emotional and sometimes physical difficulties that national policies imposed on citizens. At this early juncture, however, policymakers often acted on the assumption that it was their responsibility to overlook rather than cater to the needs of individuals. With thousands of immigrants pouring out of ships and into immigrant camps daily, and with insufficient supplies of food, shelter, clothing, health care, education, and jobs for these new citizens, Israeli leaders believed, not without reason, that the only way to handle the country's pressing needs was by the pursuit of harsh and sometimes painful policies.

In writing her letter, Edith L. fought her battle alone—but she was one of many Israelis who did so.[138] These individual struggles produced a cumulative effect.[139] Because Israel was fundamentally democratic, disgruntled citizens were able to bring their displeasure over travel policy to the attention of policymakers, who eventually revised the rules.

In analyzing citizens' letters, one of my key assumptions is that, although citizens and government officials did not always have the same interests, they did share values, conventions, and what Luc Boltanski and Laurent Thévenot have called "regimes of justification."[140] When citizens argued that they had worthy reasons for traveling abroad, they justified their need with a set of values that was built into the social order and cultural repertoire of which both citizens and policymakers were a part.[141]

Beyond the immediate aims of these citizens' letters—namely, to obtain exit permits—the letters and the authorities' replies constitute an elementary form of direct interaction between state and citizen. An examination of such correspondence thus reveals more than the nature and operation of the regime — it also casts some light on what concepts of citizenship had been internalized by Israeli Jews.

At first, citizens who sought an exit permit needed a recommendation from a government ministry. Thus, letters to the prime minister and cabinet members abound. Some letters were submitted to cabinet members as a last resort, after an application and subsequent appeal had been rejected.[142]

Such personal letters often supplement an argument or justification with a narrative of the applicant's life. They employ one or more of the following strategies: they beg for help, appeal to the recipient's compassion, or threaten to file a lawsuit or attempt suicide; or they voice a grievance and denigrate a political figure, political party, or the government at large. They convey anger, frustration, despair, longing for relatives abroad, self-pity, and anxiety.[143]

In her book on pardon tales in sixteenth-century France, *Fiction in the Archives*, Natalie Zemon Davis explains what historians look for when they read centuries-old petitions. Traditionally, historians seek the truth, which they reveal by stripping texts of their fictional elements, leaving only the true core exposed. In fact, however, it is often difficult to reconstruct the truth behind an account of events offered by a document, especially documents of certain types. Nevertheless, historians can glean from documents information about such matters as rituals, customs, attitudes toward rulers, and acts of violence and revenge. In her perusal of pardon tales, Davis spotlights the literary aspects of the documents, in particular their narrative structures. "I think that we can agree with Roland Barthes, Paul Ricoeur, and Lionel Gossman," she writes, "that shaping choices of language, detail, and order are needed to present an account that seems to both writer and reader true, real, meaningful, and/or explanatory."[144] I follow her strategy here. That is, I consider the cultural context in which the letters and petitions are embedded; uncover, whenever I can, the truth behind the case; and consider the crafting of the narratives.

JUSTIFYING THE NEED TO TRAVEL

Businessmen who needed to travel abroad applied to any one of several ministries to endorse their application. For instance, a letter asking that Israeli employees of private importers be allowed to travel to Eritrea to supervise the kosher slaughter of animals was directed to the Ministry for Religious Affairs. Israel could not produce enough meat locally, so it had to be imported, either frozen or canned. Since some of Israel's Jews required kosher meat, and since places like Eritrea had no competent local Jewish religious authorities, the slaughter of the animals whose meat was to be sent to Israel had to be supervised by Israelis.[145]

Religion aside, the cultural repertoire of established Israelis was modernist and mainly Western.[146] From lawyers wishing to take summer classes in London to kibbutz members seeking to learn the latest dairy farming techniques,[147] Israelis believed that their personal trips abroad would serve the general good. Government agencies agreed that it was to the country's benefit to allow some professionals and students to travel overseas — primarily to Western countries — for educational purposes.[148] Applicants presented themselves as professionals aspiring to excel so as to improve Israel's society and economy.

Responding to a query submitted by two young lawyers, Haim Cohn, the attorney general, expressed his hope that in the near future, aspiring attorneys of their sort would be allowed to travel abroad. He regretted to tell them, however, that economic conditions did not yet permit such travel.[149] With this reply he offered a vision of the future as a counterweight to the hardships of the moment. The reply also reflects the attorney general's vision of a normal state, in which professionalism was not only a means of serving the public good, but also a worthy end in and of itself.

The authorities may have had good reason to doubt the sincerity of this request.[150] Perhaps the lawyers really needed additional legal training in London, but it could well be that they simply wanted to take a vacation in England. It would hardly be surprising if both motivations played a role. Most applicants applying for exit permits on the ground of their work sought to present their trip as one that would benefit not only them personally, but also the state and society. What stands out in the attorney general's reply is its evocation of a dissenting value system — one centered on the individual rather than the public good. Yet this remained a vision for the future.

The dire economic situation called for a different approach, and utilitarian thinking was much more commonplace, on the part of both letter writers and respondents, than ideas of personal improvement or professional excellence. For example, the famous Jungian psychologist Erich Neumann was granted an exit permit that enabled him to participate in the Eranos Foundation conference in Switzerland in 1951.[151] However, his wife, Julia, who was also a psychologist, was not allowed to accompany him. In support of the Neumanns' application, Minister of Justice Pinhas Rosen stressed to the minister of immigration that sales of Neumann's books abroad brought hard currency into Israel's coffers and that the cost of Julia Neumann's trip would be borne by the conference organizers and thus would not take any foreign currency out of Israel.[152] This case is an example of how, until the summer of 1952, permit requests were often refused even in cases when all costs (including fares) were prepaid by individuals or organizations abroad. In fact, some such sponsored trips were used as covers for large unapproved commercial transactions that circumvented austerity, foreign currency, and tax regulations. Presumably these transactions increased activity on the black market and pushed up the exchange rate there. They may also have exacerbated the problem of smuggling foreign currency out of the country. Such dealings could destabilize the value of Israeli currency at a time when the government sought to shore up its value at an official rate.[153]

In the end, Julia Neumann was granted an exit permit, on the grounds that she would be providing her husband with material assistance and that their work would contribute to the common good. Rosen may have had in mind Neumann's prominence or social worth as a scholar and professional. But most likely he thought that evoking the general good to justify Julia Neumann's trip would cast it in the most favorable light.

However, the general good is a fluid and amorphous concept that can be interpreted very broadly and differently by both citizens and bureaucrats. For example, an official in the Ministry of Internal Affairs' Department of Journalism, Propaganda, and Cinema recommended that an exit permit be granted to a producer of a movie titled *Moledet* (Motherland) because it was being made under the supervision of the department and the Jewish National Fund (an agency of the Zionist movement).[154] The official implied that the intended trip would promote the nation's ideological values. In addition, the fact that this movie was to be sent for screening abroad suggested prospects for financial gain.

When the Weizmann Institute of Science applied via official and unofficial channels (when a representative of the institute contacted a personal connection in the Ministry of Defense) for a professor of geophysics to be allowed to travel to the United States with his family to study oil exploration, it was presented as a once-in-a-lifetime opportunity that would benefit the state. Again, the emphasis was on the ability to gain practical knowledge of value to the national economy. The request was denied.[155] It seems reasonable to presume that the reason for the rejection was the applicant's wish to take his entire family with him, including his mother. This may have been taken to mean that at worst he might be intending to emigrate, or at best that he might easily be tempted not to return to Israel. Although there was no official rule against permitting entire families to travel, there is ample data showing that not allowing it was the de facto policy. Families were deliberately divided, unless members of the family stated explicitly that they wanted to leave the country for good.[156]

Freedom to leave the country, policymakers believed, had to be balanced against the state's interest in increasing its Jewish population. As noted above, emigrants resolved to leave for good were generally allowed to do so,[157] but leaders felt it was imperative to prevent the creation of situations in which travelers who had intended to return to Israel might be tempted to remain overseas permanently.

Since obtaining an exit permit required applicants to submit a detailed account of their reasons for wanting to travel and their plans for the trip, the system almost invited the authorities to study the day-to-day activities of citizens. And once the authorities looked closely, they grew suspicious. Israelis of the 1950s guarded their privacy far less than we do today, but that does not mean that some were not disconcerted by the near-absolute discretion granted to officials and politicians to pry into their personal lives.[158] The same was true of organizations, even large and powerful ones like the Histadrut. If such an organization applied for exit permits on behalf of employees or members, it was the government, not the organization, that had the final say in deciding whether the trip was germane to the organization's goals and requirements, and which employee or member would best serve the organization's needs by being granted an exit permit.[159]

Notably, letters submitted in cases relating to business or professional education were usually briefer than private requests for exit permits. The style of the former was more ceremonial, in accordance with the etiquette of formal letter writing, and they were typed rather than handwritten. Most important, they generally refrained from seeking to provoke an emotional response in the reader. They simply offered a coherent narrative — a clear purpose and a clear justification. Applications by private individuals were different in almost every respect. However problematic and difficult it was for organizations and professionals to negotiate their way through the bureaucratic maze, it was even more complicated for private citizens, most of whom lacked contacts, organizational support, and expertise.

Private citizens who applied for exit permits offered reasons for their travel that ranged from health problems to visiting elderly relatives and marriage plans. While these may all seem manifestly private matters, the fact is that citizens felt that they ought to present their planned trips as beneficial to the public.[160] In the Israeli context, personal status issues, such as marriage and divorce, had a public aspect. As noted above, under Israeli law, these matters fell under the sole purview of the Chief Rabbinate, rather than the civilian authorities. Jewish legal strictures could require a trip abroad to lay the groundwork for a marriage in Israel. For example, a citizen seeking to remarry might be required to produce a *get* (a Jewish writ of divorce) from a spouse not living in Israel. Other more obscure rituals could also be required, such as the *halitzah*, a ceremony in which a widow releases her brother-in-law from a legal obligation to marry her. Since these were religious matters, Israelis applying for exit permits when travel was needed for such a purpose were required to obtain a recommendation from the Ministry of Religions.[161] One typical case involved an immigrant from Turkey, who wrote the ministry:

> I have a sister in Turkey (Istanbul) and a few days ago a relative of mine came to Israel and brought terrible news . . . regarding my sister, who is about to marry a non-Jew in the next few days [not clear] I had no other alternative but to apply to your office so you could give me a recommendation for the Ministry of Immigration that will enable me to get an exit permit for Turkey so I will be able to prevent my sister from carrying out this humiliating act and from disgracing our family. . . . Please believe me that the fate of my sister and the honor of my family is in your hands.[162]

Significantly, the Ministry of Religions endorsed his application.[163] After all, it was not the applicant's marital or legal status that was at stake, but that of his sister — who was not an Israeli citizen. In other words, in the eyes of the relevant officials, the boundaries of the collective were not delimited by the borders of the state of Israel. The Jewish family and the greater worldwide Jewish collective mattered.[164]

The Diaspora supported Israel both on the national and personal levels. Jews around the world donated to Israeli organizations and charities and lent political support to Israel in the countries where they lived. Furthermore, Jews in the Diaspora sent money, food, and clothing to relatives in Israel who faced shortages in the strict austerity regime imposed after independence.[165] These overseas relatives and friends were valued but, at the same time, perceived as imminent dangers to the new country because of the questionable nature of their commitment to Zionism.[166] As one commentator noted caustically:

There is another factor [encouraging emigration from Israel]. Relatives abroad. This is an interesting [psychological] complex. . . . They sometimes walk around feeling that they have not done enough for their relatives who survived Hitler's inferno or another inferno, and they have yet another sense of guilt from which no Jew in the Diaspora is free, of having sinned by not immigrating to Israel, to support the frail state that indeed needs their support. What does a person like this do? He helps his relative in Israel emigrate to his own country and settle there with a good business. In an instant he gets rid of both feelings of guilt.[167]

One of the most common reasons offered by individuals seeking exit permits was to visit relatives abroad.[168] According to the government's criteria for permitting travel, this was not considered an adequate reason.[169]

When organizations submitted requests for an exit permit, it was the stated goal of the trip and its contribution to business, the economy, the organization, and the common good of the state and society that were expected to influence the application's outcome. Ordinary citizens employed other tactics to persuade the authorities.

Many such letters contained both stories of misfortune and references to the applicant's past—as opposed to future—contributions to the Zionist cause, Jewish state, or Jewish people. As in Edith L.'s letter, individuals often offered several justifications for their planned trip, as opposed to the single one generally asserted in applications coming from the companies and professionals. Edith states that she wants to find happiness, marry her fiancé, and seek medical treatment unavailable in Israel.[170] Although she demonstrates despair, anger, and frustration, Edith's common sense is clearly evident, and her judgment is not clouded by suffering. She does not explicitly demand the right to happiness. However, she claims that as long as she is sick and unhappy, she is obviously a burden on society rather than an asset to it. It seems that she wants to prove that allowing her to depart is in the state's best interest. She clearly realizes that it is society's best interests, rather than her own, that will determine whether she may travel abroad.

The primary reason she offers for her need to travel is her desire to marry and regain her health. She seeks to establish an empathic connection with her readers and feels that she is justified in demanding the opportunity to marry. While only implicitly, Edith L. also clearly believes that she has a right to be happy and that her readers will accept this as a legitimate reason for travel. Since private letters sometimes reflect a writer's free-form internal narrative of his or her own life, it is possible that Edith's final plea—in which she argues that granting her permission to leave the country would ultimately contribute to the public good—indicates the disparity between the flow of her narrative and her sudden awareness at the end of the letter of the need to include this vital justification somewhere in the request.[171]

Another letter writer, Gershon M., a war veteran who had been wounded in an accident during his military service and subsequently suffered a major nervous breakdown, stated in a letter to the Minister of War Victims that he needed to leave the country to seek medical attention and convalesce under his sister's care in the United States: "I have been left with no succor. My health is deteriorating as every day goes by. Bad thoughts fill my mind and urge me to kill myself, but I know that I should not do so. I am a Zionist, who worked so much for the Zionist ideal, and dreamed so much about this country, is it really the case that no one is interested in me . . . [?] I plead for someone to take an interest in my fate."[172]

Letter writers cast themselves in stock roles: the feeble, the unfortunate, and the veteran who has paid his dues to society.[173] Obviously, some writers combine several characteristics. Gershon M. says he is feeble and suicidal. But he also repeatedly describes himself as a Zionist activist, apparently assuming that his past contributions to the Zionist collective have earned him the right to be heard. Furthermore, he suggests that his past commitment to the Zionist ideology and military service should earn him the right to travel abroad. Yet his narrative is rife with contradictions. On the one hand, he presents himself as worthy; on the other hand, he declares himself to be mentally ill, and thus worthless to the Zionist state. This strategy is similar to that employed by Edith at the end of her letter. Although it is not clear whether Gershon was allowed to travel (the Ministry of War Victims replied to him that the matter of exit permits was outside its purview), this contradiction presumably did not serve him well; bureaucratic logic requires clarity and coherence. Letters such as Gershon's and official responses to them make it possible to reconstruct contemporary Israeli society's scale of worth. They show that past or current work for the Zionist cause was, in fact, a prerequisite for securing an exit permit.

In theory, a substantial need, such as a genuine health problem, or a certain prospect of benefiting the state were basic values that state officials were supposed to consider when granting an exit permit. Nevertheless, in practice, when private citizens applied in writing, they often conveyed the assumption that foreign travel was a right one had to earn, or even a privilege granted to those who had proved sufficient loyalty.[174] An extraordinary story illustrates this point. Aviva K. E., a widow who had recently lost her husband on the battlefield, wrote to Ben-Gurion in the midst of the 1948 war:

> I am writing to you hoping you will assist [me in] my request. I left my father's home in Belgium and immigrated . . . in 1946. I have studied at the Hebrew University and I was a member of the Haganah. From the beginning of hostilities I took part in guard duties in and around Jerusalem. . . . During the first cease-fire I moved to Tel Aviv for health reasons . . . started working . . . and after a few days a terrible disaster befell me when my husband . . . was killed. . . . I stopped working and since then I have had a deep emotional need to see my parents and spend a short while at home. Obviously after the visit I will return and continue where I have left off. Over the past three months I have contacted various ministries. At first I encountered a lack of understanding everywhere. Later, when they finally understood my mental state, they promised to help me. But so far I have not received an exit permit. I am imploring you to understand my urgent need to travel abroad and meet my parents. I know that your daughter faced a similar misfortune and that you will understand how I feel.[175]

Aviva presents herself as a defender of Jerusalem, a student, and a worker, all roles of a loyal and worthy citizen. She articulates very clear plans: after a visit abroad with her parents, she intends to come back to Israel and benefit her country and society. The loss she experienced and her emotional state make her deserving of an exit permit at a time when such permits were granted in very limited numbers.[176] Aviva includes one fact in her letter that could be construed as a contradiction: the fact that she left Jerusalem during the war and moved to Tel Aviv for health reasons. While this could cast doubt on her loyalty and resilience, she overlooks this inconsistency.

Another case of incongruity in a citizen's account of herself is the case of Rita V. There are several documents in this case: her own correspondence, a letter written by a lawyer on her behalf, formal documents regarding the loss of her apartment and her belongings, and a letter supporting her request from the minister of justice to the minister of immigration. This correspondence suggests that, in most cases, a successful application required a life story stripped of contradictions.

> In June I requested permission to travel to Germany to visit my mother, who resides in Berlin and is very ill. . . . My mother is my only relative

who survived the Holocaust. My father and my only brother perished at Auschwitz. . . . I was informed, that the government in principle does not give such permits to visit relatives, but I strongly request that in my case the extraordinary circumstances be taken into consideration. For my sick mother I am the only one, and the last hope of her miserable life is my coming to see her before she passes away. And I too, after having had all my other close relatives taken away from me, would sacrifice everything to see my sick mother. I am afraid that if I had to inform my mother, who has been expecting my arrival for a long time, that I am not allowed to visit her, she would be unable to live with this disappointment because of her poor health.[177]

Rita added that if she were granted the right to leave for Germany, she would attempt to salvage some of the family's property in both West and East Germany. Visiting Germany was a very sensitive issue at that time, so soon after the Holocaust. In principle, Israelis were not allowed to travel to Germany, and Israeli passports included a proclamation stating that they were valid for all countries except Germany.[178]

Rita's initial application was denied. Like other citizens who received the same answer, she fought to have the decision reversed. Avraham Landsberg—a lawyer and, like Rita, a member of the Progressive Party—wrote on her behalf to Minister of Justice Pinhas Rosen, who shared the same party affiliation. Landsberg speculated in his letter that her application had been rejected because, prior to the War of Independence, she had lived with a non-Jewish Turkish national who worked for Shell Oil. When the war broke out, he had been transferred to Transjordan. Perhaps, Landsberg suggested, the authorities were suspicious that she might reestablish contact with him.[179]

Rosen took up her cause. "Rita V.," he wrote to the director general of the Ministry of Immigration, "is an honest and unfortunate woman, who barely supports herself through physical labor, after having lost all of her possessions when her apartment was destroyed and her belongings stolen in Bat Yam during the war."[180]

Thanks to Rosen's intervention, Rita was granted an exit permit.[181] Was she initially turned down because she wished to travel to Germany, or was it due to the Turkish lover who could have compromised her patriotism? Or maybe visiting an old mother who had survived the Holocaust was simply not considered a good enough reason for foreign travel? Perhaps the real obstacle was the arguments that Rita made in her letter. She wrote at length about her mother's pressing emotional need as well as her own. She was not going to get married or receive medical treatment; rather, she was concerned about her elderly mother, who was not an Israeli citizen. It looks as if her "worthier" reason for traveling—salvaging property—was tacked on just to please the authorities. Given the categories of legitimate reasons for travel laid out by the authorities, and the fact that elderly people were generally considered a burden and were therefore allowed to exit the state easily, it seems likely that catering to the needs of an elderly Jewish woman beyond Israeli borders was not a priority.

The former Turkish lover did not appear in Rita's letter or in that of Rosen. Rosen, in fact, rewrote her story, presenting Rita as a war victim who had lost not only her apartment but all of her personal belongings as well. He tried to transform her life story by stressing how much she had suffered. Depicting her as a person who had shared the burden of the efforts leading up to the birth of the state, he declared that she had proved her loyalty.[182]

In a long and detailed letter, Guta R., a widow and a sister of a Holocaust survivor, implores the authorities to allow her to travel abroad to visit her dying brother. She seems to have sensed a personal lack of social capital or service to Zionism and Israel. Rather than recount her own life story, she offers in brief the life stories of her deceased husband and another brother, both of whom had dedicated themselves to the Zionist enterprise as members of kibbutzim and the Histadrut, and through their work as pioneers. She also mentions that her son would be enlisting in the Israel Defense Forces just a few weeks later. Guta employs an apologetic tone when mentioning that the brother she wishes to visit in Sweden had not immigrated to Israel, explaining that he could not have done so because he had been diagnosed with cancer.[183] She frames her narrative to suit socialist-Zionist ideology. Like other women, especially married ones, she hides herself, her life story, and her contribution to family and society behind the supposedly real actions of the Zionist men in her life.

Joseph and Theah L., born and raised in Germany, wanted to travel to Germany to visit an elderly uncle, a Holocaust survivor, and salvage family property. They stated in their letter:

I, Dr. Joseph L., . . . made aliyah [immigrated] to this country twenty years ago, after which I established and ran the Ben-Yehuda high school in Tel Aviv. I traveled abroad in 1938 . . . as an emissary of the school and the Va'ad

Leumi [National Council, the Jewish quasigovernment in Palestine], to prepare the aliyah of children threatened by the Nazis. Since then I have not left the country.

And I, Theah L., . . . left Germany in 1932 and worked continuously in the Jewish community's hospital in Alexandria until I made aliyah in 1947. I never went abroad throughout this period.[184]

This couple touted their devotion to the Zionist project in two ways. They cited their history of public involvement and noted that they had remained in the country continuously for many years. Their letter demonstrates that applicants for exit permits realized that they needed to demonstrate that they did not suffer from "travelitis."[185] Frequent travel could be seen as a symptom of disloyalty and adherence to the norms of the Diaspora rather than to those of the rooted New Jews of Israel.[186] In a similar case, a student studying in Britain asked the prime minister to allow his wife and newborn son to join him. In his letter, he told Ben-Gurion about his military service and stressed that his wife, who had been living with him in Britain, had returned to Israel to give birth to their son, so that he could be born on Israeli soil.[187]

Government officials and most citizens shared a fundamental assumption that every Israeli had to bear some of the burden of building the new state and society. It went without saying that everyone had to make sacrifices, even if there were differences of opinion about what sacrifices could be required or expected of individuals. Jews who had lived as part of the Yishuv in Palestine before the creation of the Israeli state felt a sense of belonging to their community, perhaps even a sense of intimacy.[188] Paying one's dues to society was an expression of compliance with hegemonic values, but it was also an act of comradeship and solidarity within a small community. Because most Jews felt that they had a stake in the Zionist project, they had no compunctions about penning angry letters to officials or even about making threats. In one such case, Aharon S., a sabra (native-born Israeli) and a wounded veteran of the 1948 war—threatened, when his application to travel to France for a three-month convalescence was denied, to convert to Christianity. His letter to the minister of religions voices his frustration and anger at having, in his view, been betrayed by the society he had fought to defend.[189] This was not the only time an angry or disappointed Israeli threatened to convert to Christianity. Indeed, many did convert and received exit permits because they were no longer considered Jewish. Thus, it was an intention that policymakers took quite seriously.[190]

The letters quoted above paint a picture of a society in which citizens perceived that certain rights were conditional on the fulfillment of obligations. Such circumstances, in which rights are available only to those who can prove that they have been loyal citizens, are inconsistent with the classic liberal concept of society. The cases cited above also show that even past contributions to society could be trumped by the state's current needs, in particular for foreign currency. In this sense, Israel adhered more to the socialist model characteristic of the Soviet bloc than to the Western democratic template.[191] But the comparison with nondemocratic states can be misleading, because it is only partly valid. In Israel, citizens did not always feel bound to advertise their compliance or genuine loyalty to the reigning ideology and regime. Liberal Western ideas were well rooted in the bourgeoisie and had much currency in other socioeconomic strata as well. As a result, some citizens felt at liberty to demand their rights. For example, a father who requested an exit visa for his sixteen-year-old son to visit his uncle wrote an angry letter to the Ministry of Immigration: "I was told that if my son saw his uncle two years ago there is no need for him to see his uncle now, in my opinion these reasons are not justified. The state has no business interfering in family matters and also the state should not forbid my son to visit his uncle . . . because our country is a Western-style democratic country."[192]

In yet another case, an attorney named H. Schneider wrote to the Ministry of Defense on behalf of his client: "In my opinion, not only does the person in question have to give the young state whatever it requires, without further delay, but for its part our government and all of its representatives and institutions must protect [its] citizens' rights and help them get what they [rightfully] deserve. This is why I request that you grant my client what he demands [an exit permit] as soon as possible because he cannot do his duty if his national polity [the State of Israel] does not do its duty to him."[193] Note the reversal here: the applicant demands that his rights be respected as a condition for the fulfillment of his obligations to the state. In another case, a citizen wrote (in imperfect English) to the minister of immigration:

> From all what we have seen until now it is clear that Israel is taking the shape of a genuine totalitarian State, be it à la Hitler or à la Stalin, in many considerations of which we are going to touch only one, namely the migration policy. There are thousands of cases and even more throughout Israel where

people *have* to go for obvious reasons abroad. . . . If we shall deduct the visas granted for missionary purposes (*shlihut*) and "*proteczia*" [personal connections], we are really wondering how many visas were left for mere mortals, if any at all. . . . These people [veteran Israelis who immigrated during the prestate era] came here at their own free will with no help from the Jewish Agency here or abroad and you have no right whatsoever to dictate them to stay here when they have to go abroad. . . . These regulations have to be withdrawn and immediately, thus to prevent encroachment on the rights and liberties of the people.[194]

This writer clearly rejects the collectivist ethos and decouples rights from duties. He also clearly believes that he is speaking on behalf of other Jewish citizens.

Some Israelis did not just write to the authorities or hire attorneys to write on their behalf. They went to court — and in the courtroom the state did not always have the upper hand.[195] Other citizens complained to their relatives abroad, leading to public outcries overseas that embarrassed the new country. A few Israeli newspapers adopted the issue as their own, reporting frequently about individual cases and sharply criticizing the government's travel policy and its implementation.[196]

CITIZENS CHANGE POLICY

The letters quoted above enable us to grasp the values shared by Israelis in the country's early years and to hear the frustrations and anger of individual citizens as they employ rhetoric and various means of justification in their efforts to break through the thicket of regulations and bureaucracy that kept them from traveling abroad.

The letters display different value systems. In those penned by businessmen and professionals, the values cited are profit and professional advancement. In cases relating to personal status in the Jewish family, the values appealed to are the sustainability and future growth of the Jewish people. The private interests and, especially, the emotional needs cited by citizens wishing to connect with relatives abroad were harder to justify. In part, this was because these situations highlighted the fraught relationship between Jews in Israel and their relatives abroad. Although some government ministers thought that reuniting people with their family members was a valid reason for granting an exit permit, for the most part the government did not view this as a priority.[197] In fact, Israeli officials largely disregarded manifestly personal needs in formulating and implementing travel policies. This was eloquently expressed by K. Shabtai (the pen name of Shabtai Klugman) in the daily newspaper *Davar*:

> Two Jews, whom I very much doubt had ever met each other . . . told me the same thing using the exact same words. Here [in this country], they said, we know how to do things on a large scale: how to build a cooperative, how to establish a moshav, how to bring in hundreds of thousands of Jews. But we know nothing about taking care of a person, how to reach the individual, how to share his grief, how to lend a hand in bad times, how to cheer him up, how to buck him up . . . when the wind has blown down his shack and his spirits are low.[198]

Through their pleas, letters, and lawsuits, which together constitute a sort of unorganized collective, individual citizens were able to mitigate their country's travel policy to a certain extent. Even when their individual voices fell on deaf ears, as a collective their voices were heard and their frustration answered. In the summer of 1952, the government tweaked its policy so that Israelis whose travel fare and expenses were covered by relatives and acquaintances abroad were granted exit permits. (Those who needed foreign currency to cover their travel expenses were subject to much more scrutiny.) This change made it easier to obtain an exit permit for personal reasons than for business trips — the latter, even when expenses were covered from overseas, still required a recommendation letter from a government ministry (although criteria were loosened in these cases as well).[199]

While citizens' appeals to the authorities in Israel may resemble to a certain extent appeals in the Soviet bloc, it seems likely that there was far less dissimulation in Israel.[200] True, Israelis sensed that the authorities expected them to present their requests in the context of a Zionist narrative, and doing so necessitated concealing or avoiding contradictions between the real needs they felt and the way they thought that their cases had to be presented for their applications to be successful. But this can be interpreted in two ways. First, a kind of coercion is found in authoritarian regimes, with the citizen feeling obliged to present a story that is basically false. There may well have been many cases like that in Israel, but the second way is that in many other cases it seems likely that the letter writers genuinely felt that their appeals were opportunities to convey their devotion to their country and their personal involvement in building and defending it, thus highlighting their sense of belonging to the collective.

Up to this point, I have, for the most part, discussed policymakers and officials as if they existed in a separate sphere from individual citizens. To obtain an exit permit, Israelis needed a recommendation from a government ministry. As a result, they sent letters to the relevant officials or sometimes even to cabinet ministers. High-ranking officials were thus often, if not daily, confronted with the trials and tribulations of ordinary citizens. This was reflected in the mind-set of some policymakers. In the cabinet meeting in July 1950 mentioned above, at which the Finance Ministry's recent order to travel agents to refrain from selling tickets came up for discussion, Rosen told his colleagues: "There is hardly a Jew that does not have relatives overseas and why should it be a crime if he goes once every ten years to see his relatives? It is inhuman not to allow such a trip. We cannot shut the country's gates permanently. Such trips cannot, of course, be considered vital. Why is it vital to visit a relative? ... It [the policy] is very harsh and inhuman."[201] Rosen here expressed the resentment felt by his constituency and many other citizens. The letters thus served as a means by which the weak could influence the powerful, a way of amplifying individual voices, and a channel of communication between citizen and state. These individual appeals had a cumulative impact. In their fight to make the government more responsive to their personal needs these individual citizens demanding their rights[202] were joined by other actors — including middle-class professionals,[203] Jews living abroad, and interest groups such as travel agents,[204] political parties,[205] and segments of the press.[206]

In September 1951 the Knesset was preparing to debate the exit permit issue. Yohanan P. wrote to Israel Rokach, a member of the General Zionist Party and the Knesset, asking him to "protest also against this [phenomenon]: an entire state has become a prison or a concentration camp for the citizens, who have committed no crime and done no evil."[207]

Nearly a year later, in June 1952, a senior Israeli diplomat stationed in Brussels reported to his colleagues that Belgian Jews were jokingly referring to Israel's exit permit requirement as the "Israeli iron curtain."[208] The Belgians were hardly alone — recall that Zalman Shazar had made the same comparison two years previously. Haim-Moshe Shapira — who, as minister of immigration, was responsible for implementing the exit policy — did the same at a session of the Knesset's Internal Affairs Committee, arguing that the exit permit policy was tarnishing Israel's reputation. Another member of the Knesset at the meeting lamented the psychological damage caused by the policy.[209] Two weeks later, as part of the ongoing public debate, Eliezer Livneh, a member of Mapai and the Knesset, voiced similar sentiments in an article published in the *Jerusalem Post*: "Knowing that one may not proceed abroad at will creates a feeling of frustration and confinement. . . . The idea that a certain government department is empowered to decide whether one's journey is 'essential' or not, and by such token to determine one's freedom of movement, is antidemocratic at the root. The citizen must be left to decide whether his journey is necessary or not. Freedom of movement is vital to every free man."[210]

Cabinet ministers who overtly opposed the exit permit policy, Minister of Justice Rosen and Minister of Immigration, Health, and Internal Affairs Shapira chief among them,[211] were reluctant to enforce the letter of the law and did all they could to help citizens who, while they might not meet the formal criteria, nevertheless deserved — so the ministers thought — to travel. Shapira said so explicitly at a cabinet meeting: "I should say that when I came under severe pressure, I became a bit lenient — for instance, if someone had resided here for ten or fifteen years and had not met with his family abroad, and his family sent him a round-trip ticket, [and] the family pledged that all the costs of the visit abroad would be at its expense — maybe [the trip] was not really essential, but it was a very human [need], and when I could not face the pressure, I gave an exit permit."[212] Ministers thus bent and some-times broke rules they themselves had played a role in making. As critics of the policy, they served as a mouthpiece for the citizen's point of view, and in doing so they promoted change.

In fact, reservations about the exit permit requirement had been raised within government circles from the beginning. As early as August 1949, Wal-ter Eytan, the director general of the Foreign Ministry, wrote to his minister, Moshe Sharett, criticizing the exit permit policy. He claimed that forbid-ding travel to citizens whose relatives abroad were prepared to cover all their expenses created "bitterness toward the state and the government." He also thought that it was a public scandal that citizens with a shady background were being allowed to exit the country at a time when upstanding Israelis were having their applications to do so turned down.[213]

A year later, Eytan wrote another memo. Although he was deeply con-cerned about the weakness of Israel's currency,[214] he thought that persuasion would be a better way than regulation to reduce the appetite for foreign travel. He also recommended that reasonably priced cruises be offered to the public on Israeli liners sailing around the Mediterranean Sea—which would cost little foreign currency and offer a form of relief.[215]

. . . .

Israeli law formally recognized the right to travel as a natural right only in 1953.[216] However, most decision makers and officials had previously recognized the right to travel in principle and wished to emulate Western, rather than Soviet bloc, models of travel policy. The authorities nonetheless believed that Israel's precarious economic and security situation during its early years made limits on foreign travel imperative.

The methods chosen were ones already in place and used by other Western countries. The requirement of an exit permit relied on the British Mandate precedent, which dated from 1939. Severe restrictions on the amount of foreign currency that could be taken out of the country emulated the British model and was deemed effective.[217] Imposition of a travel tax was justified by the fact that the United States had done the same thing. On other major issues (the austerity program, economic intervention, and absence of a constitution), Israeli policymakers viewed Britain as a model. The fact that Britain allowed citizens to leave the country freely and only regulated the purchase and use of foreign reserves served as a catalyst or motivator to an easing of the exit policies in Israel.[218]

In all three democratic models, war and economic troubles tightened the ties between state and citizen. But economics and security were only part of the picture. The legislation and enforcement of travel restrictions clearly served not only to meet functional or emergency needs, but also to define the model Israeli citizen and his or her affiliation to the collective. The restrictions provided what John Torpey has termed the controlling embrace of a state in designing such identity.[219]

In the United States, travel policy, as part of the larger struggle against the internal communist threat, was one way that American society sought to draw a clear line between patriotic and allegedly disloyal citizens, whether communists or fellow travelers.[220] In Britain, compliance with both the austerity program and restrictions on foreign currency was seen as a demonstration of understanding of the country's pressing needs and an indication of patriotism and of solidarity with the state and all of its citizens.[221]

Israeli policy was revised frequently, whether via changes in the law or in regulations or simply by the use of different standards of enforcement. These changes depended on objective circumstance; subjective interpretations of the country's economic, social, and security position; the social and political beliefs of the relevant politicians and officials; foreign policy considerations; the fear of losing the votes of unhappy citizens; and Israel's ongoing metamorphosis into a more liberal society. In accordance with Western democratic ideals, Israeli citizenship was perceived, at least in principle, to be a matter of choice.[222] In this framework, it was permissible for the state to make multiple demands on its citizens — in the form of military service, high taxes, and austerity programs — as long as people could leave if they wished. At the same time, the country's commitment in principle to free Jewish immigration, along with its unsecured borders that permitted Arab infiltration, led decision makers to feel that Israel's physical and psychological borders had to be defended. The nascent society and its policymakers sought to hone its collective identity and its political and social boundaries.[223]

Relatives abroad were seen as a source of support both for Israel as a whole and for their Israeli family members in particular, but overseas family members were also looked on with concern and suspicion. David Hacohen, a member of Mapai and the Knesset, voiced such fears in a meeting of the Internal Affairs Committee in May 1953:

> I have already expressed my opinion in the past . . . regarding the exit permit [policy]. . . . I have expressed my doubts about the absolute freedom that some want to grant in this area at this time. . . . What about foreign currency abroad? How . . . will a person who goes abroad without foreign currency maintain himself? What will he do to obtain currency? The state must know how its citizens behave abroad . . . and the state is entitled to know and should know. . . . Also, state security conditions require the isolation of its citizens. In a situation where so many Israeli citizens have connections with foreign citizens we have to do all we can to thwart illicit relationships.[224]

New national entities often feel the need to justify their separation and distinction from other nations. The Israeli case presents a particularly thorny example, with the country seeking simultaneously to provide a home for all Jews and to differentiate itself from the Jews of the Diaspora.[225] Citizens who wanted to travel abroad, in particular those seeking to visit relatives or deal with marital and personal legal issues, posed a threat to this need for separation. When they presented themselves as connected, related, or close to their relatives abroad, they signified the importance of Jews living outside the country, blurring the separation between them and Israelis and linking Israel's Jews inexorably to their old Diasporic identities.

Some applicants underscored the fact that they had not left the land of Israel for a long time. Not only was this proof of their loyalty, but it may also have implied that Israel and the cultural repertoire it offered immunized them against the temptations of the Diaspora. This immunity was especially important for a state in which so many citizens were new immigrants and had had relatively little time to acculturate themselves and gain a sense of belonging to Israel. A prolonged stay in the Land of Israel also promised immunity against "travelitis," with its connotations of rootless Diasporic Jewish existence. Israeli Jews had to be quarantined, it was felt, to avoid infection with this malady.

Finally, citizens' letters were a powerful tool for conveying criticism, demanding rights, or merely voicing despair and frustration. Because Israel was a state in the making and because the regime was seeking legitimacy beyond what it garnered in the polls, policymakers based their actions not only on explicit policy but also on their individual political needs and consciences. In a democracy — even a new and imperfect one, as Israel was at the time — this pursuit of legitimacy could yield change.

CHAPTER THREE

. . . .

Craving Recognition

A STATEMENT OF personal grievance appeared in July 1949, just after the end of the War of Independence, in *Hador*, the daily newspaper published by Mapai:

> The undersigned is a new immigrant, and with great sorrow says what he saw with his own eyes: there is discrimination, and to a certain extent even disregard, toward people whose only sin is that they responded immediately to the state's call . . . after enduring all the seven circles of hell of covert immigration, deportation to Cyprus, concentration camps, and last but not least — participating in Israel's war of freedom in blood and in soul . . . I do not see an effort being made by the members of the established Yishuv to minimize the suffering of . . . the new immigrants, when all they want is to live human lives . . . and here every new immigrant still has to fight — for what? For a smidgen of warmth and emotion, for some sort of understanding of his situation, for his opposition to discrimination and condescension.[1]

The author was Avraham Avtalyon, a new immigrant from Bulgaria. Avtalyon exposed the enormous distance between the Zionist ideal and the social milieu of postwar Israel. He had expected closeness and warmth from the Jewish society that was taking him in, but he had been bitterly disappointed. Instead, he felt hurt, slighted, and frustrated. Avtalyon was just one out of hundreds of thousands destitute immigrants who experienced material hardship, contempt, and emotional distress.

In telling Avtalyon's story, the reporter who introduced him to *Hador*'s readers took the opportunity to remind them, loyal supporters of the ruling party, of how central the principle of equality was to the new country. The reporter demanded that equality be pursued in everyday life: "If I correctly understand what is written in Israel's Declaration of Independence, and the things said time and again by this new immigrant from Bulgaria ... I permit myself to ask openly: Are those responsible for public affairs really and genuinely precluding the risk that many of the new immigrants will be reduced to the status of second-class citizens? Are they doing everything to educate not only the Diaspora, but also the Yishuv, to carry out, in practice, its obligations to the new immigrants?"[2] In these two passages, both an immigrant from Bulgaria and a journalist, the latter a longtime member of the Yishuv, demand that veteran Israelis recognize that the new immigrants had no less of a stake in the new state than they did, and that the immigrants should thus by right be treated as equals. But there are differences in language and tone between the two texts. The immigrant demanded that people pay attention not only to his grievances about the actions of the state and society but also to the emotional needs of immigrants. Those responsible for his absorption into Israeli society were expected to display empathy. In making this claim, he voiced one of the important emotional aspects of the intention to establish a Jewish nation-state. Avtalyon sought more than the formal right to participate in the decision-making process. He expected to be involved in a profound, personal, and compassionate dialogue between the individual immigrant and the society taking him in. And he expected this dialogue to establish a feeling of emotional intimacy and mutual connection and — more than anything else — to give him a sense of belonging.

Immigration, Voice, and Recognition

The implication of Avtalyon's text was that the cure for his distress and loneliness was what Axel Honneth calls recognition (*Anerkennung*).[3] According to Honneth, each experience of social humiliation is accompanied by negative moral emotions such as indignation, shame, and guilt.[4] Avtalyon reported his negative experiences of being discriminated against and disparaged; he rose up against the established order and sought warmth and emotion.

One might think that the very fact that the immigrant's letter was printed in the ruling party's newspaper was an act of recognizing him and the justice of his claims.[5] But did this restore his personal dignity and provide a remedy for his dejection? Presumably not. It seems proper to view the granting of recognition as an ongoing process and not a one-time event.[6]

Since the French Revolution, the ability to voice one's thoughts has been bound up in the question of listening and the feasibility of dialogue.[7] Yet the discussion of voice in the framework of freedom of expression has largely not taken into account all the human needs that lie at the base of the demand to be heard.[8] For the most part, the right to freedom of expression is considered a negative right, aimed at removing restrictions and allowing opinions to be voiced. The right to be heard, however, is a positive right, requiring society, and policymakers in particular, to make an effort to listen.[9] It represents a human need to be recognized, a need that cannot be fully guaranteed by any law or constitution.[10] It demands that society and governing bodies see it as their duty to ensure that individuals do well and flourish in the most fundamental way — in their self-perceptions.[11]

At the foundation of the common liberal approach, which focuses on negative rights, is the atomistic concept of the individual as an independent unit who connects to other such units only in instrumental ways. The supporters of this approach maintain that social struggles are conducted only in relation to common interests.[12] In contradiction of this view, the concept of recognition is widely used in current social thinking, where the demand for recognition is seen as not only pertaining to the individual's interests but as also touching on the kernel of the individual's identity. This approach suggests that social relations effect one's valuation of oneself and one's identity. What stands out in this approach is the profound need for belonging, consideration, respect, and appreciation from the society and its policymakers.[13]

The two texts in *Hador* portray a trio of actors — immigrants, established Israelis whose duty it is to absorb the immigrants into the country, and policymakers. This chapter of the book is devoted to the relationships among these three groups and the immigrants' demand for recognition.

IMMIGRATION AND ABSORPTION IN THE 1950S

Between November 1948, when the first Israeli census was conducted, and May 1961, when the second one was held, Israel's Jewish population grew by 1,215,679 people. Of the 1,932,357 Jewish citizens counted in the 1961 census, 880,579 — nearly half — had immigrated since the state was founded (see Table 3.1).[14]

In comparison, the number of immigrants who entered Israel during this period approached the number that entered the major immigration-absorbing countries during the two decades following World War II. During that twenty-year period, the United States took in about a quarter of a million immigrants per year, Canada took in 120,000–140,000 per year, and Australia took in about 100,000 per year. Israel, a much smaller country, took in almost as many immigrants per year between May 15, 1948, and December

TABLE 3.1 · Jewish Population by Period of Immigration, 1948–61

	November 8, 1948		May 22, 1961	
	Percent	Number	Percent	Number
Place of birth				
Israel	35.4	253,414	37.8	730,446
Another country	64.6	462,567	62.2	1,201,911
Unknown	697	—a	—a	—a
Total	100.0	716,678	100.0	1,932,357
Period of immigration				
1931 or earlier	18.8	86,209	6.0	72,623
1932–39	42.7	195,841	13.5	162,322
1940–47	20.8	95,538	7.2	86,387
1948–51	17.7	81,346	49.4	593,797
1952–57	—a	—a	16.6	199,231
1958 or later	—a	—a	7.3	87,551
Unknown	—a	3,633	—a	—a

Source: Adapted from *Hashnaton Hastatisti Leyisrael* 13:52 (Jerusalem 1962).
aNot available.

1951. At this time Israel was the principal destination for Jews who left other countries: about 80 percent of Jews who emigrated from their home countries in that period immigrated to Israel.[15]

As noted in the introduction, about 690,000 immigrants arrived in Israel during this period of less than four years, and about 28 percent of them were Holocaust refugees.[16] Of the immigrants who arrived between the establishment of the state and the end of 1960, the proportion of those who came from Asia and Africa was 53.4 percent, with the rest coming from Europe and North America (Table 3.2).[17] The result was that the ethnic composition of Israel's Jewish population changed radically during this period. Eighty-five percent of the immigrants came from Europe in 1948, while only half did in the two years that followed. In 1951 the proportion of immigrants from Asia and Africa reached 70 percent (Table 3.3). These immigrants from the Islamic world came from a variety of countries. The three largest groups arriving during these years of mass immigration were from Iraq, Romania, and Poland (Table 3.4).

Once the British left Palestine and Israel became independent, it immediately opened its doors to two groups that the British had barred: Holocaust

TABLE 3.2 · Immigration to Israel 1948–61, by Year of Immigration
and Immigrant's Last Continent of Residence

Immigration	Total	Asia*	Africa	Europe*	America and Oceania	Unknown
May 15, 1948– December 1948	101,828	4,739	8,192	76,554	478	11,865
1949	239,954	71,652	39,215	121,963	1,422	5,702
1950	170,563	57,565	26,162	81,195	1,954	3,687
1951	175,279	103,396	20,382	47,074	1,286	3,141
1952	24,610	6,867	10,286	6,232	950	275
1953	11,575	3,014	5,102	2,147	930	382
1954	18,491	3,357	12,509	1,369	1,091	165
1955	37,528	1,432	32,815	2,065	1,155	61
1956	56,330	3,139	45,284	6,739	1,067	101
1957	72,634	4,230	25,747	39,812	1,410	101
1958	27,290	7,921	4,113	13,695	1,320	241
1959	23,988	3,544	4,429	14,731	1,147	137
1960	24,692	1,782	5,379	16,169	1,158	204
1961	47,735	4,149	18,048	23,375	1,969	194

Source: Adapted from Hashnaton Hastatisti Leyisrael 65:234 (Jerusalem 2014).
*Until 1995 the Asian republics of the former USSR were included in Europe.

survivors living in displaced persons (DP) camps in Germany, Austria, and Italy; and European Jews who had been captured in recent years while attempting to enter Palestine in violation of British restrictions and who had been sent by the British to detention camps in Cyprus. However, these Jews arrived only gradually because the British did not open the camps in Cyprus until 1949, and the United States also sought to bar Jews of conscription age in the DP camps it controlled from reaching Israel (although US enforcement of this policy was inconsistent).[18] Jews also arrived from Bulgaria, Yugoslavia, Libya, Morocco, Turkey, and Yemen — and after the war also from Poland, Romania, and Iraq as noted above.[19]

Immigrants of military age who arrived during the 1948 war were inducted and played an important role in reinforcing the fighting forces and in the war effort in general.[20] But at the same time immigration imposed an enormous burden on the new country's economy, its bureaucratic apparatus, and on the absorbing society as a whole. As soon as the British left, the new

TABLE 3.3 · Immigrants by Continent of Birth, 1948–51

Continent	Thousands	Total	1948	1949	1950	1951
Total	686.7*	100.0%	100.0%	100.0%	100.0%	100.0%
Asia	237.7	23.2	5.3	30.6	34.4	59.9
Africa	93.3	28.1	9.1	16.7	15.2	11.5
Europe and America	336.6	48.7	85.6	52.7	50.4	29.0

Source: Moshe Sicron, "'Ha'aliya hahamonit' — Memadeyha, me'afyeneha vehashpa'oteha," in *'Olim vema'abarot 1948–1952*, edited by Mordechai Naor, 35 (Jerusalem 1986).
*The continent of birth of 19,000 immigrants is unknown.

TABLE 3.4 · Main Groups of Immigrants, 1948–51

Country of origin	Thousands of immigrants
Iraq	123.3
Romania	118.0
Poland	106.4
Yemen and Aden	48.3
Morocco, Algiers, and Tunisia	45.4
Bulgaria	37.3
Turkey	34.5
Libya	31.0
Iran	21.9
Czechoslovakia	18.8
Hungary	14.3
Germany and Austria	10.8
Egypt	8.8
USSR	8.2
Yugoslavia	7.7

Source: Moshe Sicron, "'Ha'aliya hahamonit' — Memadeyha, me'afyeneha vehashpa'oteha," in *'Olim vema'abarot 1948–1952*, edited by Mordechai Naor, 34 (Jerusalem 1986).

government and the Jewish Agency, which had condemned the British for restricting Jewish immigration, announced that all Jews were welcome in Israel. In fact, however, the new government's decision makers were of two minds regarding both the quantity and quality of the immigrants. The numbers were greater than anticipated and beyond the new country's capacity to absorb them. In addition, not a few of the immigrants were unwell or elderly people, who imposed on the country a responsibility that it had difficulty assuming. Furthermore, a large part of the new population consisted of children. While these provided a foundation for future economic growth, they also had to be supported in the short term by a relatively small number of breadwinners.[21] The large numbers of children and elderly placed a heavy burden on the country's health, education, and welfare systems.[22]

With the exception of a few tens of thousands of people, most of these immigrants did not pay their own way to Israel. The Jewish Agency transported them to the country and, after their arrival, provided them with housing, basic equipment and furnishings, food, and health services. The state provided education at a basic level and established a state-owned housing company, Amidar, to build immigrant housing projects all over the country.[23] The combination of a huge influx of immigrants and scarce resources meant that the challenge was enormous. At the end of 1951, with the state on the brink of insolvency and increasingly unable to provide the population with minimal nourishment, clothing, and basic services, the immigration policy was changed. Immigrants from regions where Jews were not considered to be in imminent danger, such as North Africa, would have to be able-bodied and capable of supporting themselves and their families to be allowed to move to Israel. The decision was strictly enforced, and the result was a sharp drop in immigration rates (Table 3.2). The economic crisis and growing unemployment rate also discouraged immigrants from coming.[24]

The most urgent challenge was providing housing. There had been a housing shortage even before the State of Israel was established, and the immigration wave made it much worse. Between May 15, 1948, and December 1949, 341,000 immigrants arrived. About 15 percent of them (53,000) were housed in the country's cities and *moshavim*. About 10.5 percent (36,500) were taken in by relatives. A similar proportion were settled in hundreds of hastily built moshavim and labor villages, which in many cases were not connected to the water, sewage, and electricity grids and lacked paved access roads. About 4.6 percent (16,000) were absorbed by kibbutzim, and about 6,000 children, 2 percent of the total number of immigrants, were placed in the Youth Aliyah program. About 36 percent (124,000) were housed in the homes of Arabs who had left or been expelled during the war, and the rest, about 22 percent (69,000), were placed in immigrant camps. The formerly Arab neighborhoods in cities — Haifa, Jerusalem, Tiberias, Safed, Lod, Ramla, Beersheba, Acre, Majdal (renamed Ashkelon), and Yavneh, quickly filled with Jewish immigrants. From September 1, 1948, to April 1, 1949, some 90,000 immigrants were settled in these cities. Those who arrived in the early waves, mostly Europeans, were settled in former Arab homes. After May 1949, when all the vacant homes had been given out, newcomers were placed in crowded immigrant camps.[25] Since only half the Arabs whose homes stood empty had lived in cities, only some of their houses were seen by the absorption authorities as fit for habitation, despite the minimalist nature of contemporary standards. The standards crowded each immigrant family into a tiny space.[26] In 1949–50, some 200,000 newcomers went through the immigrant camps, with between 60,000 and 100,000 living in them at any given time. The average stay in the camps was three to six months. The Sha'ar Ha'Aliyah camp in Haifa was where immigrants were received and sorted. The other camps, of which there were forty by the end of 1949, provided temporary housing before the immigrants were given permanent housing in a city or rural settlement. During their time in the camps, immigrants' basic needs were provided for — not just housing but also food, education, and medical care — by the absorption agencies. The services were of low quality and thus were sharply criticized by both the absorbers and the absorbed.

The Jewish Agency found itself in a financial crisis in 1950, and as a result it decided to revise the temporary absorption program. Most of the immigrant camps were turned into what were termed transit camps (ma'abarot), and many more of these were established — by May 1952 there were 129.[27] These functioned as community settlements, with residents housed in improvised dwellings such as metal shacks, huts, and tents. Despite these poor conditions, immigrants were better off than under the previous arrangement because each family was now assigned its own housing unit rather than having to share space with other families.[28] However, the services provided were cut. Instead of receiving food in a communal kitchen, the residents of the transit camps had to purchase and cook their own food. Because of overcrowding and a shortage of resources, both the immigrant and transit camps suffered from very bad sanitation and hygiene conditions. There were not enough latrines, showers, hot water, soap, or other hygienic goods. Proper sewage systems were not installed. As a result, food was scarce and morbidity high, with epidemics breaking out frequently. The substandard living conditions and insufficient health services led to a sharp rise in infant mortality.[29]

The transit camps were meant to provide temporary shelter for a limited period. But in January 1953 they were still home to between 155,000 and 200,000 immigrants, according to different estimates. In May 1955 there were still 83,000 immigrants living in them.[30] In the period up to 1952, hundreds of new farming settlements were established, and the authorities succeeded in persuading immigrants to move to them. But conditions there were tough, and many immigrants abandoned the new communities.[31] New urban settlements, called development towns, were also established, fifteen of them by the end of 1951 (some were on the sites of previous Arab villages). At that time about 120,000 people lived in these places.[32] Like the new moshavim, these towns were for the most part located on the country's periphery. A renewed wave of immigration in 1954–56 (Table 3.2) brought in mostly Jews from North Africa, who were settled in the homes left empty by other newcomers who had left the immigrant moshavim and development towns. At this time another seven development towns were also established.[33]

The second most urgent absorption problem was the provision of food. The new country imposed rationing during the 1948 war and tightened these regulations in April 1949. The purpose was to prevent price gouging that would in turn lead to inadequate nutrition. But rationing could not solve all the problems. Because of its chronic shortage of foreign currency, the state found it difficult to acquire sufficient food for its burgeoning population and farm animals. This situation was exacerbated by other problems: there were not enough trucks that were equipped to transport fresh food; many of the new immigrant settlements were located in remote locations and lacked paved access roads; and the basic ration the state provided did not accord with the tastes and habits of many of the immigrants, especially those from the Islamic world. Special foods needed by children and babies were also scarce.[34]

Another problem was creating jobs. In 1949 the unemployment rate in the civilian workforce reached 9.5 percent. And this number did not include residents of the immigrant camps, who were considered to be wards of the state. If they had been included, the unemployment rate would have been 14 percent. On the one hand, the camps were pressure cookers in which immigrants lived in harsh conditions and did not work; on the other hand, they served as a safety valve, because when the immigration rate was at its height the country's workforce was also swelling, as discharged soldiers sought work. The camps thus held back the entry into the economy of even more jobseekers. Two years later, despite continuing mass immigration, unemployment had been reduced by employing the newcomers in construction jobs and public works, funded by printing money.[35] The unemployment figure does not show the gap between employment levels in the established and immigrant populations. In 1950 the unemployment rate among immigrants who had arrived in the previous two years was at least 14 percent. Most established Israelis—those who had arrived before 1948—had jobs. They constituted the skilled workforce that staffed the young state's expanding administration and service agencies, local government offices, and the Jewish Agency's immigrant absorption programs. The established population also filled management positions and acted as entrepreneurs in the private sector, as well as in the large range of enterprises run by the Histadrut. The force and depth of unemployment were thus much greater among immigrants than among the established population.[36] True, the level of employment increased rapidly, but because labor was in such great supply many of the immigrants were employed in government-sponsored jobs of doubtful economic value. The goal of these public works was to provide jobs for immigrants who had not found employment in the commercial or public sectors.[37] In 1952—following the adoption of a new economic program based largely on budgetary restraint, the contraction of credit, an increase in the tax burden, and a devaluation of the currency—the economy went into recession. Food prices rose steeply, and the demand for labor dropped. The immigration rate was significantly lowered. Unemployment reached 11.3 percent, a new peak, in 1953. The situation of the new immigrants, who had had difficulty being absorbed into the workforce in the first place, declined even further.[38]

In 1954 the economy began to grow again.[39] Despite the upturn, the gap between the standard of living of the established population and that of the immigrants remained salient for the rest of the country's first decade, even after the end of mass immigration. Some of the disparity can be explained by the fact that the established population was, on the whole, better educated and thus had higher earning potential than the immigrant population. Only 16 percent of the immigrants had completed secondary school, as opposed to 34 percent of the established population.[40] The educational level of Iraqi Jews and Holocaust survivors was much higher than that of the rest of the immigrants; on average, male Holocaust survivors were very close to established Israelis in terms of their level of education.[41] Especially wide socioeconomic disparities were evident not only between immigrants from the Islamic world and old-timers but also between the former and the European immigrants who arrived during the immigration wave. Immigrants from Asia and North Africa thus became by far the largest component of the population on Israel's frontiers.[42] In these areas, the level of health and education services was substandard, and jobs were hard to come by.[43]

THE IMMIGRANTS:
SELF AND PUBLIC PERCEPTIONS

Throughout the years of the mass influx of newcomers, established Israelis feared that the immigrants would limit progress in the Zionist project. Both survivors of the Holocaust and refugees from Islamic lands found that the absorbing population looked askance and down at them. The charged relations between the Ashkenazi absorbers and the Mizrahim have figured prominently in the scholarly literature.[44] As noted in chapter 1, the typical attitude displayed by this established population toward the Mizrahi immigrants was characterized by condescension, arrogance, and what we would now call an Orientalist attitude. But during the state's early years, established Israelis vigorously debated the question of whether Holocaust survivors could be worthy Israeli citizens.[45]

The image of the Holocaust survivor began to take form even before these immigrants arrived, when emissaries from the Yishuv were sent to the DP camps. In their reports home, the visitors described a mass of degenerates of low moral fiber. To the Jews of the Yishuv, the survivors seemed to have lost all claim to human respect, as well as their faith in others — reaching the point of cynicism, nihilism, and anarchy. They were, the emissaries claimed, unwilling to engage in real labor, preferring black-market speculation and the pursuit of easy money. Some in the Yishuv charged that the DPs were the survivors of negative selection. Good people, they said, did not survive the concentration camps, only those who knew how to play the system and who were prepared to betray their fellow Jews. One emissary told Ben-Gurion that if 100,000 of these Jews were to immigrate to Israel, they would destroy the country.[46] The emissaries also claimed that many of the survivors were mentally unbalanced, even though professionals in the field were divided on this point.[47] It should be noted in passing that, during the 1950s, Israeli psychiatrists did not view Holocaust survivors who were mentally ill as a distinct group. It was only at the end of the 1950s that psychiatric articles began pointing out the specific difficulties and incidence of mental illness among the survivors.[48]

More than 22,000 Holocaust survivors were drafted into the Israeli army and participated in the 1948 war, most of them in combat roles.[49] According to Tom Segev, they gained a reputation as pathetic, cowardly soldiers, prisoners of their past.[50] The cruelest manifestation of this attitude was the way they were referred to in Hebrew slang—*sabon*, meaning soap. The epithet derived from the baseless rumor that the Germans had manufactured soap from the bodies of Jews and was meant to label the survivors as cowards.[51] Survivors of the Holocaust had expected to find a warm welcome in Israel and to gain a sense of belonging to a family, which would have given them some solace for their suffering. Their encounter with the real Israel was a bitter disappointment.[52]

Like their European brethren, immigrants from the Islamic world were also the subject of negative stereotypes. They were portrayed as ignorant, backward, and primitive. In particular, Moroccans were the subject of negative characterizations. From the establishment of the state through March 1949 only 13,000 Jews arrived from North Africa, about three-quarters of them from Morocco.[53] But despite their small numbers, they stood out in a negative way. They were said to be unstable, hot-headed, impulsive, oversensitive, wild, unreliable, and, in particular, violent.[54]

It is no wonder, then, that the immigrants felt alienated and that mainstream Israelis were treating them with disrespect. Furthermore, these attitudes inevitably proved detrimental to the economic and social absorption of the immigrants, not to mention to their self-esteem. But the immigrants were hardly just passive objects on which the absorbing society acted. They took action to protest such slights and to assert their needs and rights. Indeed, the construction of their civil identities can hardly be understood if they are portrayed simply as victims. They were agents whose identities were molded not only by their absorbers but also by their own thoughts and actions. While the power relations may have been asymmetrical, the immigrants played an active role in their entry into Israeli society.

Impelled by the negative feelings they encountered and the scarcity, poverty, and poor living conditions they endured, many immigrants pushed back, demanding what they saw as their fair share of the country's resources and insisting on recognition as full and equal citizens.[55] While most scholarly attention has focused on newcomers from the Islamic world,[56] all immigrants fought to gain equality.

In the context of a democratic state, "speech" can be described as any act by which a citizen informs the regime about her concerns, her opinion about the functioning of the state, and her expectations that flaws be remedied. The act can be accomplished through political parties, labor organizations, or third-sector associations. Such messages can also be conveyed via demonstrations, lawsuits, reports in the press, and—as shown in the previous chapter—letters to a government ministry. But a citizen's act of communication need not be verbal. Voting on election day—as well as deciding not to vote—are instances of such speech. Another form of nonverbal communication lies outside the boundaries of the law, such as buying goods on the black market, squatting in buildings and refusing to leave, abandoning farming settlements set up by the authorities for immigrants, or fleeing immigrant housing projects and returning to the transit camps that the state was trying to evacuate. Violent acts against symbols of the state and establishment representatives are also kinds of communication.[57]

A large portion of the means of expression available to Israeli citizens in the period under discussion exist in nondemocratic countries as well. Ottoman subjects, for example, submitted petitions to the sultan's court. In totalitarian states, such as the Soviet Union under Stalin or communist East Germany, citizens made personal appeals to state authorities. Overt and covert forms of protest are also familiar features of colonial and postcolonial regimes.[58] But Israel was from the start a democratic country in which political parties of widely varying ideologies competed for the votes and affiliations of the immigrants. In addition, relations between the immigrants and the state were not conducted only directly between the two sides but also via the press and civil organizations. The relationship between the immigrants and the government was exposed to political scrutiny and public criticism. Furthermore, in contrast with the situation in nondemocratic countries, in Israel the government's power was limited by norms and law on the one hand and by the massive intrepid disobedience of citizens on the other hand.[59] The immigrants and the press had the ability to embarrass the government and, at least in theory, to change it.[60] The immigrants' demands compelled a response by the authorities, both because their cause was taken up by the opposition parties in Israel and because of the pressures of world and Diaspora Jewish public opinion.[61] Finally, the country's survival required continuing immigration and capital investment, and these depended on its success in providing a home and livelihood for the recently arrived immigrants.[62]

Another question also needs to be answered. What, precisely, constitutes listening? There are simple and easily defined cases. Some of the cases are a request from an ordinary citizen that receives a positive answer; a demonstration that leads to negotiation and a response to at least some of the demands made by the demonstrators; and seeing to the needs of a population that hardly has any means of making its voice heard, such as the immigrant girls who were the subject of chapter 1. But there are more difficult cases. For example, if immigrants stage a strike, and the authorities invite representatives of the strikers to negotiate, is this a case of attentiveness to their plight? Or is it an empty gesture, or perhaps simply a way to reduce their opposition or a nice way of disciplining them? Perhaps it is a bit of each. It is not always possible to classify such actions unambiguously. It is also difficult to assess how broad and deep an impression the government's acknowledgment of its citizens makes on those citizens' hearts and minds.

The Immigrants Enter the Fray

Israelis were not passive and docile citizens during the 1948 war and the period of rehabilitation that followed. As the war raged, and as the new country recovered from it, they voiced resentment of, protested and complained to, and made demands on their government.[63] The government's centralized policies, a product both of the need to fight the war as well as the economic crisis that accompanied it, were in accord with the zeitgeist — the postwar rehabilitation programs then being pursued by Western European governments, as well as with the worldviews and the cultural and institutional heritage of Israel's decision makers.[64] Such centralization led to the formation of a corps of politicians and officials in the government, the Jewish Agency, and local government who had the power — or so citizens believed — to solve their problems and to alleviate their emotional distress.[65]

ACTING THROUGH ORGANIZATIONS

One of the tactics employed by immigrants to enhance their influence and status was to establish or join organizations based on people's place of origin — what Yiddish speakers called *landsmanschaften*. These groups provided their members with mutual aid, served as their mouthpieces, and negotiated on their behalf with the authorities.[66] Such organizations have a long history in Israel, starting in the Ottoman period and growing in the Mandate period that followed.[67] The press covered their meetings as a way of exerting public and political pressure on decision makers and of presenting immigrant grievances to the authorities.[68] Leaders of these organizations proved adept at navigating and exploiting political rivalries to gain publicity for their charges in the party and independent press.[69] Immigrant representatives also met with national leaders to discuss their problems. In addition, they were successful at having some of their representatives included in the slates that mainstream parties ran in national and local elections.[70]

When, in 1953, the number of emigrants topped the number of immigrants, arousing fears that Jews were abandoning the Jewish state, the landsmanschaften seized the opportunity to claim that they were the organizations best positioned to provide for immigrant needs and to prevent emigration.[71] Large numbers of immigrants also joined the Histadrut, which provided a range of services from medical care and housing to cultural activities.[72] The interests of immigrant doctors were represented by the Israel Medical Association.[73] The political parties did their best to recruit immigrants and, through direct assistance and by supporting their claims for better living conditions, sought to gain their votes.[74] The question here is not the extent to which this provided effective representation for the immigrants or whether the relationship of the immigrants to the coalition parties were ideological or simply an instrumental arrangement that served both sides. My points are that, even if they faced a glass ceiling in some of these organizations and continued to feel discriminated against, the immigrants had available to them a variety of channels for action and that they exploited a variety of platforms to make their voices heard and to promote their interests.[75]

Before examining immigrant protests, it is necessary to place the question of recognition and rights in their historical context. At the end of the 1940s and the beginning of the 1950s that context was necessarily different from today's neoliberal ethos. The concept of the general good held by the groups that made up Israel's Jewish society underlined values like freedom from want and promoted the meeting of everyday needs such as for employment and housing. The political discourse of the time was not devoid of the demand for fair cultural representation for different groups (the parties represented in the First Knesset included not only Arab ones but also Yemenite and Sephardi ones). And both political and social battles were waged over questions of ethnic culture, particularly religious identity.[76] Yet these demands did not possess the moral legitimacy that characterizes today's identity politics. The concept of multiculturalism, so central to the contemporary discourse on equality, had not yet been articulated. The emphasis then was on the construction of a common national culture, not the recognition and fostering of separate cultures.[77]

IMMIGRANTS VOICE THEIR COMPLAINTS

Following their arrival, and throughout the 1950s, the immigrants complained about each of the innumerable defects in the absorption process. Their problems were reported on and debated in the press, both independent newspapers and those associated with political parties.[78] A few examples will demonstrate how varied these grievances were.

"Four Thousand Residents of Salameh [an evacuated Arab village on the edge of Tel Aviv, where immigrants were settled] Lack Electricity and Doctors! Before the Elections Everyone Promised to Turn the Village into Paradise — Now They've Forgotten the Address!" shouted a headline in *Yedi'ot Aharonot*, "In Salameh's dilapidated homes and crooked, winding alleys 4,000 immigrants now live from hand to mouth in crowded conditions. On the narrow sandy paths and in the courtyards piles of garbage, trash, and rotten vegetables can be seen. The entire place is pervaded by a suffocating stink," the reporter wrote. He quoted one of the inhabitants: "Until a short while ago they didn't collect the garbage at all." Despite these horrible sanitary conditions, the reporter added, most of Salameh's residents prayed for summer. In the winter, most of the roofs leaked, and the walls became saturated with water. There was no electricity and no telephone service. From 11:00 at night, when the last automobile leaves the village, the reporter said, the village was cut off from the rest of the world and there was no way to get a doctor. The residents "had complaint after complaint."[79] A correspondent for the newspaper *Herut* reported that a Yemenite woman who lived in Salameh had shown him how the room she shared with her three children was unfit for human habitation — a well yawned in the middle of the floor: "The hole is covered with sheet metal, and the woman goes out to work each day, seized with fear about what might happen to her children, that they might take the sheets off the well and fall in." Other immigrants from Yemen and Aden contended that immigrants who arrived from Europe and the Cyprus detention camps were assigned better homes.[80] Many other complaints were about housing conditions; the lack of connections to the sewer system, street lighting, and roads; and about the difficulty of making a living.[81]

Immigrants living in the Saqiya transit camp (which later became the town of Or Yehuda) complained of the lack of a telephone line and resident physician. *Kol Ha'am*'s correspondent reported: "The security situation in this village is very bad, infiltrators have already attacked it many times, and at night in particular the settlement is entirely cut off from the outside world. The Petah Tikvah police and other institutions confirmed that a telephone had to be installed immediately. One night an elderly women suddenly fell ill and needed medical care immediately. She was 'loaded' onto a donkey but died before she reached the nearest doctor."[82]

In Majdal, later renamed Ashkelon, immigrant women protested about shortages. One complained: "There aren't enough eggs and butter for the babies, and potatoes arrived today for the first time and we haven't tasted meat since we arrived here."[83] Yemenite immigrants in the Jerusalem region claimed that they received inadequate food supplies. Food was delivered irregularly, and even when the supply truck arrived, they charged, it often lacked the most basic items, such as loaves of bread for Sabbath meals.[84] A reporter for *Herut* who visited Ramla offered an eyewitness account of "a woman who was running around frantically. We approached her and someone asked her in Russian: 'What happened, Madam?' 'I don't have any bread for my children,' the woman replied in Bulgarian."[85]

Immigrants also complained about the costs of storing their possessions and moving them from shipping company warehouses to the places where they were settled.[86] The drivers who had been hired by the authorities to do this work, the immigrants charged, had organized themselves into a cartel and were demanding prices that were twice as high as rates set by the government.[87] Some immigrants never received their belongings. A newspaper reported the travails of a woman who had survived the Holocaust. She was in tears because the luggage of her eighteen-year-old niece, who had survived the horrors of the war and recently arrived in Israel, had not been located. "Overcome with disappointment, the woman and the young girl began to wander from place to place in search of her things," the article elucidated.[88]

Underneath the headline "Ramla Complains," a *Davar* correspondent wrote in April 1949 about the anger of the immigrants: "The problem of jobs has yet to be solved, and about a third of job seekers remain idle."[89] About three weeks later *Hador* reported:

> Many have not worked a single day for the last several weeks. A number of immigrants have already sold a large part of the household goods they brought with them from overseas, so they would have money to buy food.

... Outside the [Employment] Office, our correspondent [was] surrounded by scores of unemployed people who told him about their plight. All they were asking for was work, no matter how hard it might be, so that they could support their families. These people claimed that the institutions [responsible for them] were not seriously concerned with creating jobs for the inhabitants of Ramla, and that the leaders of those institutions had no conception of what was liable to happen in this city if the situation were to continue for another few days.[90]

Yedi'ot 'Aharonot reported that in Yahudiya, "new immigrants are supporting themselves by selling belongings they brought with them from overseas and ask with concern and apprehension: What will we do tomorrow? Why did they bring us here, to places where there are no workshops and factories?"[91]

In 1950, after the immigrant camps were reorganized as transit camps, the public kitchens that had supplied food to the immigrants were closed. *Yedi'ot 'Aharonot* reported that hunger then spread through the camps:

Rachel Baruch and her husband Ya'akov, from the "Yisra'el" immigrant camp, are among those "who will die of starvation." . . . They sold . . . their small home and some of their belongings and arrived in Israel eight months ago with their son and 50 lira in gold coins. The son was killed in an automobile accident four months ago. The money ran out about a month later. It is shocking to see how the parents currently live — they are old and weak. . . . The Welfare Ministry office in the camp has given them six lira since the [public] kitchens were shut down. . . . When I visited their quarter of a tent in the camp [which they shared with three other families] the elderly woman was so weak that she could not get out of her bed. The old man . . . set out to sell some old clothes at the camp's rag market.[92]

The press continued to run heart-rending stores like these for most of the 1950s.[93]

Stories about the desperate straits of the immigrants appeared in the foreign press as well, especially at the time of the mass influx of 1948–51. One such story, about the horrible conditions in the immigrant camps, appeared in the *New York Times* as early as in July 1949.[94]

Immigrants from Asia and North Africa, who were exposed to devastating prejudice, complained about discrimination throughout the 1950s.[95] They were outraged by the selective immigration policy that was instituted in the autumn of 1951, which prevented elderly and infirm people primarily from North Africa from joining their relatives in Israel.[96] They demanded to be permitted to reunite their families, and some even threatened to leave Israel.[97]

The immigrants also frequently complained of the incivility of the officials with whom they had to deal. An immigrant from Romania told *Haboker* that he was "trembling from the insult" he endured when a customs agent rummaged through the suitcase in which his wife had packed her underwear and asked him in a demeaning tone of voice whether he was smuggling cigarettes. Then, even more rudely, the agent demanded to know: "Dollars? How many dollars do you have?" The process ended with a body search of the immigrant. He encountered the same suspicion at his immigrant camp: "They would not believe that he was an electrical engineer and wanted to make him into a fruit picker. . . . They did not believe that he had not brought a treasure of gold and dollars into the country. . . . They would not believe, they suspected, insulted, and abused him."[98]

An immigrant woman said that she was expected to shed all signs of the Diaspora — to change her appearance, her clothing, and the way she spoke. She was resentful of the bad reputation attributed to the immigrants: "Your newspapers trumpet how awful the new immigrants are — they are strange, alienated, do not want to learn Hebrew. People pour out all their insults and bad language on the immigrants. . . . And why are [established Israelis] so unwilling to put themselves in our places, grasp the bitter truth, and realize that 'the other side' plays a big role in all the ills created by our special situation?"[99]

PUBLIC PROTEST

Immigrants did not just rely on intermediaries to voice their grievances, they also mounted direct protests. Even before the war was over, immigrants demonstrated throughout the country — in cities, immigrant camps, and evacuated Arab villages in which immigrants had been settled. After the establishment of the transit camps in the spring of 1950, they demonstrated in the camps as well. The Moroccan-born poet and political activist Sami Shalom Chetrit has claimed that the Israeli establishment viewed such protests as criminal activities,[100] but in fact the response of the authorities was varied, and demonstrations frequently led to negotiations between the demonstrators and policymakers. I should note that Mandate law allowed peaceful gatherings and processions by up to fifty people. However, at his discretion, the district commissioner could issue an announcement requiring the public to apply for a permit prior to organizing protests of more than fifty people. The police could then issue a permit, deny it, or impose certain restrictions on the protesters.[101]

I examine here a few protests that took place from February to October 1949 and were reported in the press. Most of them centered on housing, unemployment, and inadequate or inappropriate provisions.

In February 1949, immigrants who had been settled in or moved to vacated Arab homes in Jaffa were told to leave rickety structures that were in danger of collapse. Refusing to return to the immigrant camps where they had been housed, they staged a demonstration in Tel Aviv.[102] In April, survivors of the Holocaust living in Givat Aliya, a neighborhood in Jaffa, were ordered by the city's military governor to vacate wooden shacks in which they had opened small businesses. They were not offered an alternative location for their shops. So they staged a march, bearing a sign saying "Leave us alone. Do not destroy the wooden stores from which a few miserable ailing and weak people make a living. If you do not listen to our cry, blood will flow." According to one newspaper report, "all the demonstrators entered the governor's building and a department chief agreed to meet with a delegation and negotiate."[103]

Demonstrations by unemployed immigrants were common sights throughout the country in the first half of 1949.[104] In February, March, and April jobless immigrants demonstrated in Safed, Ramla, Netanya, Jerusalem, Jaffa, Tiberias, Yahud, and Lod.[105] In April, inhabitants of Lod protested not only the lack of work but also shortages of electricity, bread, and flour and the fact that their homes were not connected to the water supply.[106] That same month, immigrants in Ramla went to Tel Aviv to hold a rally in front of the building that housed the Knesset's sessions and government offices. They were received at the Labor Ministry, where officials promised to find jobs for the unemployed and, in the meantime, to waive charges for rent and electricity, for those who had it.[107] The label "revolutionary innovation" was attached to these demonstrations by the Israel Communist Party newspaper *Kol Ha'am*, which claimed that, as a result, "sealed ears and locked money boxes have opened . . . IL [Israeli lira] 70,000 have been allocated to public works in Lod and Ramla."[108] In a telegram sent in May 1949, the mayor of Safed informed the prime minister that unemployed residents of his city were planning to send a protest delegation to the government offices in Tel Aviv. He asked that the government send a delegation to Safed. He noted that the situation there was dire and that he feared "horrible consequences that could also lead to bloodshed."[109] In July, 600 people from Ramla staged another demonstration in Tel Aviv. Following a clash with the police in which six of their number were injured, two of them severely (four policemen were also injured), they staged a sit-down strike in front of the government offices.[110] It ended only when Minister of Labor Golda Myerson (who later changed her name to Golda Meir) visited the demonstrators at midnight and promised to create hundreds of jobs for the unemployed.[111] A similar strike planned by immigrants in Lod was averted when Myerson learned of the plans in advance and the next morning sent a delegation of officials to try to calm tempers and look into the needs of the immigrants, in the hope of finding a solution.[112]

In October, job seekers demonstrated in Netanya and stormed the municipal building. The municipal secretary (a person comparable to a city manager in the United States) spoke to them and asked that they appoint a delegation to represent them. The mayor conferred with officials of the city's labor bureau and with an engineer from the state's Public Works Department. It was decided to employ the immigrants in the paving of the road from Netanya to Tel Aviv, using manual labor instead of bulldozers. The mayor also decided to employ more people in public works in the city. When informed of this plan, the job seekers dispersed.[113]

Demonstrations like these were aimed at compelling the authorities to provide for other urgent immigrant needs as well. In April, residents of the immigrant camp at Pardes Hannah rallied, demanding not just work and housing but also better provisions.[114] They went on a hunger strike, refusing to eat for twenty-four hours (or, according to a report in the Histadrut's daily newspaper, *Davar*, skipped the main meal of the day) to protest the inadequate quantity and quality of the food supply and the fact that the menu did not agree with their ethnic preferences. They also protested living conditions and their lack of certainty about their futures.[115] In contrast with the common memory of the immigrants of this time, one in which established Israelis wielded unrestrained control over the newcomers, this contemporary report and others like it indicate that the established Israelis lived in great trepidation of outbreaks of immigrant rage and were concerned about the spreading protests and the living conditions of the immigrants. A *Davar* correspondent spoke to the director of the Pardes Hannah camp and reported that "while the storm has subsided for now, institutions and authorities must remove all causes of resentment that can be eliminated. [The director warns that] 'A single match can cause a horrible eruption.'"[116] Finance Minister

Eliezer Kaplan visited the camp following the protest. *Kol Ha'am* criticized him for showing an interest in the immigrants only after they had taken such severe measures.[117] A similar strike took place in the immigrant camp in Netanya that same day, for similar reasons. A protester there told a reporter from *Haaretz* that the food rations did not supply him with the minimum number of calories he needed to survive.[118]

In September, people in an immigrant absorption facility in Hadera staged a protest against the substandard food given to them there. A Jewish Agency delegation arrived, accompanied by the police, to examine the provisions. The delegation concluded that the immigrants were right and promised that the food would be improved.[119]

Protests also followed tragic events. Following the sudden death of a twenty-four-year-old immigrant in June, 400 immigrants from Tripoli, Libya, demonstrated at Beit Lid against the unsanitary conditions there. They dispersed after authorities promised a thorough investigation of the cause of the young man's death.[120]

VIOLENCE

Some demonstrations turned violent. In April, *Haboker* reported that jobless protesters, both immigrants and army veterans, had forced their way into the Histadrut building in Haifa, where they smashed furniture in several offices.[121] In May, workers in Jerusalem occupied the Jewish Agency building to demand housing, claiming that officials there were discriminating against them. The police were called to disperse the workers, but subsequently the agency began negotiating with the protesters.[122] That same month demobilized soldiers, most of them immigrants, demonstrated in Haifa; city officials agreed to meet with them. The latter believed they had persuaded the immigrant soldiers that officials were doing the best they could for the soldiers. But the officials' success was only temporary: the next day the protesters returned.[123] During the second demonstration, a fight broke out that left a number of demonstrators and policemen injured. Some of the demonstrators met with Jewish Agency representatives, and, the police force held a press conference to explain its policy on dispersing demonstrations. Eight demonstrators were arrested and charged with "disorderly assembly, resisting the police, damage to property, and assault and battery."[124] Several months later, when they were tried, a police officer was called as a witness. He said he had received a head injury, lost consciousness, and required medical attention. He added that, during the protest, the demonstrators shouted "Fascists!

Nazis!" at the policemen.[125] Subsequently, on July 27, another officer argued in his testimony that the police understood how the unemployed felt and had dealt with them with great restraint rather than brutality. He also claimed that a Jewish Agency official had asked the protesters to choose representatives who could take part in negotiations, but that in response they smashed furniture and shouted, "We won't leave, there'll be a revolution here!"[126] The trial ended with the release of three of the defendants for lack of evidence. The others were required to post a surety of 50 lira to guarantee their good behavior for a year.[127] Such lenient verdicts and sentences show that the court preferred to end the affair quietly.

In June, residents of Yavneh held a demonstration after a malfunction in the pumping system had left them without water for three days. About seventy inhabitants of the town had come down with dysentery. According to contemporary reports, protesters attacked a Jewish Agency official, who required medical care. Representatives of the demonstrators, expanding on their demands, insisted on being allotted a guaranteed number of workdays sufficient to support their families. They were invited for talks at the Workers Council in nearby Rehovot. Workdays were assigned, and the representatives were promised that the water problem would be resolved immediately.[128] At the end of August, North African immigrants living in Hadera's immigrant housing attacked two officials of the General Labor Bureau who had proved unable to provide jobs. One suffered facial wounds, the other stab wounds. *Hatsofe* reported that the bureau's officials had been subject to threats for several weeks because they were unable to provide work for all those demanding it.[129] Labor Bureau workers feared for their personal safety, and some asked to be transferred to other locations.[130]

An official report on unemployment issued by the Ministry of Labor on the period from April until June 1949 stated that "the situation in places where immigrants are concentrated is extremely severe and approaches the boiling point."[131] The offices of Labor Minister Golda Myerson and Prime Minister David Ben-Gurion were inundated with telegrams and other messages from immigrants describing their plight.[132] Riots, demonstrations, strikes, petitions, letters, appeals to newspapers, and violence were all means the immigrants used to respond to their lack of work and other problems throughout Israel's first decade.[133] In the recession year of 1953, the situation grew worse.[134] A writer for *Ma'ariv* reported that despairing young Moroccan immigrant army veterans were demanding their right to work "by pounding on the table." The writer added that "right now the tension in the Beersheva

Labor Bureau is so high that work routines are no longer in place; the officials are afraid to report to the office and the Labor Bureau offices look as if they had been hit by a bomb."[135]

Officials at the agencies responsible for providing housing to immigrants were also subject to violence:

> The Jewish Agency Housing Department has turned into a dangerous outpost — people shout, hit, strangle, and make every threat in the world. . . . Three helpless officials see to the absorption of large numbers of immigrants . . . the interaction is generally brief and sharp, at the drop of a pin desks fly like feathers. . . . When he heard an official give the curt reply "Right now there isn't any [housing]," a man began shouting: "I must slaughter you!" He was already feeling in his pockets . . . the official panicked. His face paled. Grappling with the immigrant, he was wounded in the right hand.[136]

Another immigrant, a woman who had survived the Holocaust, strangled an official who was himself a Holocaust survivor.[137] Far outnumbered, policemen also often became the victims of violence.[138]

THE ESTABLISHMENT'S RESPONSE

When the demonstrations and violence were just beginning, the absorbing agencies, including the Jewish Agency and the government, were perplexed. They blamed the communists for fanning the flames. Yet they did not deny that the conditions the immigrants lived in were harsh or that the organizations responsible for them needed to do something to allay their suffering.[139] One way to discomfit the government and other responsible authorities, such as the Jewish Agency, was to tell the story outside Israel. Immigrants and their political allies overseas, as well as those who had left the country, used the international media to vilify the authorities.[140]

The term "catastrophe" was repeatedly used at two meetings of the Mapai Secretariat in April 1949 that addressed housing and employment. It was applied to the immigrant camps and to other places where newcomers had been settled. Zalman Aharonowitz — then a member of the Knesset and general secretary of Mapai, and later a cabinet minister under the Hebraicized last name Aran — declared that "the fact that the camps in this country, in which there are tents, house people in worse conditions than [those of Jewish refugees in territory under British control] in Cyprus or in American camps in Germany is, in the opinion of all, inconceivable."[141] Eliyahu Dobkin, a senior Mapai official who headed the Jewish Agency's Youth and

Pioneering Department, was also appalled by the situation in the camps: "It is said that there are 500,000 or 600,000 people in the tent camps and that there is room for another 20,000. All these numbers are not just numbers. It is a crime to hold people in such living conditions. It is the beginning of a catastrophe. . . . I will not describe here the living conditions in the camps . . . it is a horror that I saw nothing like in any [other DP] camp. This is the immigrant's first encounter with the country. This is how he sees it. This is where he is encountered."[142]

Giora Yoseftal, who headed the Jewish Agency's Absorption Department, reported that rates of unemployment were especially high in Haifa and even worse in Ramla, Acre, and Lod, with a quarter of the workforce in the latter three cities were out of work. The situation in former Arab villages was similar.[143] Beba Idelson, a member of the party's Knesset faction, shared with her colleagues her impressions from a visit she had made to the immigrants who had been settled in Ramla and Lod: "People are going from house to house, preparing demonstrations and a petition to the prime minister. They are doing this because of the lack of work there."[144] All the speakers at the meeting voiced their fears that a wave of protests was about to begin. Pinhas Lavon, secretary general of the Histadrut and a member of the party's Knesset faction, declared that if immigration were not reduced,

> We will face the likelihood of a huge explosion. As one of the members has said — during this year the material may become concentrated enough for a counterrevolution in Israel. . . . Each day that people are not taken out of the camps becomes a situation in which a detonation is inevitable. The members who deal with immigration matters say that they are flabbergasted by the relative calm that prevails in the camps. I fear that they are living under an illusion. It is apparently quiet on the top, but below natural forces of destruction are converging, and one fine day a hundred thousand such people will be concentrated in the camps with no way out, and they can amass over a month, they'll rise up . . . it could be an explosion that will sweep away the government and the Knesset and the military police all at once. Without agonizing over it too much, we have to do everything to get past the danger point.[145]

But Ben-Gurion responded coolly to his colleagues' fears of a collapse of the social order, refusing to get upset. The employment situation was not that terrible, he maintained, and he warned against panic: "People can live for years in tents. Whoever doesn't want to live in them shouldn't come."[146]

Ben-Gurion was the greatest supporter of mass immigration. He used his authority, political skills, and charisma to keep the gates of the state open.[147] Facing the rising tide of panic among his colleagues, he must have felt compelled to respond as he did. He had other concerns. To the displeasure of party colleagues who demanded that the army open its bases so that immigrants could be housed in them, he defended the hold of the Israel Defense Forces on their bases. When criticized for this position, he responded: "The bases should be checked. That will be done. But we will not throw the army out. There's no need for that. Before we risk the use of force, [consider that] the army can shatter our regime if we throw it out [of its bases]. . . . What force can throw out the army?"[148]

Ben-Gurion seems to have been more anxious about his government's stability than about an immigrant uprising.[149] He thus played down the immigrants' struggle: "It is not a hundred percent clear right now if we have a country, because it is fighting desperately for its survival, and the war is not against a demonstration in Ramla, that's nothing, let them demonstrate."[150] Idelson, who had seen the suffering of the immigrants firsthand, responded: "And it's not important if Ben-Gurion thinks we are exaggerating. I don't know what exaggeration is. It is enough to see the people living and suffering." Apparently seeking to get the plight of the immigrants placed higher in her party's priorities, she added that the problem was giving the country bad press among the world's Jews, especially in the United States.[151] The debate then moved on to the question of who was administratively responsible for the situation and the lack of funds. The Jewish Agency asked for the state's help in finding funds to meet immigrants' needs. The agency proposed that a tax be imposed on Israeli citizens to fund the construction of public housing. Despite the fears that immigrants' fury could throw the country into crisis, and despite the compassion and the shame that many of the speakers at the meeting felt regarding the immigrants, the discussion was conducted largely as a matter of budgetary policy and in the context of a larger debate about the division of powers between the Jewish Agency and the government. Given the lack of any means of estimating how many more immigrants were likely to arrive, the severe shortage of funds, logistical difficulties, and political jockeying between Mapai and its opponents on the right and left, the ruling party's leaders were in a bind. They tried to meet immigrants' needs, but they were also painfully aware that every penny invested in state-sponsored work programs as relief for the newcomers was a penny that could not be invested in the construction of vital infrastructure such as permanent housing and job-creating economic development. Thus, they sometimes preferred to work to create a future in which the immigrants would be citizens in a thriving Jewish state instead of addressing their immediate troubles.[152]

At some of the protests recounted here and at many others, representatives of the Jewish Agency, the Histadrut, and local governments, as well as members of the Knesset and state government officials, met with demonstrators or their representatives to assuage their anger, bridge differences, and find at least partial solutions to their problems.[153] But in many other cases the immigrants were dealt with harshly: they were forcibly evacuated, returned to their camps or housing, and compelled to move from one location to another. The police were violent or imposed collective punishments.[154] Throughout the 1950s the government used two tactics with the immigrants: conciliation and negotiation on the one hand, and the repression of protest on the other hand.[155]

IMMIGRANTS MEET POLICYMAKERS

The immigrants' plight was debated again and again in the Knesset.[156] But they did not always need intermediaries to speak for them. Some of them took matters into their own hands and went to the Knesset themselves to complain to its members. At the end of July 1949 immigrants mounted a violent demonstration in Tel Aviv in front of the Knesset building. They broke down the gate and entered the yard, battling policemen who were called to disperse them, and a number of demonstrators and policemen were injured. Knesset Speaker Josef Shprinzak termed it a siege. "This house," he declared, "cannot be in a constant state of receiving delegations on every complaint, every trouble, and every issue or slogan, that gather around them a clique of wild demonstrators." But he left the door open to receiving delegations as long as they did not besiege the building.[157] There was nothing new in this. Delegations had been received at the Knesset before this incident and would be received after it. The record of one such later visit has survived. In this instance, a group of Iraqi Jewish immigrants from the Saqiya B transit camp arrived at the Knesset on November 5, 1951. They asked to meet the Speaker, but he was not available. Akiva Govrin—a member of Mapai and then chairman of the Knesset's Labor Committee—and Moshe Rosetti, the Knesset secretary, met with the immigrants. An interpreter was brought in, as the immigrants spoke in Arabic. On the face of it, the fact that the committee chairman took time away from his duties to speak with visitors who had not made an appointment seems impressive. But the conversation that followed gives a different impression. Govrin and Rosetti made a point of giving the five members of the delegation, which included one woman, a chilly reception. Fearful, as Israeli officials at the time generally were, of communist provocation, they did not even respectfully greet the visitors. Instead, Govrin immediately asked, "Who sent you?" Undeterred, the group's spokesman, Shaul Hayak, responded, "No one sent us, we came of our own accord because we were fed up with everything in the transit camp."

Rosetti chided them: "We do not make a practice of receiving delegations in this manner, the practice is to write us a letter requesting an interview with the Speaker. . . . The Knesset Speaker is busy now and cannot see you. However, since you are already here, I have invited Mr. Govrin . . . who will listen to you, and afterward look into the matters that you place before him, and we will inform you of the results subsequently."[158]

The immigrants, who had arrived in Israel only five months previously, had brought a letter with them. Salim Elwya, one of their number, submitted it to Govrin. Signed by 757 residents of the camp, it was addressed not only to the Speaker, but also to the prime minister, the Jewish Agency, and the Histadrut Executive Committee. It spelled out the immigrants' demands: for clean water; sufficient provisions, bread in particular; and the prevention of price gouging. They also wanted bus service and a paved road to connect the camp to the main road. Furthermore, they asked that a doctor serve the camp and that sufficient medicines be supplied. They also requested that a telephone line be installed, as well as electric lighting, and that there be sufficient classrooms so that all the children could attend school. The record of the meeting ends with Govrin's promise to examine the complaints and to send a response to the members of the delegation.[159]

Note that the immigrants displayed impressive organizational ability. A large constituency had chosen a committee to represent them. The delegation, certain of its power, had arrived with a clear list of grievances and determined to further the interests of the camp. They were not overawed when they met these top officials. They presented themselves as citizens entitled to equal access to resources. Though they were received coldly, even rudely, by Govrin and were preached to by Rosetti, the two officials sat with the immigrants' representatives and heard what they had to say. The record shows the ambivalence that both elected and appointed officials felt toward immigrants. On the one hand, officials felt that they had a fundamental if unwritten duty to meet with these citizens. This felt obligation is key to understanding the culture of the Israeli government at the time. On the other hand, they suspected the immigrants' motives and reprimanded them for not making an appointment.

The meeting itself amounted to an act of recognition, with the immigrants received as citizens. Yet alongside this formal display of recognition, the record shows that the officials did not entirely accept the immigrants' demand for equal treatment. Clearly there was some dichotomy between the dismissive attitude of the officials (who may have been fatigued by their inability to help these petitioners and many others who had come before them) and their sense of duty to the public. They fulfilled their formal obligation by holding a conversation, but they made a point of showing their displeasure and impatience. We may presume that the delegation's members sensed that their interlocutors were not entirely supportive of them. The suspicious question that Govrin fired at them at the start no doubt exacerbated their frustration, sense of isolation, and feelings of being discriminated against.

Nevertheless, they did not come as supplicants but as citizens asserting their right to receive fair treatment from their government. Since visits by immigrants to the Knesset or the president were not rare events, and since they seem to have been considered as effective modes of action, I maintain that the effectiveness of such encounters should not be measured only by their immediate outcomes.[160] Even if relief was slow in coming, whether because of the limited capabilities of decision makers or a slipshod bureaucracy, it is necessary to understand how immigrants understood the significance of their efforts and the importance of meeting with decision makers.

For quite a few immigrants, then, leaders, decision makers, and officials did not occupy some distant realm. Using the right methods and learning the best means to reach them, immigrants were able to make leaders accessible and at times even sway them by persuasion, public action, and violence. When decision makers met with immigrants, the latter were able to gain an impression of the former without being overwhelmed by awe. The immigrants were able to level a good measure of criticism at the people who had power over their lives. At times the dismissive attitude of officials could be frustrating. It could prompt immigrants to cease efforts to influence them, or in some cases to give up or even emigrate. But as the immigrants grew better at formulating their criticisms and needs, they were able to make demands for fair distribution of resources, equality with established Israelis, and recognition in more powerful ways. Fighting for rights is, after all, at the heart of the experience of citizenship, and public activity thus hones and deepens the feeling of being a part of one's society. As James Tully has written, "Participation is a strategic-communicative game in which citizens struggle for recognition and rule, negotiate within and sometimes over the rules, bargain, compromise, take two steps back, start over again, reach a provisional agreement or agree to disagree, and learn to govern and be governed in the context of relatively stable irresolution where the possibility of dissent is an implicit 'permanent provocation' which affects the negotiations."[161]

Tully posits that what shapes and holds individuals and groups together as citizens is not the ability to reach a certain kind of agreement, but rather the free activities of participation themselves.[162]

THE IMMIGRANTS SAY NO

There was another channel for change: active resistance. In September 1948, while the war was still in progress, immigrants broke into and squatted in the homes of Arabs who had fled Jaffa.[163] In May 1949, approximately 150 discharged soldiers, most of them immigrants, did the same in another building in Jaffa, after they received no response to their demands to be provided with housing. The military police evacuated the squatters by force, and many of the latter were injured. According to some reports, a few of the intruders tried to kill themselves by leaping from windows.[164]

In September 1949, a group of sixty immigrants living in the Etzion immigrant house in Jerusalem sent telegrams to the prime minister, Knesset Speaker, interior minister, and Histadrut Executive Committee, the text of which reached the press. The immigrants complained that Jewish Agency officials were trying to force them out of the house and move them to a former British military camp in Talpiot, a neighborhood in the southern part of the city. The petitioners refused to move into barracks there and claimed that Jewish Agency workers had, under police protection, taken away their beds and forced them to sleep on the floor. They also charged that the police had broken into their rooms and removed all their belongings. The immigrant house had cut off their electricity and water supplies. The immigrants declared that they would leave the immigrant house only if they were allowed to move into stone houses in the city, as they had been promised a transfer to permanent housing.[165] A month later, in October, a demonstration was staged by immigrants and discharged soldiers who had been served evacuation notices from homes where they were living, in Jerusalem's Mamila neighborhood. The protest turned violent. The director of the government housing department in Jerusalem was injured when the tenants slated for ejection, who had squatted in the neighborhood illegally, demanded alternative housing.[166] Such incidents, in which tenants refused to comply with or resisted orders to leave housing they had been given or taken of their own accord, continued throughout the decade to come.

Immigrants sent to settle in the Lachish region, southwest of Jerusalem, engaged in both strident and quiet resistance. Strident forms of resistance included demonstrations, protests, and appeals to the press. Quiet ones included noncompliance with the regulations governing the moshavim in which they found themselves—for example, by employing wage laborers, working outside the village, leasing out farmland, and planting crops other than those the villages had been assigned to raise.[167] Another sort of evasive resistance was simply abandoning such settlements. The departments responsible for settlements viewed such actions as a direct threat to their ability to govern.[168]

At least at some times and in some places, immigrants were subject to rules that did not accord with the democratic standards of the time and certainly not with immigrants' expectations. For example, the residents of immigrant camps were at first forbidden to work. Some immigrants—those residing temporarily in immigrant camps—were offered only secular education for their children, despite their desire for religious instruction. Many, dependent on public housing, were not allowed to choose where to live. At times they were also denied the choice of what work to engage in. This was especially true of the unemployed and those whose immigration had been funded by the Jewish agency, who were compelled to settle in some of the moshavim.[169] Some scholars have argued that such restrictions on immigrants' freedom and their dependence on governmental and quasigovernmental institutions placed the immigrants in a subordinate position. Smadar Sharon argued that some immigrants felt like subjects of an autocracy rather than citizens of a democratic country.[170] Faced with restrictions, some immigrants seemed to have fashioned for themselves an identity that placed them outside, separate from, and opposed to Israeli society, even as they engaged in little open resistance.[171]

At the same time, the infrastructure of democracy—party rivalry, a multiplicity of media outlets, the difficulties of bureaucratic coordination, and the large number of bodies with responsibility for the newcomers—gave the immigrants the foundation they needed for legitimate democratic action.[172] There is thus no basis for the claim made by some writers that covert and tacit resistance—the weapon of the weak—was all that was available to the immigrants and all that they used. On the contrary, immigrant citizen protest took place openly and on an almost daily basis. They played the cards that democracy dealt them and understood the power of their votes, in particular. They also discovered that voicing their demands loudly was a better way of getting what they wanted than politely waiting for promises to be kept.[173]

The fact that they knew that they had to be outspoken to get what they wanted is clearly shown by those immigrants who defied the authorities by mounting demonstrations or refusing to comply with their demands, only days after arriving in the country. In one case reported in *Lamerhav*, six newly arrived immigrant families insisted on spending an entire night in the bus that brought them to a new neighborhood built on the hillside above Tiberias, refusing to occupy the apartments in a temporary housing unit that they had been assigned to by the Jewish Agency. The families acted on the advice of earlier immigrants who had been living in the structures for the past three years. The new families stridently insisted that they receive housing in permanent structures, and in the end the Jewish Agency acceded to their demand. Nine other immigrant families arrived in Tiberias after categorically refusing to settle at Avivim, a new moshav on the northern border. They, too, refused to disembark from the bus that brought them there, and the Jewish Agency finally gave in and sent them to a city.[174]

In a March 1951 article, Amos Elon, a correspondent for *Haaretz*, described a sit-down strike by Yemenite immigrants who were resisting a directive to move from their tent camp, which was located close to good farmland, to permanent houses that they themselves had built, but at a site where the soil was poorer: "And the homes have been built. But the Yemenites remained — in tents; suddenly the village organized for 'resistance.' The larger number refused to enter the houses, and the minority didn't dare say a word. . . . After three months of unproductive negotiations, Mr. Levi Eshkol, head of the Jewish Agency's Settlement Department, had to come in person as the head of a delegation to persuade the immigrants to give up their rickety tents and enter the houses."[175] On top of economic hardship came the frustration that resulted from unemployment, placement in nascent farming settlements, and the humiliation they felt at being assigned make-work and treated as unskilled laborers.[176]

A study of the development of public protest in these years found that immigrants organized to demand more food (that is, food they could eat), better living conditions, the right to choose their permanent place of residence, better medical care, the right to send their children to schools that fit with their religious views, fair wages, and of course jobs. Most of their protests were reactions to the harsh socioeconomic conditions confronting a poor country in its initial years, problems that the authorities had no resources to address. The study counted seventy-three instances of protest in 1949. This number included the protests of the entire Jewish population, not just immigrants, but nevertheless, it seems low. The spring and summer saw four to five immigrant protests each month, suggesting that immigrants alone staged at least fifty protests over the course of the year.[177]

However, it is important to note that the overt acts of resistance had value beyond resolving burning issues of the moment. They should be seen as acts of democratic citizenship. The problems were severe. Nonetheless, the protests were aimed not only at solving them but also at forcing the authorities to listen to the protesters and grant them recognition.

The Demand to Live with Dignity

The demands, like those of Avraham Avtalyon, did not concern only living conditions and the allotment of resources; they also had to do with social standing, respect, and identity.[178] The immigrants had material needs, and they felt that they were not respected. This latter phenomenon was particularly acute during their initial days in the country. Here is one description of the series of humiliations immigrants had to endure at the Sha'ar Ha'Aliyah selection camp[179] at the hands of camp workers associated with Mapai:

> Girls arriving at Sha'ar Ha'Aliyah are subject to humiliations at the hands of the police and camp staff. Some are given preferential treatment by receiving a room and a food card with improper intentions; the dining hall is crowded, but instead of providing explanations to the immigrants that they must follow instructions and avoid congestion, the police are used to eject them by beating them; there is no one to explain to the immigrant how to arrange his affairs and how to act to avoid unnecessary trouble; immigrants are treated with contempt; . . . the established workers left . . . leaving only workers who are themselves new immigrants and who have, overnight, turned into policemen and givers of orders; the treatment of the immigrants is hurtful and repugnant. . . . Their first encounter with the country is, for them, a huge disappointment. . . . The nurse also treats the immigrants with scorn, and the doctor offers no attention to the immigrant who seeks him out; a regime of orders and beatings prevails at the camp.[180]

The resistance displayed by the immigrants expressed not only their refusal to accept the prevailing order and their desire to change it, but also what should be taken as their rejection of the disdain with which they were treated. Immigrants staged hunger strikes at a number of camps in 1949. These were both the desperate cries of people who had no other means at their disposal and a potent performance of a refusal to accept the food that the government and the Jewish Agency had decided they should eat. Hunger strikes were strikes for a physical need, food, and they counted as an absolute refusal to accept things as they were.

A lively debate ensued among Israelis regarding the immigrants' demand that they not be treated with contempt. Immigrants were quoted as protesting the emotional injustice being done to them. But as in Avtalyon's case, established Israelis too voiced their frustration at the failure of some of their compatriots to exhibit proper behavior toward the newcomers. In March 1949, *Al Hamishmar* published an interview with an elderly immigrant from Shanghai who said quite simply: "The official can't give me an apartment, and he is not much help in finding me a livelihood, but why is he so rude? After all, a pleasant word doesn't cost money." After reporting this statement, the journalist told his readers:

> I gazed at the old Jew and his wife and I was ashamed for the entire Yishuv. After all, that official, that rude man, is one of us. We, the Yishuv, assigned him to care for the new immigrants. We placed him in the country's show window . . . but I did not empower him to be rude. . . . Of course it's understood that every new immigrant is going to have a tough time before he finds himself. But these adjustment troubles should be in the nature of heat rash, which the Israeli climate, not the Jewish Agency, gives the immigrants. It comes and goes and leaves no marks. But rudeness is worse than heat rash, it's like chicken pox—even after it goes away it leaves marks, if not on the face, than on the immigrant's soul.[181]

A writer for *Haboker* offered his readers an account of how the immigrants felt, following a trip he had made to the Jordan Valley. The residents of the transit camps there felt rejected. He reported that they told him: "established Israelis don't want us. We aren't good enough for them." The reporter asserted that these accusations must be exaggerated and were perhaps completely unfounded. But he understood that "the fact isn't really important, what's important is the feeling the immigrants have."[182]

In conclusion I offer one more example, a particularly heart-rending one. A few months prior to the Saqiya B transit camp delegation's journey to the Knesset, another group from that camp and its sister camp, Saqiya A, went to Tel Aviv to demonstrate. The immediate cause was the injury of an immigrant from Saqiya B, Yitzhak Shaharabani, during a disturbance that had taken place next to the employment bureau at the camp. The injuries were serious, and the twenty-two-year-old Iraqi immigrant's life was in danger. The demonstrators demanded better treatment from the Jewish Agency: "We do not want good food or clothes. Not luxury apartments, either. We know what the situation in the country is. But treat us like human beings, see that we are suffering and miserable people. Because if you don't want us, why did you bring us here? For officials to kill us like dogs?"[183]

Despite the anguish of their absorption process, it is clear from this passage that the immigrants were not seeking to become the masters of their masters. They did not expect that—not in 1949; not at the time of the Wadi Salib riots of 1959; and not years later, when the Black Panther movement took up the cause of this same population. The great majority considered themselves loyal Israelis. They sought to become partners in shaping the social order. They yearned to feel equal, to belong—they asked for recognition.[184] An examination of the sources from that period also shows that the absorbing population and institutions did not seek to yoke the immigrants to their own goals and purposes and turn them into second-class citizens—that is, established Israelis did not aspire to lord it over the newcomers.[185] Despite cases in which established Israelis displayed scorn and rejection of the immigrants, the national ethos, which proclaimed the brotherhood and equality of all Jews, moderated this alienation felt by the newcomers. Despite the discrimination the immigrants suffered from in the 1950s, they remained justifiably hopeful of achieving recognition and equality.[186]

Listening to the Immigrants

"It is necessary that people feel that they have come among brothers who are concerned and who take care of their problems. But what is the situation now? They have the feeling that they are abandoned and neglected, as if they have come to an alien country. . . . The Diaspora has arrived here and we are neglecting it, at times neglecting it in a 'criminal way.'"[187] This incisive charge was pronounced by the historian Ben-Zion Dinur at a meeting of writers and intellectuals convened by Prime Minister David Ben-Gurion in March 1949, just after the war ended. The purpose of the meeting was to discuss how intellectuals could be involved in immigrant absorption. This meeting and its outcome will be discussed below.

As I have shown, the government — while doing its best to provide for the immigrants' material wants, although falling short — neglected no less important but intangible needs. The impersonal nature of modern bureaucracy virtually ensured that the newcomers' encounter with the absorption apparatus would engender and entrench the feeling that they were being treated with contempt and rejection.[188] In response to this, Ben-Gurion appealed in 1952 to all civil servants, army officers, lawyers, policemen, and other officials to change their behavior. His detailed and utopian portrait of an ideal attentive government worker testifies to the fact that, in reality, most of them were the opposite:

> One should never disregard the most precious thing that the country stands on — *the citizen, the living person.* The civil servant necessarily meets, on a daily basis in his work for the state, living human beings whose needs are provided for by the state. . . . The living person who appeals to the civil servant does not see the country as a whole — he sees the state's delegate, and on that basis judges the state. The civil servant has not done his duty if he is only loyal to the state, if he does not make contact with the living person who applies to him as the state's emissary — with sympathy, with love, in full identification with and intuitive understanding of his pain, his wants, his plight, his deepest resentment, as well as his shortcomings and flaws. . . . The civil servant cannot do his duty if he views the person turning to him for help and guidance only as a number in his orderly card file — rather than as a living person. . . . The civil servant cannot do his job without *love of both his fellow man and his fellow Jew.*[189]

With the goal of mitigating the disaffection between the absorbing agencies and the immigrants, Yehuda Borla, one of the writers who attended the postwar meeting with Ben-Gurion, proposed that the educated elite place itself at the service of the newcomers and serve as a conduit for their voice:

> I find it necessary to remark that there is a great deal of indignation and resentment, that a number of matters in the country are not as they should be. A person who has the ability to write a few lines in the newspaper . . . writes in the newspaper. And another can't write . . . bears the resentment in his heart and spreads it among others. But it also happens that things are written and read but do not get corrected. We thus need to create some sort of platform for the people, a "People's Voice Platform," in which principally a number of writers, scholars, and cultural figures will serve; each grievance

from the voice of the people will come to them, in writing or orally, and they will serve solely as intermediaries, to direct the complaints to the necessary place, so as to get all injustices corrected.[190]

Seeking to bridge the cultural chasm between established Israelis and immigrants and to find solutions to the latters' wide range of problems, writers, teachers, public figures, and artists founded an organization called 'Im ha'Oleh (meaning "with the immigrant"). Its members visited immigrant camps and neighborhoods, met immigrants, and lectured before them in an array of languages.[191]

They were not alone. Throughout the 1950s, many other organizations worked to mediate between the immigrants and both the absorbing society and the authorities.

Some paid workers who were part of the absorption apparatus of the state or the Jewish Agency, as well as some soldiers, also felt a sense of responsibility, identified with the immigrants, and stood by them. I propose to view the individuals and organizations that helped and listened to the immigrants — volunteers, employees, and enlisted men and women — as a network of listeners. The network included women who worked in health and medical organizations and operated in a professional capacity in immigrant communities and also those who sought to help the immigrants as volunteers in the framework of women's organizations and the Moshavim Movement (the umbrella organization that united the comunal farming villages known as moshavim).[192] Students and members of youth movements operated in a similar way as part of the Shurat haMitnadvim organization, with the goal of creating direct contacts between established Israelis and immigrants in transit camps, immigrant neighborhoods, and immigrant moshavim. These volunteers visited immigrant families on a weekly basis, catalogued their needs, and offered help. They intervened when salaries were not paid, made needed contacts with medical personnel, helped immigrants receive loans or discounts, and provided them with vocational training. When living arrangements needed to be found for the elderly, the volunteers took the initiative. They advocated for immigrants' rights before the authorities.[193]

Longtime members of the Moshavim Movement mobilized to provide assistance to immigrants by sending instructors to the immigrant farming villages. The older generation spent about two years serving in this capacity, after which members of the movement's younger generation took their place.[194] The movement also sent emissaries to speak with immigrant settlers and to study the organizational difficulties faced by the new immigrant moshavim.[195] In addition to volunteers who worked as part of organizations, there were individuals who acted on their own initiative.[196] Lawyers offered legal aid to the indigent.[197] Volunteers taught Hebrew to immigrants living in the large cities.[198] A network of volunteers in the Jerusalem region taught Hebrew and mathematics for years in the transit camps located in the city and in nearby immigrant settlements. When civilian agencies and organizations proved inadequate to the task of absorption, the Israel Defense Forces sent soldiers to work in transit camps and outlying settlements. At least a few of the soldiers, especially women, established personal relations with the immigrants.[199] Members of the Knesset and cabinet ministers also visited immigrant communities.[200] For some people, such as Idelson, these visits impelled them to seek more ways to aid the newcomers. Much of the work among the immigrants was focused on providing practical assistance. But contemporary testimonies indicate that friendships also formed between people on the two sides, especially between immigrant women and established Israeli women who served as teachers and counselors.[201]

A spectrum of attitudes can be discerned among established Israelis who aided immigrants. At one end were Israelis who viewed the immigrants as equals and felt a personal obligation to help them. At the other end were those who viewed the newcomers as indigents—inferiors whom they were duty-bound to help.[202] Religious Israelis were particularly attentive to the remonstrations of observant immigrants and worked to provide for their religious needs. However, these Israelis also at times took advantage of the plight of observant immigrants for their own partisan political ends.[203]

Was this network of listeners attentive to the immigrants' troubles out of empathy and acceptance of them? The answer to the question depends, of course, on context and circumstances. However, more often than not, even the most empathetic Israelis found the culture of the immigrants to be alien. That meant that they had limited understanding of and sympathy for at least some of the newcomers' problems.[204] The act of listening had not only cultural boundaries but also political and personal ones, which determined how the absorbers perceived the immigrants and their needs.[205] Nevertheless, at the very least it is clear that in spite of their patronizing attitudes, Orientalist biases, and arrogance, this network of listeners—and not a few policymakers—understood that the lives of the immigrants had to be enhanced and that their physical and social isolation needed to be ameliorated.[206]

Counselors working at newly established moshavim where newcomers were settled adopted the point of view of the immigrants, asserting that they had been discriminated against in comparison with immigrants who had been settled in urban neighborhoods. This was particularly the case with the younger generation of counselors, who displayed a lack of confidence in the bureaucracy that dealt with the immigrants, blaming it for the newcomers' miserable circumstances. These counselors exceeded their authority, circumventing their superiors and doing all they could to help the immigrants.[207] As with counselors and workers in the transit camps in the country's periphery, officers, soldiers, and even government and Jewish Agency officials responsible for immigrants developed an identification with their charges and censured the absorbing agencies for their negligence.[208] A report sent by an army commander to his superior officer displays such empathy: "They feel . . . an oppressive loneliness and are becoming increasingly aware that they were dumped in a bleak and desolate place, without any oversight, without guidance, and without any prospects for the future."[209] Another example comes from the secretary — that is, the director — of the Ajur transit camp in a request he made to Minister of Labor Myerson to accelerate the paving of a road to the camp. "We see that the spirit of the people here is not strong," he explained. "Could the Minister of Labor . . . relieve the anguish of want . . . and the isolation that the people of the camp feel."[210]

The network of listeners identified with the difficulties faced by the immigrants and waged battles with the absorption agencies to promote the interests of the newcomers.[211] To the extent that they could, they helped provide the immigrants with their material needs — workdays, warm clothing, sufficient food, education and health services, and infrastructure like electricity and water. At times they also provided emotional warmth and sympathy.[212] In exchange, they expected the immigrants to adapt to their new country's culture and mores — to make themselves like the people who were helping them.[213] The absorbers thus sought to shape the immigrants in their own image. This attitude grew out of the self-confident national cultural repertoire that had taken form during the Yishuv period.[214]

At the same time, and despite the dominant status of the new Hebrew culture, absorbers sometimes revised their modes of action in response to immigrants' cultural needs and desires.[215] The demand of the network of listeners for remedies for the immigrants' material and emotional state contained a demand to grant the immigrants recognition. This second demand grew out of a universalist perspective: the immigrants, the absorbers claimed, were human beings (and Jews) just as they, the representatives of the dominant culture, were. The network of listeners did not stipulate recognition of the uniqueness and richness of the cultural spectrum that the immigrants represented.[216] Yet even in this regard the beginnings of a change were evident. This can be seen in an article bearing the title "Who Will Learn from Whom?," which was printed in a collection published to mark the tenth anniversary of the immigrant moshavim in 1959. The author, Rivka Guber, one of the senior Moshavim Movement activists, confessed to acting with European arrogance toward the immigrants and to not acknowledging the value of the variegated cultures of the newcomers from the Islamic world. She warned her colleagues against creating a hierarchy in which the new Israeli culture was privileged over the cultures brought by the newcomers.[217]

JOINING THE ADVOCATES OF CHANGE

Immigrants' demonstrations, hunger strikes, vandalism, attacks on officials, and abandonment of settlements all made an impression on policymakers and volunteers and came up for discussion among those who made decisions.[218] Periodicals published by the establishment were full of criticisms of the deficient living conditions of the immigrants and insults to their dignity and feelings.[219] In spite of their anxiety that the regime's legitimacy might be undermined, Mapai decision makers identified with the immigrants.[220] At a meeting of the Mapai Central Committee on March 5, 1950, Minister of Labor Golda Myerson told her colleagues:

> I do not understand the people of the camps. Why have they never gone . . . to Pardes Hannah and broken all the windows in the houses around them. Were I and [Member of the Knesset Shmuel] Dayan living in camps like these — we would certainly be breaking windows. I would at least. They are not required to understand our difficulties. . . . What will we do with hungry people when there are tens of thousands [of them] in the country? We anticipate next year seeing 55,000 job seekers in the [Labor] Bureaus. What will we tell them? We'll explain to them that they need to perform productive labor? They are prepared to do that. Will we explain to them that it's better to work in industry than on the roads? They are prepared to do that. We won't feed them by explaining economic theory to them. . . . They are not asking for anything except work and food. . . . It may well be that we just don't have the strength to make this business work. We're going to come out of the business one way or another, or we'll go to hell. If we have

to, we'll go to hell. I want to go by constructing housing, creating jobs for people rather than by having people die in the camps.[221]

As noted, acts of protest by immigrants were not met only with punishment. Negotiations were held with immigrants, and in at least some cases they were granted additional assistance. This was also true in the case of those who sought to leave the immigrant moshavim. The archives contain long lists of the names of immigrants who sought to leave the farming villages and show how their cases were handled by officials. Most such applications were approved, and the applicants were provided with alternative housing. Over the course of a few years, efforts were also made to improve economic and social conditions in the moshavim so as to reduce the incentive to leave.[222]

The absorption of the immigrants into Israel's democracy was rife with contradictions. On the one hand, the immigrants enjoyed a broad freedom of expression and had access to the media. They were a presence in the public space; negotiations were conducted with them; and they were able to frighten the authorities, who were anxious about losing control. When unemployed immigrants demonstrated, it was seen as an important expression of their rights, and not just by the parties of the left. "They want to be constructive brothers in the homeland, not to stand in line at the welfare office. They want to adjust, to integrate, to lend a hand to the enterprise of constructing [the nation]. Their demonstration is justified—it is not a demonstration of the despairing, but of people demanding justice," asserted *Hed Hamizrah*, speaking for immigrants who demonstrated in Ramla in July 1949.[223] Nevertheless, it is clear that despite their access to the public arena and their use of their political power, and despite the encouragement they received from the network of listeners, substantial disparities of power and status separated the immigrants from their absorbers. The immigrants' use of their voices as citizens brought them into the ranks of the advocates for change. In other words, their struggles can be seen as a sort of rite of initiation through which they entered the ranks of Israel's citizenry. Yet this achievement did not produce an adequate response to their economic and social plight. In particular, it did not relieve the emotional distress that became the formative influence on their self-awareness. Even if some of their material needs were met in response to their demands, and even if they began to sense that they had the power to act to change their lives, they still felt the lack of "a smidgen of warmth and emotion," the absence of real understanding of how they felt, as

Avtalyon so well put it. What they did not get was recognition and a sense of feeling that they belonged.

Not all immigrants raised their voices.[224] In every society and at every time there are pockets of silence. This is especially true in the case of people who have just arrived in a new country in great distress. The essence of my claim is that the immigrants had at their disposal a plethora of channels for expressing their opinions, making demands, and demonstrating opposition. In other words, the immigrants, taken as a whole, were not a silenced group — they were a speaking one. Not only was their voice heard, but the absorbers could not disregard either their vocal or their nonverbal protests.[225] Thanks to the democratic nature of the country and the immaturity of the regime, the immigrants comprehended what channels were open to them. The waves of protests and the most common responses to them show that many of the immigrants acted fearlessly. Consequently, even though many of them had no past experience of democracy, their modes of action display, overall, an understanding of the nature of a multiparty democratic polity.[226] At least some of them had no familiarity, prior to their immigration, with how to speak out publicly, freely, and intrepidly. Thus the very option of raising their voices in protest, the experience of liberation exemplified by the removal of obstacles to speech, was of great import.[227] This rapid internalization of democratic life may provide some explanation of the wave of protests that broke out in the months that followed the 1948 war.[228]

Patterns of public expression and protest, along with the way officials and society in general responded to them, were thus established during this initial encounter. By the mid-1950s the model was in place — immigrants would demonstrate, and then a delegation of them would negotiate with the authorities.[229] Thanks to the network of listeners and the fact that at least some policymakers were also attentive to the mood of the newcomers, a dialogue between the two sides began to take form.[230] From the network of listeners' contacts with the immigrants sprang an initial web of relations. One reservation should be added, however: the relations were of varying emotional depth. At most, in the case of the absorption apparatus and the Israeli population as a whole, they were merely correct.

The social gap between absorbers and newcomers and the latters' feelings of alienation were not unremarked by policymakers, and as already shown, they were not unremarked by the country's founding father, either. As early as August 1949, in a talk he gave to the command staff of the Youth Corps (in Hebrew, Gadna), Ben-Gurion shared his impressions of the Israeli society then taking form:

> The first thing I learned and which stunned me is the huge distance, I could almost say the abyss, between the Yishuv's management echelon and the majority of the nation. . . . Those who stand at the head of all the parties and every municipality, the Histadrut, youth movements, and so on — they are a single echelon, one could almost say a *nation*. And there is a second nation, that which lives in the poor neighborhoods, the suburbs of Jerusalem and Tel Aviv, and now also in Jaffa, Ramla, Lod, Tiberias, and Safed . . . that is another nation entirely. . . . These two nations almost never meet. While all of us repeat "all Jews are brothers," and each of us is so dedicated to the nation and concerned about the nation, . . . that is an *abstract* nation. . . . But those simple flesh-and-blood human beings who live in shacks . . . in dark houses without illumination, often without sufficient food — they do not know *that* nation. We do not live with it.[231]

In using the first person plural, Ben-Gurion did not except himself. He took himself to task as well as others for being distant and alienated from the immigrants. He clearly understood what the immigrants needed, and he asked the members of his audience to devote themselves to the immigrant absorption enterprise in its most profound sense — the creation of solidarity and equality: "The children, adults, and elderly . . . every living human being who is in fact part of that abstract concept . . . what we're talking about is that we need to be in contact with him and to provide for him and connect to him, and display reciprocal responsibility for him, and to be ashamed if he has less education than me, if he lives in worse conditions than I do, if he cannot know what I know. . . . Our duty is to turn it into a dynamic reality, for it not to be just a framework, but real."[232]

A year and a half later, in March 1951, Amos Elon portrayed in *Haaretz* the polarization between immigrants and established Israelis. He asked acquaintances of his whether they knew any new immigrants personally. He found that, with the exception of family members, no personal ties had been established between old-timers and newcomers. He declared that, in fact, there was "a second Israel behind the screen of corrugated metal shacks, right under our windows, in hearing distance of a cry of 'Shalom.'"[233] The situation he described was widespread, but it hardly represented the entire picture.

· · · · · · · · · ·

Despite the understanding that decision makers showed of the difficulties and suffering of the immigrants, the force of the waves of protest of 1949 and their prominence in the media and political discourse made many policymakers feel that they were threatened. Aware of the huge disparity between the situation in the field and the hopes for an exemplary society that were part and parcel of Zionist ideology (even if different brands of Zionism saw that exemplary society in different ways), policymakers feared they would fail at the huge task that had been assigned to them: the establishment of a functioning state and a cohesive society. At these difficult moments, when the absorption apparatus was overextended, only one resource remained available to policymakers, Ben-Gurion first and foremost among them. It was the hope that by working together they could overcome the difficulties, just as they had, at heavy cost, defeated Israel's enemies.[234]

The immigrants, in contrast, confronted a huge gap between the hopes that had led them to Israel and the reality they encountered there. They struggled for their very subsistence and encountered alienation, scorn, and discrimination. Most of all, they felt that their voice was not being heard. Although they shouted in the city squares and conducted negotiations with the government, their protests were covered by the press, and they had a network of listeners, most of the immigrants of the 1950s seem to have felt that no one was paying any attention to them. At that primal historical postwar moment, relations between immigrants and established Israelis and between new citizens and the governing apparatus varied widely. There was undoubtedly a huge gap between the volume of immigrants' shouts and the extent to which they were listened to. This is especially evident in the instrumental nature of the negotiations conducted with angry demonstrators, in which there was often no real dialogue. Nevertheless, the immigrants' vigorous presence in the public arena and their ability to make their demands and on occasion obtain satisfaction, demonstrates that despite the pain, disappointment, and hurt they felt, they not only did not lose their voices in the process of immigrating, but in many cases gained a voice for the first time.[235]

In his well-known book *Exit, Voice, and Loyalty*, the influential economist Albert Hirschman offered a model of the conduct of individuals in relation to organizations and states. He claimed simply that when an organization or state declines or deteriorates (or, it should be added, when individuals sense that this is happening), citizens have two options. One is exit — that is, leaving the organization or country. The other is voice — that is, remaining in the framework while criticizing it, with the goal of changing the way the organization is run. The concept of loyalty serves as the deciding or moderating factor when the citizen makes her choice between these options. The greater her loyalty to the organization or state, the greater will be her inclination to criticize the existing situation while remaining in the framework, as opposed to simply leaving.[236] The immigrants of the 1950s used their voices. Only a small minority left the country or closed themselves off and constructed a contrary or alternative identity.

The Zionist ethos promised equality to all Jews and contained the sense that a long-standing historical injustice was being repaired in the new country. In the new State of Israel, every Jew was supposed to be of value by virtue of being a member of the community.[237] The new identity was meant to be based on a sense of self-respect that Jews had found hard to maintain in the face of the contempt and hostility with which they had been treated by non-Jews in the Diaspora.

These ideals, and the great achievement of the founding of the state, were powerful forces in shaping the feelings of the young country's citizens. The immigrants felt they had been deceived when they had been led to believe that after arriving in Israel they would become equal members of the Israeli collective.[238]

Ben-Gurion was profoundly aware of the immigrants' full range of human needs, and of the duty the absorbers owed to the newcomers. But the great majority of established Israelis did not attend to Ben-Gurion's entreaties. The recognition they granted the immigrants was largely an abstract, theoretical one. In Honneth's terminology, Israeli society granted the immigrants ideological recognition.[239] Immigration was viewed as vital to the state, and the new arrivals were immediately granted citizenship. But they were not fully integrated into society in the political sense.[240] Their demand for full recognition, warmth, and a sense of equality (including the material manifestations of such equality) was not met.[241] That kind of recognition also came with conditions: they were expected to change and to contribute to the nation. The standards for meeting these measures were set by the absorbers.

Nonetheless, the fact that the immigrants were invested with political rights granted them the capacity for taking action to change their status. This action brought them much frustration, but on occasion it also gave them a sense of achievement and some limited measure of power to shape their fates. They used it to constitute their citizenship, expressing their confidence that they would someday become full and equal citizens in every sense of the word.

CONCLUSION

· ·

The establishment of the Jewish nation-state created a space in which Jews could strive to constitute rights and freedoms and create a common civil identity. All Jews could participate—women and men, immigrants and old-timers, policymakers and ordinary citizens. True, most decision makers and core groups in the established population were committed in theory to the democratic principles embodied in the country's Declaration of Independence. They sincerely wished to live in accordance with the universalist principle of fundamental human equality.[1] But the path toward realizing this egalitarian vision was strewn with failures brought on by political constraints, ideological contradictions, economic and security challenges, bureaucratic failings, and the full range of human weaknesses.

This new democratic space became a battlefield for ideologies and religious beliefs, normative cultural systems, interests, and sensibilities. It teemed with civil and political activity that pitted clear-cut but opposing ideological positions against each other. Most salient was the contention between the socialist left and the liberal-capitalist center and right. However, the struggle was also fed by intuitive responses to disappointment, suffering, pain, heartbreak, discrimination, and restrictions on freedom. Despite a pervasive sense of uncertainty, in terms of both the new country's economy and its security, political and civil activism was grounded in optimism. Many Israelis maintained a dogged faith in the ability of the members of the nation to work together to build a good, modern, and enlightened society that would benefit human beings as individuals. This was the case even if not all aspects of modernity and progress were adopted in equal measure, and if some of the contours of the future society remained in dispute.

The state of rights in Israel at this time reflected all these factors, including political power relations and the values of the parties in the governing coalition. Mirroring rapid changes in historical circumstances and lessons learned in practice, it also expressed the work of agents of change from civil society, and manifested, to a certain extent, the voices of citizens. At the same time that new rights were constituted, such as the right to childhood, some freedoms were restricted, such as the freedom of movement. On the one hand the state endeavored to shrink the gender gap, while on the other hand gender differences were entrenched when the new state reaffirmed the standing of religious law in personal affairs. Immigrant citizens strove to lower the social barriers that set them apart from established Israelis, but at the same time some immigrant groups acted to enshrine gender hierarchies. Established Israelis formed networks of listeners and opened their ears and hearts to the immigrants with the goal of facilitating their absorption, while at the same time constituting and reinforcing cultural hierarchies. Thus, within the boundaries formed in close association with emerging Jewish nationalism, categories of nation, gender, culture, ethnicity, religion, class, and seniority in the country served as the basis for simultaneous and contradictory struggles. On the one side, the goal was the pursuit of equality; on the other side, the perpetuation of social hierarchies.

Power differentials between the Ashkenazim and the Mizrahim, between the labor movement and the bourgeoisie, and between men and women were defining features of Israeli society from the start. I have shown, however, that these dichotomies were less rigid than scholarship has thus far claimed, that the barriers between groups were permeable, and that relations between these groups changed to a certain extent over time.[2] A common national identity and the sense of solidarity and belonging engendered by that identity reduced the distinctions between groups. However, these sentiments also served as a smoke screen that made it possible to deny the existence of such distinctions. Other extenuating factors were the grant of a basic (even if extremely limited) suite of housing, education, and health services; the difficult security situation, requiring cooperation among citizens in the face of external threats; and the civil equality embodied by the grant of political rights. Even weak groups, such as the immigrants, had an arena in which they could voice their anger and fight to improve their position in society, demand equality, and defend their freedom. They, too, acted in the public arena and, in doing so, participated from the beginning in the creation of Israel's civil identity — despite the fact that, at least at first, they felt less a part of the state than did the established population, and certainly than that population's elite.[3]

The vociferous cultural process of constituting the national community broadened democracy and encompassed (at least in part) children, women, and immigrants. Yet, at the same time, it silenced the voice of the Arab minority.

The difference between the intensity of the Jewish civil experience and the meagerness of the minority's civil affiliation carried with it a certain advantage — that of marginality. Muslim and Christian religious institutions and the advocates of the patriarchal tradition of the Arab minority certainly did not find fault with the regime's limited motivation to consistently and vigorously enforce progressive principles on Palestinian girls by preventing early marriages. In this, the Israeli state, like the Mandate regime that preceded it, acted inconsistently. On the one hand it passed progressive legislation that ostensibly applied to all its citizens, but on the other hand it did not enforce the law within the minority population. From the perspective of both today's multiculturalist currents and the Ottoman tradition of recognizing the autonomy of religious institutions, this negligent enforcement could be seen as an accommodation of differences. But given the spirit of the time, it should also, and perhaps primarily, be seen as a manifestation of exclusion: Palestinian girls were not part of the nation in formation and thus did not receive the same protections that Jewish girls did. Theoretically, the Israeli state was committed to full equality, as embodied in the grant of Israeli citizenship to the country's Arab inhabitants. Albeit slowly and grudgingly, it issued these minority citizens Israeli identity cards.[4] But the blood spilled and animosity produced by the long Jewish-Arab conflict, and the welding of Jewish national identity to Israeli civil identity, erected high barriers between the two peoples. The mantle of rights and freedoms that protected Israel's citizens did not cover them all equally: the part that cloaked the Arabs had many more holes in it.[5]

The battles for rights examined in this book, chosen for their diversity and the wealth of information they provide, reveal some of the more profound aspects of the experience of citizenship in early Israel — those that touched on people's ways of life and granted them control over their bodies and surroundings, as well as those that touched on their inner beings, the essence of their self-awareness. Citizenship is not just a formal identity expressing an inborn connection to a particular state, nor is it simply the sum total of the legal rights and freedoms enjoyed by a country's citizens. Citizenship is part of people's most intimate conception of themselves, forged in the depths of their souls. It is constructed of beliefs and opinions and collective memory; it is crafted out of emotional identification and fraternity, as well as frustration and injury. Its form is constantly changing as a result of day-to-day experience, and it crystallizes both in public activity motivated by mobilization in the name of the state and in protest activity fed by rage and a critical attitude toward the state and its government. Citizenship takes shape as an individual writes a letter to a cabinet minister requesting assistance in obtaining a permit to travel outside the country, participates in an angry demonstration in front of the Knesset, or helps extricate a girl from an underage marriage.

The civil identity of Israelis, like that of the Yishuv, was not uniform. On the contrary, it was sufficiently flexible to contain both liberal and socialist ideas, religious and secular approaches, and an entire range of contradictory standards in the area of gender relations and family values. The identity of both the established elites and of many of the new immigrants was centered on a common core: an aspiration to establish an exemplary, free, and cohesive society in which all Jews would feel self-confident and proud of their material and cultural achievements. This core also included an expectation that individuals would in large measure bow to communal needs, especially in everything connected with defense and security. The new Israeli identity also included expectations that time would meld Israelis, old and new, into a unified if heterogeneous culture (even if the values of that common culture were hotly debated) and that a measure of intimacy would be achieved among the members of the imagined community.

During these early years, many Israelis felt as if they had a common fate, but they also realized that much divided them — politics, ethnicity, and Jewish religious practices and beliefs. For many of the newcomers, democracy and its values were new and alien. Yet precisely because of the population's ideological, religious, and ethnic diversity, and despite the novelty of democratic experience for many of the newcomers, the country's democratic foundation served as a bridge over troubled waters.[6] The fights for rights discussed here display the determination of both citizens and policymakers to shore up this foundation and expand the mantle of citizens' rights and freedoms, like a patchwork quilt sewn out of variegated and sometimes clashing concepts of freedom, equality, and fraternity.

Once the Israeli leadership decided not to promulgate a written constitution that could instigate a paradigmatic legal shift, this quilt of citizens' rights and freedoms was constrained by previous traditions. Among these were religious beliefs and the religious autonomy of the Ottoman and Mandate regimes; Mandate emergency laws that significantly curtailed freedoms; and the heritage of Mandate governance, which bequeathed to the Israeli state a great deal of utilitarian leeway in the area of law enforcement.[7] At the same time, the recent and distant past served as an inspiration for expanding the scope of citizens' rights. The distant past, in the form of the ethics of the biblical prophets, served as a lodestone; while the Mandate, which incorporated many modern elements such as a revision of the status of children in society, served as a precedent. Israeli decision makers, who had been brought up on liberal values before they moved to the Jewish state in formation; the progressive tradition exemplified by women's organizations; and labor Zionism's socialist roots all contributed to the constitution of social and civil rights.

During its initial years, the Israeli state found itself in the grip of phenomena pushing it in contradictory directions. It was overwhelmed with concerns about its fundamental military, economic, and political security, which often prompted decision makers to act unbendingly and arbitrarily, out of fear of losing control. At the same time, paradoxically, the weakness of the state and its bureaucratic apparatus led decision makers to display flexibility and enter into dialogue with discontented citizens.

Finally, the expansion of rights was accelerated by a vision of the future that was based on a modernist (if sometimes contradictory) conception of progress. It emerged in a series of resolutions settling competing ideas representing progressive, socialist, liberal, universal, and particularist ways of thinking. Even when a particular goal was broadly shared—for example, the prevention of premature marriage—there were sharp disagreements about the proper pace of change and the right way to bring it about. The struggle between differing political, religious, and social outlooks meant that change happened slowly. In fact, even when a decision was made—for example, in the form of a piece of legislation—battles over the issue at hand did not subside. This slowed the extension of rights and freedoms.

The actors in the fights for rights that I have examined in this book were decision makers—cabinet ministers, members of the Knesset, judges, and experts—and civil society organizations and volunteers, as well as ad hoc alliances of interest groups and individual citizens. These ranged from a courageous girl who ran away from her husband and asked for help from women's organizations to Supreme Court justices to a citizen threatening to sue to legislators laboring for years to amend a law, and from immigrants staging a hunger strike to volunteers mobilizing to help newcomers. The positions, actions, and feelings of state agents on the one hand and citizens on the other hand exemplify opposing interests and points of dispute but also show that a complex web of mutual interactions emerged. Despite the fact that decision makers held power, while individual citizens in general, and immigrants in particular, were weak, the two sides interacted constantly and intensely, whether directly or through the mediation of bureaucrats, journalists, political rivals, and reformers. The result was a dynamic and emotionally charged web of relations. Leaders sometimes lorded it over citizens, seeming to be insensitive and blind to the plight of individuals and groups. Officials could treat citizens and immigrants with resentment, discrimination, and scorn, observing procedures with overly bureaucratic strictness. Yet as I show here, many officials also responded to these supplicants with sympathy and empathy, doing all they could to help.

Demands for policy changes came from every direction. The middle class, feeling that its autonomy and freedom were unjustly impeded by the travel restrictions instituted by the government, fought to revise those restrictions both through a public and political campaign and through individual direct interactions with officials. Letters written by citizens to government leaders and officials protested these policies and castigated their authors and enforcers, but those letters were also part of a dialogue involving both disagreements and fluctuating points of agreement. The letters of recommendation that were required for an exit permit put decision makers in direct contact with the human beings behind the dry statistics, confronting them with the inner worlds and biographies of individual citizens. While many applications were turned down, the pressure exerted by government ministers to grant exit permits, and the fortitude and agency displayed by citizens, sometimes got applications approved even when they did not accord with the government's official policy. Finally, ongoing and cumulative pressure, along with varying historical and political circumstances, led to changes in the law, expanding the freedom of movement of Israel's Jewish citizens until this freedom was stabilized for a long period at a point of national consensus.

Despite their economic and social disadvantages, the immigrants were not passive victims. They quickly displayed their awareness and capacity for organization, not to mention their talent for exposing the regime's vulnerable spots and limited reach. Their protests, which placed the government on the verge of losing control, forced policymakers to give in to at least some demands. Some decision makers realized that citizens required a measure of relief from the vicissitudes of daily life — in other words, that the immigrants needed room to breathe. The fact that emigration remained an option for disgruntled citizens and newcomers forced cabinet ministers and officials to find ways to reduce public discontent. The mobilization of a network of listeners to the immigrants shows that the latter could both voice their critique of the regime and be heard. It serves as evidence that the immigrants and at least some established Israelis shared an expectation that a just society could and should be instituted — even if there were disparate ideas about what constituted justice.

Alongside constructive practical action, Israeli society in its early years was full of hopes, dreams, and expectations. The great discrepancy between the exemplary society that Israelis hoped for and the actual sorry state of affairs did not prevent many from using that vision as a standard by which to measure the society in which they lived.

Children and teenagers enjoyed a special and prominent moral standing in the value system of the Yishuv and the early state. This grew out of Zionism's ideological gaze toward the future and the fact that children were seen as the citizens of tomorrow. It was also basic to the modern progressive views of women's organizations, doctors, and welfare workers. The battle to raise the marriage age centered on young girls whose voices reformers sought to listen to and broadcast. These actors worked long and hard to save such children. Unless one sees it in its larger context, the campaign cannot be understood. The defense of children served for these core groups as a litmus test for the morality of the entire Zionist enterprise and for the authority of the new state. The voice of children played a unique role in public discourse. It expressed and reinforced the status of childhood and children in society. When a child raised his or her voice, it was not merely as the child of his or her parents. In the spirit of the time, children belonged to the nation as a whole, and the entire country was responsible for their lives and futures. As in the battle to raise the marriage age, the voice of children could serve to underline the alien culture of some of the immigrants, but it was also a way to include them in Israeli society. Unlike adult immigrants, children did not generally express anger or frustration and did not threaten decision makers. Rather, their voices made moral demands that could not easily be ignored.

In conclusion, I offer an example taken from *Davar*, the newspaper of the Histadrut, which was controlled by the ruling party, Mapai. The article, from October 1956, offers the impressions of the correspondent, Rachel Adiv, after a visit to the "big area," a dilapidated and war-wrecked border region between Tel Aviv and Jaffa where immigrants lived. She offers a picture of people living in filthy hovels, with open sewage running between homes, and despondent inhabitants. Among the spectrum of voices she quotes in her piece are the voices of children. One girl called out to her:

> "Lady, give us a different house." ... "But a good and pretty one, with electricity, pretty and decorated, and there should be a shower, too" — "And a nice

and clean bathroom and where you can see at night," a dark-haired boy adds for his part — "And there should be a yard, with light in it," says the third boy — "And there should be a flower garden and hoe" — and "What do you call it, oh, what do you call it?" — the first girl, the group's spokeswoman, says again — "that thing you open and close, you must know" — "A curtain, a curtain," the bony boy suddenly and joyfully remembers.[8]

Electricity, a shower, a flower garden, and a curtain — in short, a decent childhood — are the modern cultural foundation that children demand to share. Adiv spends most of her article depicting troubles and shortages. But the children she quotes describe what should be, what exists in their imagination. The little details they offer create a possible and different reality, one in which the national home provides all comers with equal living conditions and civil status. It is a national home where everyone feels at home. Their innocent comments highlight the disparity between the ideological imperative of national solidarity and the lack of equality. It shows the great distance between early Israeli society's values of freedom, justice, and public welfare and the actual society in which Israelis lived. Yet it contains a kernel of hope for the future. That hope is intimately linked up with the young age of the country itself, young like the children quoted in the article. The greater part of its life lies before it.

Israeli democracy, like other contemporary ones, did not in its early years live up to the promises of equality, freedom, and fraternity on which it was founded. At the time, many Israelis sensed that an intolerable gap yawned between the hopes that accompanied the founding of the state and the reality they lived in. Yet this gap did not paralyze the new society. On the contrary, the force of the vision and the enormity of the distress motivated them to act for change. The test of a new democracy is not merely the extent of the equality that it grants its citizens, but rather the political, socioeconomic, legal, and public infrastructure that it establishes and that allows weak and excluded groups to fight to gain equal rights and freedoms. Whatever its injustices and flaws, Israeli democracy in its early years offered its citizens a worthy dream and tools for making it a reality.

NOTES

. . . .

Introduction

1. Etz-Hayim 5716, 2:354.
2. BGA, Minutes Division, "Divrey sofrim," March 27, 1949, 21.
3. *Davar*, May 14, 1948.
4. *Davar*, October 3, 1948. For information about Berger, see Bareli 2007, 261–62 and 265.
5. Zamir 1994, 326.
6. For discussion of the links among rights, states, and nations, see Moyn 2010, especially 12–13, 29–31, and 41–43.
7. Migdal 2006, 8.
8. Sicron 1986, 31–32.
9. Kimmerling and Migdal 1999, 146.
10. Palestinian Arabs constituted the majority of the inhabitants prior to the 1948 war, but during the war some 700,000 Palestinians fled or were expelled (Morris 2010, 438).
11. See, for example, N. Kedar 2009, 145–47; Z. Drori 2000, 141–45, 148, 161, and 169; A. Shapira 5757, 259–62.
12. Azaryahu 1995; Almog 5756; Liebman and Don-Yihya 1983, 94–116.
13. BGA, minutes division, "Divrey Sofrim," March 27, 1949; R. Shapira 2011, 30–31.
14. See, for example, Horowitz and Lissak 1990, 58; N. Kedar 2009, 141 and 170–71; Peleg 1998, 244.
15. Wasserstein 2003, 1 and 18–19.
16. In comparison, see Ury 2012, 214–15.
17. Shachar 5763, 572.
18. N. Kedar 2009, 171–72; Kimmerling and Migdal 1999, 149; Robinson 2013, 41–44.
19. Kimmerling and Migdal 1999, 145–46. In Israel, national affiliation was favored over the territorial concept of citizenship. See Weiss 2001, 47 and 50.
20. T. Segev 1984, 12–13.
21. Morris 2010, 429–36; Penslar 2013, 225.
22. Emmanuel Sivan equates these figures to the fatality rate of Russian recruits during World War I (1991, 19–25).
23. Ibid., 52–53.
24. Barkai 2004, 773–77; Penslar 2013, 225 and 245–46.
25. Segev 1984, 12; Harris 2014, 69–73; Chazan 2014; Ben-Porat 1988, 36–41.

26. Horowitz and Lissak 1990, 25.

27. Hacohen 1994, 183–94.

28. Gal 2002, 101–3.

29. T. Segev 1984, 125–28 and 140.

30. Lissak 1999, 58–65; Rozin 2011, 180–81.

31. N. Gross 1999, 333.

32. Rozin 2011, 3–64; Hagiladi 2011, 149–337.

33. Picard 2013, 69–94.

34. Barkai 1990, 70; N. Gross 1997, 142.

35. T. Segev 1991, 180–225.

36. Rozin 2011, 189–90.

37. N. Gross 1997, 142–43; Picard 2013, 187. See also chapter 3, table 4.

38. YEA, 40–8, minutes, November 18, 1951; Kemp 2002, 61–62; Y. Tsur 2002, 85; IDFA 16–392/1955, report, December 10, 1953, and 3 Kislev 5714 (November 10, 1953); Lissak 1999, 85–87.

39. Morris 1996, 44–84 and 113–28; CZA S100/78/1, minutes, March 7, 1952; ISA, GVM 5, 21:67, March 29, 1955.

40. Morris 1996, 199–254, 299–304, and 59–362; Tal 1998, 209–34. Following the deal, France, already a major supplier of arms to Israel, agreed to increase the quality and the quantity of the weapons it sent and to rush shipments (Heimann 2015, 30–32).

41. A UN force was stationed in the Sinai Peninsula after this campaign (Bar-On 2001, 225–51).

42. From a trove of scholarly work, here is a sample: A. Shapira 5757, 260 and 264–66; Sela-Sheffy 2003; Bondy 1990; Cohn 2005; Lahav 1999, 141–47 and 150–53; Klein 1997, 53; Silber 2008, 212–13.

43. M. Tsur 1999, 5.

44. Aronson 1998; Rozin 2008, 96, 112, and 116.

45. The nature and character of the basic laws were not known then, even to the lawmakers themselves. See Rubinstein and Medina 1996, 1:283; Gavison 5758, 61; Rozin 2002a, 30.

46. Sharfman 1993, 40–45; Goldberg 5753; Aronson 1998, 25–26; Friedman and Radzyner 5767, 8 and 91–93. For a comprehensive and elaborate discussion of Ben-Gurion's republican worldview, see N. Kedar 2015. For a cultural explanation of the decision, see Rozin 2007.

47. Much has been written about this decision. See, for example, Gavison 1985; Friedman and Radzyner 5767; Zidon 1966; Sprinzak 1986, 63–75; Negbi 1987, 25–46; Aronson 1998; Aronson 1999, 299–315; Neuberger 1997; Yanai 1990; Goldberg 5753; Gavison 5758; Rubinstein and Medina 1996, 1:47–53 and 367–68; Barak 1992; N. Kedar 2013.

48. Much has also been written about this controversy. On the involvement of third-sector organizations, see, for example, Kabalo 2007. On the worldview of the justices, see, for example, Olshan 1978; Lahav 1999; M. Shaked 2012; Cohn 2005. On the worldview of politicians, see, for example, Bondy 1990.

49. Ewick and Silbey 1992, 740–41.

50. Rozin 2008, 98 and 103.

51. E. Gross 2000, 79–83.

52. See, for example, *Davar*, September 29, 1959. For a critical view, see Peled and Shafir 2005, 88–90 and 96.

53. Lahav 1977 and 1991; Negbi 1995; Likhovski 1999, 28–29; Barak-Erez 1999; N. Kedar 2007.

54. See, for example, N. Kedar 5766; Khenin and Filc 1999; A. Kedar and Yiftachel 2000; Berkovitch 1999; Lahav 1993; Zameret 1997.

55. See, for example, Mautner 2008 and 5768; Sela-Sheffy 2003; Shamir 2000; Likhovski 2006 and 2007; Barak-Erez 2007; Bilsky 1998.

56. Ewick and Silbey 1992, 733.

57. De Certeau 1997, 16.

58. See, for example, Y. Shapira 1977 and 1996; Ram 1993; Peled and Shafir 2005; Kimmerling and Migdal 1999; Hever, Shenhav, and Mutzafi-Haller 2002. In this context, see also a discussion of the gap between the image and reality of Mapai, the ruling party, in Bareli 2012.

59. See de Certeau 1997, 19.

60. Kabalo 2007, 22–25; Rozin 2011, 3–38.

61. Krampf 2010.

62. Rozin 2012, 181.

63. Likhovski 2007.

64. Migdal 2001a 19–20, and 2001b, 108.

65. Zameret 1993, 47-48.

66. BGA, Minutes Division, MCLJC, July 13, 1949, 5–6. Ben-Gurion differentiates between moral rights and legal rights.

67. N. Kedar 2005.

68. Zameret 1993, 26.

1. The Right to Childhood and the Age of Marriage Law

1. Yehudit Wienner, *Kol Ha'am*, July 7, 1950.

2. Immigration from Yemen had three stages. Between December 1948 and March 1949, 5,000 refugees from Yemen and 2,000 Jews from Aden immigrated to Israel. The major part of the operation commenced in spring 1949, and approximately 35,000 Yemenite Jews had immigrated to Israel by the end of that year. Between the end of 1949 and the fall of 1950 another 10,000 immigrated (Meir-Glitzenstein 2012, 13–14).

3. PLA, IV104–83–47, letter, November 16, 1949. In the Knesset plenum on January 24, 1950, Maimon evinced frustration, saying that "for many months I have been demanding in the Constitution, Law, and Justice Committee to submit a bill criminalizing child-marriage" (KM, 4, January 24, 1950: 639).

4. See Ajzenstadt 2010, 68–71; Margalit-Stern 5766, 120.

5. Sicron 1986, 35.

6. The Yemenites accounted for 6.5 percent of all immigrants arriving in the first five years after the founding of the Israeli state. See T. Segev 1984, 181–82; Meir-Glitzenstein

2012, 245–56; Rozin 2011, 145 and 163–64. See also BGA, Correspondence Division, letter, November 27, 1950.

7. Gaimani 2006, 53–55.

8. Biale 1997, 149 and 160–66; Stampfer 5747, 75. See also Zalkin 1998, 244; Bartal 1998, 229.

9. E. Greenberg 2010, 151–54; Fleischmann 2003, 60; Shilo 2001, 62–64 and 199–201; Avishur 1990, 1:32–35; Laskier 1983, 33; Simon 1992, 46; Eraqi Klorman 2004, 2:207–8. For a comprehensive survey of marriage ages in Jewish communities in the Islamic world see Stahl 1993, 62–70 and 84–86. Attempts to raise the marriage age were not always successful (see Y. Chetrit et. al. 2003, 45–49; Stahl 1993, 71; Bashan 2005, 18–19).

10. Melamed 2004; Melamed and Shenhav 2008; Portugese 1998, 176 (quoted by Melamed 2004, 78).

11. Layish 2006, 16–25.

12. Treitel 1994.

13. ISA, OPM, G5587/4, letter, November 7, 1949; ibid., memorandum, August 30, 1949.

14. ISA, OPM, G5587/4, letter, November 9, 1949.

15. Women indeed went by their husbands' surnames, but in those years Ashkenazi and Mizrahi intermarriage was rare. See *Hashnaton Hastatisti Leyisrael*, 5716, 7:28, and 5717, 8:27. For data on fertility rates based on country of origin, see Halishka Hamerkazit Lestatistika, 1965, 37–39. About the allocation of birth prizes, see ISA, OPM, G50/340, G5588/1, G5588/3, G5587/4, G5588/20, and G5588/23. Some of the files included women's addresses as well as their names. On the decision to extend the benefit to Arab women, following their appeals, see ISA, OPM, G5587/4. See also *Herut*, October 24, December 5, and December 23, 1949; *Hatsofe*, February 11, 1951; *Davar*, November 4, 1952.

16. Sicron 1986, 34–35; Y. Tsur 2000b, 108–13.

17. Berkovitch 1999.

18. Leissner 2009, 24.

19. Ajzenstadt and Gal 2001, 9.

20. Hok Habituah Haleumi (National security law) (Tikun) (no. 4) 5719–1959, 68, *Sefer Hahukkim* No. 287, 9 Av, 5719, August 13, 1959, 160.

21. Melamed 2004, 94.

22. Key 1909.

23. Lengborn 1993; Cunningham 1997, 163–64.

24. Trattner 1999, 109.

25. Cunningham 1997, 160–62. See also Trattner 1999, 109–10.

26. Zelizer 1994, 5.

27. Ibid., 6.

28. Ibid., 14.

29. Gordon 1990, 187–88.

30. Koven and Michel 1990, 1078 and 1108; Braudo 2008, 3 and 5; Baker 1990; Ladd-Taylor 1994, 74–91.

31. Shilo 2013, 297.

32. This is in contrast to the situation in the United States, where maternalists and feminists no longer cooperated after the ratification of the women's suffrage amendment to the US constitution in 1920. See Ladd-Taylor 1994, 104–05; Shilo 2013, 142–48; Margalit-Stern 2006, 374–84; Ajzenstadt 2010, 63–66.

33. See, for example, Shilo 2010.

34. Margalit-Stern 2011, 174–77.

35. On the prominence of the maternal discourse in the discussion of women rights, see Berkovitch 1999. On the prominence of the national discourse about the construction of motherhood and child care and the medicalization processes, see Shilo 2013, 257–58; Razi 2010; Stoler-Liss and Shvarts 2011. Similar trends can be seen in Syria and Lebanon (Thompson 2000, 141–48). On feminist discourse, see Lahav 1993.

36. Margalit-Stern 2006, 23. Hadassah, the American women's Zionist organization, established a chain of well-baby and well-mother clinics following World War I (Shvarts 2000). The physician Rosa Welt-Straus, an American suffragist who immigrated to Palestine in 1919, brought her values with her and headed the Union of Hebrew Women for Equal Rights — which became the key player in achieving both the women's vote and the criminalization of child marriage in mandate Palestine. See Shilo 2013, 148–55. Regarding women's organizations' international connections, see ibid., 267–77; CZA, J75/40, memorandum, August 16, 1949, and letters, March 29 and May 11, 1951.

37. CZA A 255/475 "Palestine women's council."

38. Ibid.; Likhovski 2010, 390.

39. CZA, J 75/3 (1920–47), memo, 1923. On the status of women of Yemenite origin, see Margalit-Stern 5766.

40. Eisenman 1977, 50.

41. Goitein 1957, 215–16; Layish 2006, 17.

42. ISA, GoP CS, M 15/273, letter, July 18, 1932; Likhovski 2010, 387.

43. About the ethnic aspect of the union, see Ajzenstadt 2010, 80–81. See also Margalit-Stern 5766.

44. For example, in a letter to the Chief Rabbinate (YTA 3/3–15, letter, July 16, 1943). In the letter the Union of Hebrew Women for Equal Rights asked the Chief Rabbinate to accustom men, during the rabbinical court sessions, to show respect to women, avoid derogatory names such as prostitute (*zonah*) or son of a prostitute (*ben zonah*) and, of course, to avoid violence against women outside the courthouse. See *Haisha*, Nisan 1, 5686. About the periodical, see Diskin 2011.

45. Hirsch 2011, 106–7; Rozin 2005; Ajzenstadt 2010, 68–71; Leissner 2011, 365.

46. Gerber 2009; Hirsch 2011, 118–19; Razi 2009, 166; Rozin 2002b.

47. ISA, GoP CS, M 15/273, memorandum, June 24, 1928.

48. Ibid., memorandum, March 6, 1930. In Egypt in the late nineteenth century child marriage became a medical concern. Medical experts warned against sexual intercourse and pregnancy of young girls. See Kozma 2011, 38.

49. Ibid., letter, March 19, 1930.

50. See, for example, Likhovski 2002.

51. Amin 2002, 129–32; Kashani-Sabet 2011, 68 and 70.

52. Likhovski 2010, 389.

53. Ibid.

54. ISA, GoP CS, M15/273, letter, April 1932.

55. ISA, GoP CS, M15/273, note, June 16, 1932.

56. This kind of consultation had taken place in India. See Nair 1996, 73.

57. ISA, GoP CS, M15/273, letters, August 4, 1932, and September 25, 1932.

58. Ibid., letters, July 20 and September 25, 1932, and January 25, 1933.

59. Ibid., report, February 12, 1933. See also Moors 1995, 21–22.

60. ISA, GoP CS, M15/273, memorandum, February 20, 1933 See also ibid., letter, October 30, 1932. Like Assaf Likhovski (2010, 388), I maintain that the data the superintendent used to support his claims are unreliable. Furthermore, the superintendent openly acknowledged that he had not included in his census an explicit question about the respondents' ages at marriage, and he admitted that there was no systematic registration of marriages in Palestine.

61. ISA, GoP CS, M15/273, memorandum, February 20, 1933.

62. ISA, GoP CS, M15/273, 6 July 1934.

63. Ibid., letters, July 20 and September 25, 1932; E. Greenberg 2010, 151–53; Fleischmann 2003, 60.

64. *Haisha Bamdina*, December 19, 1949. See also Likhovski 2010, 392.

65. Likhovski 2010, 390.

66. See, for example, Gluzman 2007.

67. Here are a few examples: *Haaretz*, December 7, 1948, December 14, 1949, and June 20, 1950; *Herut*, December 14, 1948; *Hapo'el Hatsa'ir*, February 7, 1949; *Kol Ha'am*, March 8, 1949; *'Al Hamishmar*, March 8, 1949; *Mibifnim* 13 (4), April 1949, 695–98; *Hamevaser*, July 22, 1949; *Haboker*, October 13, 1950; *Molad*, 7 (41–42), September 1951, 290–291. For more examples, see ISA, S71/171.

68. CZA, J75/34, letter, January 27, 1948; CZA, J75/34, memorandum, September 1948; *Haaretz*, September 14 and 28 and November 9, 1948. See also *Haaretz*, November 2 and 30 1948.

69. Margalit Shilo reports that the umbrella organization was formed in 1927 (2013, 181), whereas Bat-Sheva Margalit-Stern dates it to 1936 (2014, 456). I wish to thank Bat-Sheva Margalit-Stern for sharing a draft of her article with me prior to its publication.

70. Kabalo 2008, 18–33; Margalit-Stern 2014, 464–66.

71. In addition to the Age of Marriage Law, the Knesset passed a mandatory education law in 1949, a law guaranteeing equal rights for women in 1951, a child labor law in 1953, an apprenticeship law in 1953, and a women's labor law in 1954. The Welfare Services Law of 1958 guaranteed the right of minors to child support, and an amendment to the rules of evidence in 1955 provided safeguards for protecting the mental health of children when they were required to testify in court. Paid maternity leave and public funding of birth costs were also mandated by law. See CZA, J40/75, letter, June 15, 1951, and letter, March 14, 1951; Hurwitz 1959; Harris 1997, 249; Lahav 1991, 483.

72. *Davar*, February 1, 1949.

73. A. Shapira 2014, 181.

74. Margalit-Stern 2014, 461–62.

75. CZA, J75/36, letter, February 9, 1949. See also *Haisha Bamdina*, December 19, 1949. A copy of this article was found in the records of the Chief Rabbinate (ISA, CR, GL 13/8560).

76. Such marriages were either annulled or ended when the husband was persuaded to grant the girl a divorce. Below I use the term "dissolved" for either option because the sources are often unclear which is meant.

77. YTA, 2/1–15, letters, June 17 and December 21, 1923; ibid., 2/2–15, letter, September 1, 1930.

78. See, for example, YTA, 1/3–15, letter, January 30, 1927; ibid., 2/4–15, letter, July 24, 1932. The latter file (4/2–15) contains a vast correspondence about this subject.

79. YTA, 2/6–15, letters, n.d., and April 28, 1935.

80. Stoler-Liss and Shvarts 2004; Rozin 2005.

81. CZA, J40/75, letter, April 17, 1951.

82. A. Maimon, 5718, 221–22.

83. *Haaretz*, January 31, 1950; *Hakol*, August 28, 1950; *Hatsofe*, September 1, 1950; CZA S71/64; ISA, MoJ, G8004/19, report, May 9, 1950, 91–93.

84. Gaimani 2006.

85. ISA, CR, GL8560/13, letter, December 4, 1949.

86. The regulations were passed 18–21 Shvat, 5710 See ISA, CR, GL8560/13, memorandum, 17 Tevet, 5710.

87. On the struggle between the Chief Rabbinate and the Yemenite Jews, see Radzyner 2010, 188–90.

88. ISA, CR, GL8560/13, memorandum, January 6, 1950, and letter, December 21, 1949.

89. ISA, K 5/26, minutes, February 8, 1950, 14.

90. ISA, CR, GL8560/13, newspaper clipping, December 16, 1949, and letter, Kislev 28, 5710.

91. ISA, CR, GL8560/13, letter, January 31, 1950. See also *Haaretz*, February 29, 1952, CZA, S71/932.

92. ISA, CR, GL8560/13, letter, January 31, 1950.

93. Eraqi Klorman 2004, 2:295–96.

94. *Haisha Bamdina*, December 19, 1949.

95. *Haboker*, May 24, 1950. See also *Haboker*, August 9, 1950.

96. KM, 4:651, January 30, 1950.

97. ISA, MoJ, G 8004/19, report, May 9, 1950, 91–93.

98. ISA, CR, GL8560/13, letters, May 9, May 5, May 17, and May 25, 1950, and June 11, 1950.

99. ISA, CR, GL8560/13, letter, May 28, 1950. I have omitted the names of the people in question to protect their privacy.

100. *'Al Hamishmar*, May 16, 1950.

101. ISA, CR, GL8560/13, letters, June 11, 1950, 1 Tamuz, 5710, June 30, 1950.

102. *Haboker*, May 24, 1950.

103. Ibid.

104. KM, 4:619, January 24, 1950.

105. Ibid.

106. Zameret 1993, 32–48; Don-Yihya 2008, 160–64 and 178–86.

107. Deliberations in the Constitution, Law, and Justice Committee began on December 7, 1949, and attracted much public attention (*Davar*, December 8, 1949). See also *Davar*, January 4, 23, and 31, March 13, and June 14, 15, and 22 1950; *Herut*, January 12, 1950; *'Al Hamishmar*, January 31, 1950; *Hapo'el Hatsa'ir*, June 20, 1950; Daykan 1950.

108. A census conducted in November 1948, on the eve of the arrival of the first group of immigrants from Yemen, revealed that women ages 15–19 were substantially more likely to be married if they had been born in Asia or Africa than if they had been born in Europe or Palestine. However, there are no data regarding the exact age at marriage. The information is based on a 10 percent sample of the census's registration cards analyzed several years later (Gil and Sicron 5717, 61). Only starting in 1956 was the age at marriage (relevant to data collected for 1954) included in the annual statistical yearbook. It was reported that among those who had married before they became sixteen, 27 were male and 153 were female. In the following year it was reported that 22 grooms and 230 brides under sixteen had married in 1955 (*Hashnaton Hastatisti Leyisrael* 7:27, 5716; 8:26, 5717). See also ISA, MoH, G 4291/12, bill, 5710/1949.

109. KM, 4: 38, January 24, 1950.

110. ISA, OPM, G 5423/1, letter, December 25, 1949, and explanatory notes for a bill, 1949.

111. ISA, MoH, G4291/12, letter, December 15, 1949.

112. Letter, January 1, 1950.

113. Lewis 2005, 86.

114. The reform movement that emerged in the United States at the beginning of the twentieth century and that then spread to Europe sought to eliminate poverty, crime, and mental illness by drastic preventive measures. In 1935, a branch of this movement was founded in Palestine. Whether the Israeli branch nurtured eugenic ideals is debatable. See Zalashik 2008, 83–95; Margolin and Witztum 2014. See also Razi 2009, 123–25; Katvan 5773, 88–93.

115. KM, 4:638-39, January 24, 1950. On the medical establishment's viewpoint, see Katvan 5773, 86–97.

116. KM 4:638-39, January 24, 1950.

117. These were steered by Haim Wilkenfeld (later Tzadok), then the deputy attorney general. The committee sessions were nearly the opposite of the politically charged and emotional debates on the Knesset floor. For example, Wilkenfeld said: "The purpose of the criminal law is not to prevent everything that is undesirable or that contradicts one's moral or aesthetic senses. There are many things that seem to us morally defective, but we do not [necessarily] justify intervention by the criminal law. The criminal law interferes only in matters which inflict harm on the entire public. Therefore, there is no need to set an optimal marital age, but rather only to prevent cases which pose a threat to the general welfare" (ISA, KR, K5/26, MCLJC, March 8, 1950, 5).

118. KM 4:638-39, January 24, 1950.

119. Bondy 1990, 440.

120. KM, 4:639, January 24, 1950.

121. Melamed 2004, 78–80; Melamed and Shenhav 2008, 142–43.

122. KM, 4:466–67, January 30, 1950. See also ISA, Central Bureau of Statistics, GL3558/8, report. Melamed and Shenhav refer to this report, by Professor Roberto Bachi, a demographer. It should be noted, however, that despite his Orientalist tone when he points to the large gap between the birth rates of two opposing groups — "women from Austria and Yemen" — Bachi demands that a major effort be made to reduce poverty among the latter and to improve their education.

123. KM, 4:640, January 24, 1950.

124. KM, 5:1619, June 5, 1950; ibid., 5:1706, June 13, 1950.

125. ISA, KR, K26/5, MCLJC, February 15, 1950, 10 (my emphasis).

126. ISA, KR, K26/5; MCLJC, February 15, 1950, 10. On another occasion Maimon called the marriage of a girl to a forty-year-old man "a murder" (KM, 4:640, January 24, 1950). See also KM, 5:1619, June 5, 1950.

127. Margalit-Stern 2014, 471–75.

128. KM, 4:653–63, January 30, 1950. See also ibid., 4:1728, 5, June 14, 1950.

129. KM, 4:649, January 30, 1950; ISA, KR, K5/26 MCLJC, February 15 and March 1, 1950, and March 15, 1950, 3.

130. MSA, 2–11–1950–7, minutes, May 14, 1950.

131. Ibid.

132. KM, 6: 2416, August 1, 1950.

133. KM, 5:1703, June 13, 1950; ibid., 5:1705–1704; ibid., 5:1728, June 14, 1950; ISA, OPM, G1/5423, letter, June 24, 1950.

134. ISA, OPM, G1/5423, letter, June 20, 1950.

135. KM, 4:655, January 30, 1950.

136. KM, 4:650, January 30, 1950; ibid., 662, ISA, KR, K5/26, MCLJC, May 30, 1950, 2. A similar discussion had taken place on January 3, 1950, at a cabinet meeting. Minister Bechor-Shalom Sheetrit claimed that because of early puberty and to boost birth rates, the marriage age should be set at sixteen (ISA, GVM 1, 17:50–51, January 3, 1950.)

137. *Davar*, March 13, 1950.

138. KM, 4:659, January 30, 1950; ibid., 661–62.

139. KM, 4:665, January 30, 1950. For data regarding the rate of high-school students' graduation during Israel's first decade, see Molcho 2009.

140. KM, 4:657, January 30, 1950.

141. KM, 4:659, January 30, 1950.

142. KM, 4:662, January 30, 1950.

143. KM, 4:651–52, January 30, 1950.

144. KM, 4:657, January 30, 1950.

145. MSA, 2–11–1950–7, minutes, May 14, 1950.

146. Picard 2013, 168–71.

147. Y. Tsur 2000b, 110–11, and 2002.

148. KM, 4:640, January 30, 1950.

149. ISA, KR, K5/26, MCLJC, February 15, 1950.

150. KM, 4:653, January 24, 1950. See also Ada Maimon's words in ibid., January 24, 1949, 640.

151. On the various images of the "enlisted" child and the "private" child, see Darr 2013, 227.

152. KM, 4:653–54, January 24, 1950. For a comparison to India, see Goyal 1988, 4–5.

153. KM, 28:25, December 7, 1959.

154. KM, 28:23, December 7, 1959.

155. See Procacia 1951.

156. Nevertheless, there was some discussion about Arab women in Israel and in neighboring countries. See, for example, *Haisha Bamdina*, October 5, 1949, and February 27, 1950. See also A. Maimon 5718, 227.

157. KM, 4:660, January 30, 1950; ISA, KR, K5/26, MCLJC, February 15, March 1, and March 15, 1950; KM, 5:1729–30, June 14, 1950.

158. Treitel 1994, 436.

159. Ozacky-Lazar 2002. See also Bialer 2006, 167.

160. ISA, IP, L5/2271, letter, February 27, 1952.

161. Ibid., letters, June 11 and 23, 1952.

162. Ibid., letter, November 13, 1952.

163. Ibid., letter, November 25, 1952.

164. Ibid., letter, December 21, 1952.

165. In the Acre subdistrict alone, multiple investigations were held, and dozens of criminal files were opened. See ISA, IP, L29/26.

166. ISA, PMAA, GL27/17100, letters, October 22 and 28 and December 21, 1952, and February 26, 1953. In one such case, the attorney general maintained that not only the clergymen who officiated at an underage marriage should be brought to trial, but also the responsible bishop. But the Foreign Ministry prevailed, ruling that proceedings against church officials who had allegedly violated the law should be held in abeyance. See ISA, IP, L2277/8, letters, February 5 and 26, 1953.

167. Bialer 2006, 164–65.

168. ISA, IP, L8/2277, letters, July 10 and August 2, 1953; ibid., L29/26, letter, September 14, 1952; Ka'adan 2013, 76.

169. A national census in 1961 found that a huge proportion of Muslim women had married under the age of seventeen. The data do indicate a significant drop in the rate of Muslim women who married under the age of fifteen between 1951 and 1961. But Aharon Layish (2006, 16–18 and 25) and Andrew Treitel (1994, 433–35) have noted that the number of underage marriages was probably greater than indicated in the census, because many marriages were not registered and ways were found to circumvent the law. See also Halishka Hamerkazit Lestatistika 1964, 34–35.

170. *'Al Hamishmar*, December 21, 1951. See also Layish 5749, 137. The police were not eager to investigate charges of bigamy among Bedouins and in general were even less inclined to press charges relating to the Age of Marriage Law. Chief among the reasons was the expensive X-ray examinations required to determine the bride's age.

Attorney General Haim Cohn also discouraged these efforts, insofar as the Bedouin population was concerned. See ISA, PI, L12/2478, letters, May 18 and December 12, 1956. See also Boimel 2007, 217–19; Ka'adan 2013, 61.

171. For comparison to India, see Harel-Shalev 2009, 1265–67.

172. The law stipulated mandatory registration for all inhabitants, without exception. Parents were responsible for the registration of children under the age of sixteen. If births, deaths, marriages, divorces, and changes of address were not reported within thirty days, the punishment could be a prison sentence of up to three months, a fine of 100 Israeli lira, or both (*'Al Hamishmar*, March 13, 1950).

173. ISA, IP, L2478/17; ibid., L2478/18.

174. ISA, PMAA, GL17100/30, *Haaretz*, July 29, 1954. See also ISA, IP, L29/26, letter, December 1, 1953.

175. ISA, PMAA, GL17100/30, letter, June 14, 1951.

176. Guber 1962, 310; ISA, MoH, G4291/12, letters, September 5 and 23, 1951.

177. ISA, MoH, G4291/12, letter, September 23, 1951.

178. PLA, IV104–83–47, letter, January 8, 1951; KM, 8:827–28, January 22, 1951.

179. ISA, MoH, G4291/12, letter, December 31, 1951; *Haaretz*, February 29, 1952; *'Al Hamishmar*, November 11, 1955. See also Katvan 5773, 94.

180. Layish 2006, 19.

181. *Ha'olam Hazeh*, January 8, 1958.

182. Layish 2006, 18–20. See also ISA, PMAA, GL17100/27, *Haaretz*, January 17, 1955; Treitel 1994, 435–36.

183. *Haboker*, October 23, 1951, CZA, S71/195. See also *Herut*, April 26, 1961; *'Al Hamishmar*, December 21, 1951; *Haboker*, October 23, 1951, CZA, S71/195.

184. *Ha'olam Hazeh*, October 24, 1956.

185. *Ma'ariv*, December 29, 1953.

186. *Yedi'ot 'Aharonot*, July 29, 1950, CZA, S71/195; *Davar*, July 25, 1951. See also *Ma'ariv*, November 13, 1960, and January 7, 1964.

187. CrimC (TA) 134/56 *The Attorney General v. Eliezer Ben Kapelyoto*, PM 5717(21–22) 131–132 (1957) (ISR).

188. CrimA 53/57 *Kapelyoto v. Attorney General* 11 PD 498.

189. Another Yemenite depfendent who married an eleven-year-old girl was also sentenced to six months in prison (*Davar*, July 25, 1951). For a similar sentence see CrimA 117/51 *Shar'abi v. Attorney General* 5 PD 1675.

190. *Ha'olam Hazeh*, August 18, 1955.

191. Ibid.

192. Ibid.

193. See, for example, *Ma'ariv*, December 29, 1953; *Yedi'ot 'Aharonot*, July 29 and August 11, 1950, CZA, S71/195; *Ha'olam Hazeh*, April 6, 1960.

194. ISA, MoJ, GL21978/9, letter, January 5, 1956. The letter was filed separately under internal office communication inside the archival file.

195. *Din veheshbon shel hava'ada leheker ha'avaryanut bekerev hano'ar* 1956, 17, 22–24; Reifen 1961, 46–48.

196. BGAO, box 95, Ma'abarot, letter to Mrs. P. Berda, 1954; KA, minutes of the

Public Services Committee, 21 G, minutes, March 11, 1958, 2. Marriage did not provide protection against prostitution. See ISA, LAW, B5164/66, HCJ 66/65 *Salzberg v. Inspector General of Police* 19(4) PD 310.

197. Reifen 1961, 47–49, and 1978, 138–39.

198. For a discussion of the paradigm shift in the Supreme Court's ruling in the 1980s, see Mautner 2008, 160–68.

199. CA 501/81 *Attorney General v. Doe* 35(4) PD 430. Barak's ruling was quoted in CA 741/85 *Attorney General v. Zohara Sakora* 39(4) PD 651; CA 730/87 *Modzgavershvili v. State of Israel* 88(2) Takdin Legal Database 627; File No. 20080/97 Family Court (Haifa), *Doe v. Attorney General* 97(1) Takdin Legal Database 4204; File No. 81670/99 Family Court (Tel Aviv), *Doe v. Attorney General* 2000(1) Takdin Legal Database 381; FCF (Tel Aviv) File No. 90400/00 Family Court (Tel Aviv), *Doe v. Attorney General* 2000(3) Takdin Legal Database 221.

200. CA 501/81 *Attorney General v. Doe* 35(4) PD 430.

201. Ibid.

202. Ibid.

203. See CA 94/4736 *Angel v. Attorney General* 94(3) Takdin Legal Database 319, section 5 of Supreme Court Justice Meir Shamgar's ruling.

204. Even in 1978, Supreme Court Justice Haim Cohn allowed a girl to marry before she reached the legal age due to her parents' dire economic circumstances and the family's overpopulated dwelling. See CA 690/77 *Hanipes v. State of Israel* 32(1) PD 531.

205. For example, a case of two families of Georgian origin that were joined by marriage was discussed in court, as a result of a violent attack. Although the girl in this case was seventeen and a half at her marriage, the court considered the marriage to be premature because a month after the wedding, the couple was seeking a divorce. The families wrangled. A relative of the defendant said: "This girl had lost and she is missing her virginity, and in Georgia they would kill him [meaning the husband]." A relative of the plaintiff said: "You took the virginity of his daughter, and for that in Georgia they would have killed [you]" (CrimA [BS] 04/8049 *State of Israel v. Kakyashvili*, 2005[1] Takdin Legal Database 3230, section 2 to judge Zloczower's ruling). From these few sentences spoken in court in 2004 we can see that the girl's extended family still had full possession of her body, well-being, and life.

206. *Hakol*, August 29, 1950, CZA, S71/64.

207. *Hatsofe*, September 19, 1950, CZA, S71/64.

208. ISA, MoH, G4291/12, letter, March 3, 1954.

209. Ibid., letter, March, 3, 1954.

210. ISA, MoH, G4291/12, summary, December 14, 1953; ibid., letter, March 1, 1954. See also *Davar*, March 13, 1950.

211. ISA, MoJ, GL21978/9, memorandums, May 12, 1953, and January 1, 1956.

212. ISA, MoJ, GL21978/9, bill, July 20, 1956.

213. ISA, GVM 7, 17:37–40, August 26, 1956.

214. Ibid., GVM 8, 7:47–48, May 18, 1958.

215. Ibid., 50; see also 48

216. Ibid., 48 and 51.

217. The age of consent for extramarital relations was set by the Mandate government in late 1926. See ISA, GoP CS, M15/273, letter, December 23, 1933. This struggle continued during the 1960s. See *Ha'olam Hazeh*, November 15, 1962.

218. KM, 28:10–11, December 1, 1959; ibid., 28:26 and 29, December 7, 1959, .

219. KM, 29:1929–33 and 1943, July 20, 1960.

220. ISA, OPM G5423/6, letter, October 31, 1954.

221. Cover 1983, 4.

222. Rigger 1952, 261.

223. Ibid., 271–72.

224. Ibid., 262–64.

225. *Ma'ariv*, January 22, 1958, and November 13, 1960; *Davar*, July 25, 1951, and November 20, 1957.

226. ISA, KR, K26/5, MCLJC, May 30, 1950, 2 (Zerach Warhaftig).

227. McAdams 2000, 341. See also Sunstein 1996; Flynn 2005; Feldman 2009, 178–86.

228. *Davar*, December 13, 1955; Rozin 2008, 238–40; Tivoni 1982, 167–68.

229. Kafri 1962; Ahrak 1964. Mazal Ahrak emigrated from Yemen in late 1948; she was trained as an instructor and a kindergarten teacher by Shoshana Basin (Basin 1964, 262; Priver 1964).

230. Basin 1964, 263. See also Guber 1962; Kafri 1962; *Herut*, June 26, 1952; Ben-Itto 2008, 254; *Haahot Beyisrael*, March–April, 1949. It appears that not all counselors intervened to rescue girls from premature marriages (Levy 1962, 299).

231. Katzir 1984, 225–29; Terri 5754, 316–18. See also Shar'abi 2002, 132–35 and 206–8 and 2005, 214–16.

232. *Haisha Bamdina*, December 19, 1949.

233. *'Al Hamishmar*, May 16, 1950.

234. *Ha'olam Hazeh*, December 30, 1954.

235. *Ha'olam Hazeh*, October 24, 1956, and August 28, 1957.

236. *Kol Ha'am*, July 7, 1950, CZA, S71/195.

237. *Davar*, July 25, 1951.

238. In interviews recorded many years later, Yemenite women who married in Yemen remembered that when they were called to see their future husbands for the first time, they were in the middle of playing with other children. This shared memory reflects, as their interviewer suggests, a desire to postpone the marriage and extend their childhood. See T. Cohen 2005, 146–7.

239. *Zmanim*, September 27, 1954.

240. Quoted in Rimerman and Amir 1971, 132. See also *Ha'olam Hazeh*, May 12, 1955.

241. YTA, 15–3/2, letter, July 7, 1932.

242. Azmon 2001, 144. See also Khan, interview with Rachel Azgad, recorded on June 28, 1984, 20; ibid., interview with Helena Goldstein, recorded on May 6, 1984, 3.

243. KM, 4:640, January 24, 1950. See also *Ha'olam Hazeh*, May 17, 1961; *Haisha Bamdina*, December 19, 1949; CrimA 64/51 *Attorney General v. Ben Abud*, PM 5(21) 113.

244. See, for example, *Haaretz*, April 4, 1950; YTA, 4/3–15, monthly newsletter, Av 5710, 8–9. See also Gordon 1990, 179–83.

245. Spivak 1995, 54.

246. For more on the struggle during the British Mandate era, see Likhovski 2010, 392. On the Indian struggle, see Mayo 1998, 45–48; Sinha 1993. See also Melman 1998, 98.

247. Yaron Tsur has argued that the approach of established Israelis to the immigrants was dichotomous, influenced both by the optimism of Zionism, which viewed the Mizrahim as partners in the national enterprise, and by the colonial order that viewed them as inferiors. See Y. Tsur 2002, 81–85. See also Rozin 5772.

248. See, for example, Tene 2005; Rozin 2006a.

249. See Y. Tsur 2000a. See also Nofech-Mozes 1967, 202–3.

250. On legislation and its meaning, see Likhovski 2010, 377–78.

251. *Davar*, July 29, 1960. Horowitz later became an eminent sociologist.

252. Bareli and Kedar 2011, 23–24 and 30–31.

253. At a cabinet meeting in 1958, before the bill to amend the Age of Marriage Law was sent back to the Knesset, Prime Minister David Ben-Gurion pressed the ministers leading the two sides of the debate, Haim-Moshe Shapira and Pinhas Rosen, to reach a compromise. This meant appeasing religious groups and traditionalist men in general. See ISA, GVM 8,7:49, May 18, 1958.

254. Melman 1998, 99.

255. Priver 1962a; Priver 1962b; Ahrak 1964; Sofri n.d., 66–79 (I would like to thank the author's grandson, Omer Aloni, for sharing this book with me); Pinkus 1971, 184–85.

2. *The Right to Travel Abroad*

1. Many full names are not disclosed in this chapter, to protect people's privacy.

2. ISA, MoJ, G5674/10, letter, November 5, 1950.

3. Yehudai 2013, 16.

4. Torpey 2000, 4–20; Salter 2003, 78; Higgins and Leps 1998. On theoretical aspects of mobility, see N. Cohen 2010, 19–22.

5. Whelan 1981, 637.

6. Dowty 1987, 195. On the origins of Soviet mobility restrictions in imperial Russia, see Boim 1975, 7–8.

7. "Passport Refusals for Political Reasons" 1952, 172–73; Kutler 1982; Turack 1972, 9–12; Parker 1954, 871.

8. *Kent v. Dulles*, 357 U.S. 116 (1958)

9. Dowty 1987, 128–29, note 5; Turack 1972, 11 note 6; *Aptheker v. Secretary of State*, 378 U.S. 500 (1964).

10. Mahony 1989, 63 and 65–68; Parker 1954, 868.

11. *New York Times*, October 20, 1959; *Burlington (NC) Daily Times News*, June 11, 1957; *Charleston Gazette*, June 5, 1957; *Time*, June 17, 1957.

12. ISA, MoI, G2243/10.

13. To an extent, the situation was better in the United States and Britain, as it was possible for citizens of those countries to travel to certain destinations even without a passport. See Williams 1974, 648–49; "Passport Refusals for Political Reasons" 1952, 171–73.

14. N. Gross 1999, 348–49.

15. ISA, MoI, G2243/10.

16. *Hashnaton Hastatisti Leyisrael*, 13:32, 1962.

17. Ibid., 32:111.

18. Yehudai 2013, 288–89.

19. *Haaretz*, July 17, 1951.

20. KM, 31:1731, May 16, 1961.

21. McCarthy 1990, 65 and 179.

22. Suppl. 2 to the *Palestine Gazette* (extraordinary), 914, August 26 1939 (Proclamations), 677; *Palestine Gazette*, December 28 1939, 1218.

23. IDFA, 580/1956–389, letter, March 11, 1953; ISA, GVM 1, 27:55, July 26, 1950.

24. *Official Gazette*, August 17 and August 25, 1948, ISA, MoJ, G5671/14; ISA, MoI, G 2242/4, memo, August 25, 1948; IDFA, 580/1956–389, regulations, n.d.

25. ISA, MoJ, G5671/14, memo, May 31, 1949; IDFA 580/1956–387, letter, February 2, 1949; I. Greenberg 2006, 133–34.

26. Naor 2009, 21–38.

27. ISA, OPM, G5552/20, letter, August 23, 1949. See also Bar-On 2006, 480–84.

28. Naor 2009, 42–45.

29. IDFA 121/1950–181, letter, December 12, 1948; Naor 2009, 42.

30. *Haaretz*, June 19, 2005.

31. The powers of the minister of immigration under the emergency regulations were not transferred to another minister after the dismantling of the Ministry of Immigration in 1951, although in fact the minister of the interior administered the regulations (without proper authority) until the 1953 and 1955 amendments to the law granted him that authority under regulations 3(c) and (d). During the interim, first, and second governments, Haim-Moshe Shapira was minister of immigration. He also served as minister of the interior. See *Official Gazette* 17, August 25, 1948 (Appendix Bet) 81; *Official Gazette* 33, November 19, 1948 (Appendix Alef), 45–46.

32. HCJ 3/51 *Es-Said v. Minister of Immigration* 5 PD 1075.

33. ISA, MoJ, 5671/15, circular, October 30, 1950.

34. ISA, OPM, G5552/20, letter, August 23, 1949.

35. ISA, MoJ G5671/14, letter, July 28, 1949.

36. ISA, MoJ G8003/18, letters, July 3 and 7, 1951.

37. *Bauer v. Acheson*, 106 F. Supp. 445 (D.D.C. 1952); Turack 1972, 10; Parker 1954, 872.

38. ISA, MoJ, G5671/15, circular, October 30, 1950, and MoI, G2242/7, letter, August 1949.

39. During World War II, formal restrictions were imposed and exit permits were required for British citizens, in addition to restrictions resulting from the war itself. See ISA, GoP CS, M230/4, letters, July 5 and September 3, 1943, and telegram, April 24, 1943.

40. ISA, OPM, G5421/10, letter, September 23, 1949.

41. ISA, OPM, G5421/10, minutes, October 27, 1949, and letters, November 13 and December 25, 1949.

42. ISA, OPM, G5421/10, memo, "sikum maskanot hapgisha . . ." (n.d.).

43. ISA, GVM 1, 27:48–49 and 55, July 26, 1950; GVM 1, 22:87–89, April 12, 1950; ISA, OPM, G5421/10, letter, December 25, 1949; GVM 1, 31:37–38, September 14, 1950; Henry n.d.

44. ISA, MoJ, G5674/10, letter November 28, 1950.

45. N. Gross 1999, 325 and 331–33; Rozin 2011, 4.

46. ISA, GVM 1, 22:88, April 12, 1950.

47. ISA, GVM 1, 22:89, April 12, 1950.

48. ISA, MoJ, G5671/14, letter, May 3, 1959; ISA, OPM, G5552/3824, memo, May 5, 1959.

49. ISA, GVM 2, 12:18, August 14, 1951. See also ISA, MoI, G2245/102/3. Ministers did not deny that the various fees were intended to curb foreign travel. See KM, 17:170, November 24, 1954.

50. ISA, MoJ, G5671/15, circular, October 30, 1950; ISA, GVM 1, 27, July 26 1950.

51. *Haaretz*, July 17, 1951.

52. ISA, MoJ, G5671/14, letters, February 11, March 24, and June 25, 1952.

53. ISA, GVM 1, 27:43, 26 July 1950.

54. ISA GVM 1, 31:37–38, September 14, 1950.

55. ISA, GVM 1, 27:47–51, July 26, 1950.

56. Ibid., 41.

57. Ibid., 51.

58. Hacohen 1994, 20–22 and 65–68.

59. ISA, GVM 1, 27:45, July 26, 1950,; see also 53.

60. Ibid., 51, 43; ISA, MoJ, G5674/10, letter, July 10, 1950.

61. ISA, GVM 2, 12, August 14, 1951; MoJ G5671/14, letter, June 2, 1952. Tourists also needed to obtain an exit permit before leaving. See ISA, MoI, G2242/1, Kuf/410.

62. ISA, MoJ, G5671/14, bill, 1951.

63. ISA, GVM 1, 27:49, July 26 and 27, 1950; *Haaretz*, July 17, 1951; ISA, MoJ, G5674/10, letter, November 11, 1950; ISA, OPM, G5421/10, letter, January 13, 1950.

64. ISA, MoI, G2242/(5) V 410, minutes, June 4, 1952.

65. ISA, MoI, G2242/14, letter, February 11, 1953, and G2242/37, letter, March 4, 1953.

66. HCJ 111/53 *Kaufman v. Minister of Internal Affairs* 7 PD 534.

67. Ibid. See also Motion 41/49 *Shimshon Factories of the Land of Israel for Cement-Portland* 4(1) PD 143; *Shachtman v. Dulles*, 96 U.S. App. D.C. 287, 225 F.2d 938 (1955); "The Passport Puzzle" 1956, 264.

68. HCJ 111/53 *Kaufman v. Minister of Internal Affairs* 7 PD 534.

69. ISA, MoI, G2243/9, letters, January 20 and 24 and March 25, 1955.

70. ISA, MoI, G2243/9, memo, April 12, 1953, and G2242/37, circular, February 28, 1955.

71. ISA, MoI, G2242/37, letter, March 9, 1955; ibid., MoJ, G8003/18, letter April 27, 1953.

72. ISA, MoP, G6836/6 (1/3), memo, June 20, 1954; ibid., bill, September 12, 1954.

73. ISA, MoJ, G8003/18, letter, August 27, 1953, and circular, August 25, 1953.

74. See Table 2.1; *Hashnaton Hastatisti Leyisrael* 1961, 12: 83 and 102; *Hatsofe*, December 25, 1953; *Ma'ariv*, October 10, 1953; CZA, A 430/210/B/2 memo, November 11, 1953; Yehudai 2013, 253.

75. KM, 17:1817–18, June 7, 1955.

76. ISA, MoI, G2242/37, letter, June 2, 1955, and G2242/6, letter, June 17, 1955.

77. Abramov 1995, 36.

78. Tal 1994, 75–83.

79. ISA, MoJ, G8003/18, report, February 16, 1956.

80. *Davar*, August 8, 1955, CZA, S71/930.

81. *Davar*, August 10, 1955, CZA, S71/930.

82. Bar-On 1992, 13–27.

83. ISA, OPM, G5552/3824, letter, December 15, 1955. See also *Yedi'ot 'Aharonot*, December 25, 1955.

84. ISA, OPM, G5552/3824, memo, December 18, 1955.

85. ISA, MoI G2241/8, memo, October 16, 1955.

86. KM, 19:844–45, January 23, 1956.

87. Ibid., 845.

88. Ibid., 845–46.

89. Ibid., 852–53.

90. ISA, MoI, G5552/3824, letter, March 14, 1956.

91. KM, 20:1415, March 12, 1956.

92. KM, 20:1414–16, March 12, 1956,.

93. ISA, MoI, G5552/3824, letter, March 14, 1956.

94. ISA, MoI, G2242/37, letter, July 17, 1956.

95. Ibid., letters, August 31 and November 15, 1956.

96. *Ma'ariv*, January 27, 1956, CZA, S71/930; ISA, OPM, G5552/3824, letter, August 29, 1956; ISA, MoI, G2242/6, letter, July 25, 1956, and G2242/37, letter, August 31, 1956.

97. Bareli and Cohen 2008.

98. For a similar case, see Yehudai 2013, 253.

99. ISA, MoI, G2245/102/3, *Official Gazette*, 650, November 2, 1956.

100. ISA, MoI, G2242/37, letters, November 13 and 21, 1956.

101. ISA, MoI, G2242/13, letters, March 10 and June 14, 1957.

102. ISA, MoI, G2245/102/3, letter, August 7, 1957; ISA, MoJ G8004/1, letter, May 15, 1959. At the time, the fee was 30–40 liras.

103. ISA, GVM 9, May 28, 1961, in ISA, GSO, G12969/11, 49–51; KM, 31:1897–900, June 5, 1961.

104. ISA, MoJ, G8004/1, letter, September 29, 1961; ISA, MoP, G6836/6 (3/1); KM, 21, December 4, 1956, and 22:2218, June 24, 1957, and 44:164, December 14, 1965,.

105. Zilbershatz 1994, 90–91.

106. KM, 17:1089, March 15, 1955.

107. Ibid., 14: 2430, August 19, 1953.

108. Morris 1996, 44–83.

109. KM, 20:2416, July 25, 1956.

110. For a collection of newspaper clippings on this subject, see CZA, S71/930.

111. Vorm 1963, 180–82; *Davar* September 13 and December 3, 1953; *Herut*, December 24, 1953; *'Al Hamishmar*, November 15, 1953, and January 4, 1954; *Hatsofe*, December 25, 1953; Har-Even 1989, 51–52; Liebermann 2006; Y. Cohen 1990; Lamdani 1983.

112. Confino 2008, 140. See also Hirschman 1978, 103.

113. Dowty 1987, 57–58. See also Green 2005, 279–82.

114. See, for example, ISA, MoI, G2242/14, letter, February 10, 1953.

115. Yehudai 2013, 199–200 and 245–49.

116. ISA, MoI, G2242/14, letter, July 27, 1953; Green 2005, 282.

117. ISA, MoI, G2242/14, G2243/9; GVM 1, 27:41, July 26, 1950; KM, 13:939, March 11, 1953; *Davar*, December 17, 1953; *Haaretz*, July 23, 1952.

118. Such as when potential emigrants were of an age when they would soon be subject to conscription in the army, See ISA, MoI, G2242/37.

119. Yehudai 2013, 250.

120. ISA, MoI, G2242/37, letters, March 9, 17, and 22 and October 2, 1953; ISA, MoJ, G8003/18, letter, January 4, 1953; ISA, OPM, G5552/3824, letter, March 3, 1956.

121. IDFA 580/1956-389; ISA, MoI, G2243/5. See also Rozin 2006b, 95. Even during the deliberations regarding the phrasing of the Universal Declaration of Human Rights, the Soviet Union objected to the comprehensive wording regarding the right to travel abroad and return to one's country, demanding that this section, to all extents, be devoid of any real content. See Whelan 1981, 641–42.

122. KM, 13:942, January 11, 1953.

123. Ibid., 19, January 23, 1956, 846–47.

124. Ibid., 17, November 24, 1954, 170 and 173.

125. Rozin 2002a, 87–90; ISA, MoI, G2245/102/3; Alterman 1973; *'Ashmoret*, September 20, 1950; *Hador*, January 2, 1951; *Dvar Hapo'elet*, July 21, 1950; KM, 13:941, March 11, 1953.

126. ISA, MoI, G2245/102/3; ISA, MoJ G8004/1.

127. See the approach advocated by the General Zionists for an amendment to the emergency regulations in 1956, and statements by Beba Idelson (Mapai), in KM, 19: 851, January 23, 1956.

128. Rozin 2006a; Zameret 1997, 83–86 and 133–59.

129. Likhovski 2007, 665–70.

130. Aschheim 1982, 108–10; A. Shapira 1992, 29–33; Hirsch 2006, 37 and 49; Zalashik 2006, 10; Gluzman 2007, 34–36.

131. For some presentations of the Jew as a wanderer or of leaving Israel as a disease, see *Herut*, April 23, 1953; *Davar*, March 20, 1951; KM, 14:2428–29, August 19, 1953. For examples of the use of the word "root" as a verb, see *Hapo'el Hatsa'ir*, May 27, 1952; *Davar*, March 11, 1955.

132. KM, 14:2428, August 19, 1953.

133. For a fascinating view of the Wandering Jew myth, see Maccoby 1986.

134. Hirsch 2006, 45.

135. This expression has its origins in Jewish sources. It also exists in Yiddish and German (Rosenthal 2009, 344).

136. On time separation and rites of separation, see Zerubavel 2003, 87 and 95.

137. ISA, OPM, G5552/21, letter, June 25, 1949. Spelling mistakes and grammatical errors in the quote are as they appear in the original.

138. Hundreds of similar documents were found in the Israel State Archives. After careful examination, I have chosen some examples.

139. Mary Fulbrook (2005, 7) claims this was also the case in the German Democratic Republic (East Germany).

140. Boltanski and Thévenot 2006, 17.

141. Resnik and Frenkel 2000, 105–8. For a further discussion, see Fridrich-Silber 2001.

142. ISA, OPM, G5552/18, discussion summary, July 16, 1950. See also ibid., G5552/21, letter, September, 26, 1951. The need for a recommendation sometimes created an opportunity for bribery, and it is likely that personal contacts were misused so that some individuals could profit. See *Yedi'ot 'Aharonot*, June 20, 1952.

143. For a comparison with the situation in the Soviet Union in the 1930s see Fitzpatrick 1996.

144. Davis 1987, 3.

145. ISA, MoI, G715/5, letter, May 27, 1952; ISA, MoR, GL6326/18, letters, December 25, 1951, and January 10 and 15, 1952.

146. Hirsch 2006, 3–4.

147. ISA, JCMG, G277/52, letter, December 6, 1948.

148. Boltanski and Thévenot explain the role of experts in their discussion of the "industrial polity" (2006, 118–23). See also Resnik and Frankel 2000, 106–7. And see, for example, ISA, OPM, G5552/21, letter, June 21, 1949; ibid., MoIM, G2242/7, letter, June 25, 1950.

149. ISA, MoJ, G5674/10, letter, May 25, 1951.

150. In contrast, Jeremy Brooke Straughn's work (2005) on petitions (*Eingaben*) submitted to the East German authorities highlights the possible — or rather plausible — discrepancy between the personal views of citizens and their behavior.

151. The Eranos conferences, initiated by one of Carl Gustav Jung's students, brought together many of the key thinkers of the twentieth century. See Eranos Foundation 2015.

152. ISA, MoJ, G8003/18, letter, August 15, 1951. See also ibid., letter, August 5, 1951.

153. See, for example, *Hador*, November 2, 1952.

154. ISA, MoI, G715/5, letter, August 28, 1951.

155. IDFA, 580/1956–387, letters, January 11 and December 1949.

156. See, for example, ISA, OPM, G5552/20, letters, July 13 and 14, 1948; ISA, OPM, G324/32, letter, September 30, 1949; ISA, OPM, G5552/22, letter, December 6, 1948. In one case, Rosen — writing on behalf of a certain applicant — stated explicitly that his wife would not join him abroad. See ISA, MoJ, G5671/14, letter, June 23, 1950.

157. ISA, MoI, G2242/37, circular, March 4, 1953. The policy created a substantial inequity between those seeking to emigrate and those seeking to travel and then return.

See, for example, ISA, MoI, G2242/(5) V 410, minutes, June 4, 1952. See also ISA, MoI, G2242/37, letter, July 25, 1956.

158. See, for example, ISA, MoJ, G8003/18, letter, May 22, 1955. The High Court of Justice was able to intervene and reverse the ministers' decisions. See HCJ 3/51 *Es-Said v. Minister of Immigration* 5 PD 1075.

159. See, for instance, ISA, MoJ, G8003/18, letters, June 4 and 11, 1952; IDFA, 580/1956–389, letter, August 17, 1948.

160. An example is students pursuing academic studies in areas needed in Israel but not yet available there. See ISA, MoI, G2242/14, letter, August 12, 1954; ISA, OPM, G5552/22, letter, October 11, 1949.

161. ISA, MoR, GL6326/18, letters, June 3 and 5 and July 27, 1951, and January 18, 1952.

162. Ibid., letter, August 6, 1951. A sworn statement by a witness named Bechor Shaul, from the same date, was originally attached to the letter.

163. ISA, MoR, GL6326/18, letter, August 6, 1951.

164. The fear of losing people who could convert or marry non-Jews was indeed significant. See, for example, ISA, MoR, GL6326/18, letter, September 21, 1953.

165. *Davar*, August 28 and September 14, 1949, and October 31, 1950.

166. ISA, MoI, G2242/14, letter, February 10, 1953.

167. *Davar*, December 3, 1953.

168. For example, see ISA, OPM, Gimel 5552/22, letters, December 14, 1948, June 2, 1949, and July 26, 1950.

169. ISA, GVM 2, 12:18, August 14, 1951. See also ISA, OPM, G5552/20, letter, August 23, 1949.

170. ISA, OPM, G5552/21, letter, June 25, 1949. For additional examples, see ISA, MoJ, G8003/18, letters, July 23 and September 9, 1951.

171. See Straughn 2005, 1613.

172. ISA, MoR, GL6326/18, letters, June 22 and July 5, 1949.

173. Fitzpatrick 1996, 81.

174. ISA, OPM, G324/32, letter, September 30, 1949.

175. ISA, OPM, G324/32, letter, October 20, 1948. Ben-Gurion's youngest daughter, Renana, had a boyfriend who was killed during the war (personal communication with one of her relatives who wishes to remain anonymous, April 21, 2008).

176. ISA, OPM, G324/32, letter, October 31, 1948.

177. ISA, MoJ, G5674/10, letter, October 30, 1950.

178. For a photograph of such passports, see Dankner and Tartakover 1996, 84. In 1953 it was still very hard to get an exit permit and a passport that allowed a visit to Germany. See, for example, ISA, MoI, G2242/37, circular, May 7, 1953. The negotiations on the reparation agreement between Israel and West Germany were conducted in the Netherlands, because Israelis did not consider a visit to Germany an option. See also Yehudai 2013, 82.

179. ISA, G5674/10, letter, January 28, 1951.

180. Ibid., letter, February 18, 1951.

181. Ibid., letter, March 16, 1951.

182. The same kind of rewriting technique can also be detected in ISA, MoJ, G5671/15, letter, June 13, 1950, and report, February 5, 1950.

183. ISA, OPM, G5552/22, letter, August 4, 1950.

184. ISA, MoJ, G8003/18, letter, April 23, 1953.

185. See ISA, MoJ, G5674/10, letter, November 5, 1950; ISA, GVM 1, 27:47–51, July 26, 1950.

186. Some requests were denied on the ground of multiple previous journeys abroad. See ISA, G8003/18, letter, July 27, 1951.

187. ISA, OPM, G324/32, letter, September 30, 1948.

188. This feeling of shared responsibility was sometimes manifested in advice given by ordinary citizens to ministers in matters related to their ministries. See, for example, ISA, MoI, G2242/14, letter, February 5, 1953; ibid., G2242/102/3.

189. ISA, MoR, GL6326/18, letter, May 17, 1951.

190. Yehudai 2013, 290–97.

191. One model was that of post-1961 East Germany. See Fulbrook 2005, 239–41.

192. ISA, MoJ, G8003/18, letter, May 22, 1955.

193. IDFA, 580/1956–387, letter, September 20, 1948. Schneider was probably unaware of the fact that the authority to grant exit permits had been transferred to the Ministry of the Interior a month earlier, in August 1948.

194. ISA, OPM, G5552/22, letter, May 9, 1949.

195. ISA, OPM, G324/32, letter, March 4, 1949; HCJ 206/51 *Vacht v. Ministry of Immigration*; HCJ 112/51 *Afteweitzer v. Minister of Immigration* (unpublished); HCJ 162/52 *Lamberger v. Minister of Internal Affairs* (unpublished); in ISA, MoI, 2242/5(410), HCJ 3/51 *Es-Said v. Minister of Immigration* 5 PD 1075.

196. See, for example, *Haaretz*, January 14 and February 21, 1952, and July 25, 1956; *Ma'ariv*, April 12, 1953, and January 27, 1111/5356.

197. ISA, GVM 1, 27: 44–45 and 53, July 26, 1950.

198. *Davar*, December 3, 1953.

199. ISA, MoI, G2242/3(410), letter, June 28, 1952. See also ibid., letter, March 24, 1952.

200. See, for example, Fitzpatrick 1996, 95–98.

201. ISA, GVM 1, 27: 44–45, July 26, 1950.

202. See, for example, ISA, MoI, G2242/14, letter, February 10, 1953; TAMA, 7 (14)-7, letter, August 31, 1951; ISA, OPM, G5552/22, letter, May 9, 1949.

203. ISA, GVM 1, 27:47–51, July 26, 1950.

204. CZA, Eliyahu Elyashar Private Archive, A 430/81; *'Al Hamishmar*, August 22, 1956; ISA, MoI, G2242/13, letter, August 22, 1956.

205. See, for instance, ISA, MoI, G2242/14, letter, February 23, 1953.

206. See, for example, *Herut*, April 17, 1953; *Haboker*, April 20, 1952; *Jerusalem Post*, June 24, 1952.

207. TAMA, 7 (14)-7, letter, September 1, 1951.

208. ISA, MoIM, G2242/410/3, letter, June 2, 1952.

209. ISA, MoIM, G2242/3 (410), minutes, June 4, 1952.

210. *Jerusalem Post*, June 24, 1952. See also *Yedi'ot 'Aharonot*, June 20, 1952.

211. ISA, OPM, G5421/10, memorandum, October 27, 1949, and letter, November 13, 1949; ISA, GVM 1, 22:87–89, April 12, 1950, and 27:51, July 26, 1950. Other ministers who criticized the policy were Minister of Foreign Affairs Moshe Sharett and Minister of Education Zalman Shazar.

212. ISA, GVM 2, 12, August 14, 1951. See also ISA, MoJ, G5674/10, letter, January 12, 1951.

213. ISA, OPM, G5552/20, letter, August 23, 1949. The entire diplomatic staff abroad was apparently swamped with appeals by local citizens requiring their assistance to obtain exit permits for Israeli citizens. They were instructed not to interfere except in extraordinary circumstances. See ISA, OPM, G5552/21, circular, February 21, 1949.

214. Minister of Finance Eliezer Kaplan explained a year later why the Israeli currency was weakening. See ISA, GVM 1, 27:47–49, July 26, 1950.

215. ISA, OPM, G5552/18, letter, August 10, 1950. See also ibid., G5552/21, circular, February 21, 1949.

216. ISA, MoI, G5671/14; HCJ 111/53 *Kaufman v. Minister of Internal Affairs* 7 PD 534.

217. This was the case despite the relief granted to British citizens in 1959; when the need arose again in the 1960s, Britain reimposed the restrictions. Oliver 1971.

218. See, for example, ISA GVM 1, 27:48–49, July 26, 1950.

219. Torpey 2000, 10–13.

220. An excellent example is the case of Abba Hillel Silver, an American rabbi and Zionist leader whose passport was revoked and then — after the intervention of acquaintances in the State Department — reinstated. Silver wrote to the director of the US passport agency, depicting himself as one among many "loyal Americans highly recommended by an impressive list of leaders in American political, educational, and religious life whose Americanism was beyond question" (AHSA, mf3/270, June 3, 1955). See also Z. Segev 2004, 110–11.

221. For a critical and ironic view of this loyalty, see Greene 1971.

222. Whelan 1981, 639; Hirschman 1978, 102.

223. Rozin 2007.

224. ISA, MoJ, GL21986/54, minutes, May 2, 1953.

225. Even-Zohar 2010, 167.

3. Craving Recognition

1. *Hador*, July 5, 1949, CZA, S71/192.

2. Ibid.

3. Brunner 2008, 11.

4. Honneth 2008, 51. See also Van Den Brink 2011, 168.

5. Honneth 2008, 50.

6. See Bader 2007.

7. Rosenfeld 2011, 331–33. See also Spivak 1988.

8. Rosenfeld 2011, 328.

9. The right to petition the government for the redress of grievances was well established in England and colonial America. This right was separate from speech rights (Spanbauer 1993, 19). Later the right to petition, which was transferred from a colony to a federal democracy, was subsumed into the freedom of expression (Higginson 1986; G. Mark 1998, 2154–55). However, this right was not considered a way to achieve social belonging or recognition. It did not require the government to make a proactive effort to hear citizens.

10. Poole 2007, 114.

11. Honneth 2008, 12–14 and 18–19.

12. On the distinctions among various types of liberalism, see Mautner 2013, 7–8. See also Barber 2003, 177.

13. Brunner 2008, 12–14 and 18–19; Zurn 2005, 91–92; Taylor 1994. See also Pinchevski 2006, 412–15.

14. *Hashnaton Hastatisti Leyisrael*, 13:52, 1961.

15. Sicron 1986, 32.

16. Ibid., 31; Yablonka 1994, 9–10.

17. *Hashnaton Hastatisti Leyisrael*, 13:98, 1961, and *Hashnaton Hastatisti Leyisrael* 65:234 (Jerusalem 2014).

18. Hacohen 1994, 12–16.

19. Ibid., 54–66; Y. Tsur 2001, 253.

20. Yablonka 1994, 80.

21. Sicron 1986, 37–38.

22. Lissak 1999, 43.

23. Hacohen 1994, 2–8, 112–15, 121–25, and 179.

24. Rozin 2011, 126–29.

25. Lissak 1999, 24–25.

26. Barkai 1990, 34.

27. Hacohen 1994, 326.

28. Lissak 1999, 24–27.

29. Rozin 2011, 154–60 and 167; Hacohen 1994, 190–94.

30. Lissak 1999, 32.

31. Ibid., 33–35 and 85; Y. Tsur 2002, 85; Morris 1996, 122–27.

32. Efrat 1997, 109–11.

33. Picard 2009, 198–99.

34. Rozin 2011, 14–19 and 157–59.

35. Lissak 1999, 96.

36. Barkai 1990, 41.

37. Ibid., 42–43.

38. Ibid., 61–70. See also Tsoref 2010, 242, Table 10.

39. Barkai 1990, 75.

40. Sicron 1986, 39–40. See also Lissak 1999, 46–58.

41. Yablonka 1994, 12; Sicron 1986, 40.

42. Lissak 1999, 85; Picard 2009, 202–10.

43. Lissak 1999, 96–101.

44. See, for example, Lissak 1999, 58–65; Y. Tsur 2000a; Hever, Shenhav, and Mutzafi-Haller 2002.

45. Yablonka 1994, 62–69, especially 68–69; Meir-Glitzenstein 2009, 82–83. See also IDFA, 535/2004-353, report no. 23, September 22, 1949, 6.

46. T. Segev 1991, 107, note 35, 495.

47. Ibid., 104–107. See also Zalashik 2008, 114 and 148–51.

48. Zalashik 2008, 140.

49. Ibid., 80.

50. T. Segev 1991, 162.

51. Ibid., 167. This claim was later disproved by Hanna Yablonka (1994, 151) and Ya'acov Markovitsky (2005, 535).

52. Yablonka 1994, 133–34.

53. Y. Tsur 2000a, 134.

54. Ibid., 142–43; Lissak 1999, 59–61.

55. Lissak 1999; Y. Tsur 2000b and 2002; Shaked 5758. On the perception of colonialist relations in this context, see Sharon 2012, 110.

56. In 1949, 47.3 percent of immigrants were of Asian or African origin, and 52.7 percent of European or American origin (Table 3.3). See S. Chetrit 2004, 95–99; Hofnung 2006, 33–34; Lehman-Wilzig 1992, 42–47; Yehudai 2013, 268.

57. T. Segev 1984, 291–98; Rozin 2011, 26–28, 39–51, and 147; Hagiladi 2011, 249–340; Morris 1996, 121–28; Lotan 1995, 98. Some examples of violence will be discussed below.

58. See, for example, Ben-Bassat 2013; Fitzpatrick 1996; Straughn 2005; Scott 1990; Viola 1996; Bhatia 2004. For other manifestations of criticism and change, see Kozlov 2013.

59. M. Mark 2010, 24 and 84–86.

60. Weitz 1995, 129–30.

61. See, for example, KM, 14, July 29, 1953, 2065; Don-Yihya 2008, 142–46; New York Times, May 8 and July 19, 1949; Zameret 1993, 47–48.

62. Yehudai 2013, 81–82.

63. For a discussion on the immigrant organizations during the 1948 war, see Kabalo 2010a; Naor 2009, 186–200.

64. N. Gross 1997, 138–39.

65. Michael 1974, 19–21; N. Gross 1999, 325–29; A. Shapira 5757, 259–61.

66. See, for example, ISA, MoW, G6161/23, letter, June 8, 1951. See also, ISA, MoI, G2276/30, letter, May 21, 1951. I do not distinguish between registered and ad hoc or nonregistered organizations. For more information about the public role of landsmanschaften, see CZA, S71/1749.

67. Kabalo 5769.

68. *Herut*, October 9, 1952; *Haboker*, November 30, 1953, CZA, S71/1749; *Herut*, November 14, 1957, CZA, S71/3050.

69. *Haboker*, April 15, 1954; *Yedi'ot 'Aharonot*, January 13, 1954; CZA, S71/1749.

70. *Davar*, March 24, 1955; *Herut*, March 24, 1955; *Zmanim*, May 14, 1954, CZA, S71/1749; Bareli 2007, 67; Rozin 2008, 86.

71. KM, 15, November 11:107, 1953. See also *Yedi'ot 'Aharonot*, August 13, 1954, CZA, S71/1749, *Haboker*, October 5, 1954; *Davar*, October 5, 1954, CZA, S71/1749; *Herut*, September 8, 1958, CZA, S71/3120; KM, 27: 2654, July 22, 1959.

72. *Hador*, June 30, 1953; *Davar*, October 4, 1953, and March 31, 1955; *Davar*, June 24, 1953, CZA, S71/1749; *Hador*, May 30, 1953, CZA, S71/1749; *Davar*, September 29, 1949, CZA, S71/192; ISA, MoW, GL2145/6, report, August 1949; ISA, MoA, G 2436/20, letters, January 21 and April 13, 1952.

73. *Haaretz*, November 15, 1949; *Davar*, November 15, 1949. See also Rozin and Davidovitch 2009, 71.

74. *Hatsofe*, November 2, 1949, CZA, S71/197; Bareli 2007, 67 and 70–72.

75. *Hed Hamizrah*, July 1, 1949. The industrialist Bruno Landesberg, who immigrated from Romania, described the arrogance of the old-timers when he looked for a job (G. Drori 1998; KM, 5:1668, June 7, 1950).

76. Don-Yihya 2008; Zameret 1993, 23–28; Y.Tsur 2014, 403–6.

77. Shavit 1992, 2:56–57.

78. Discussions of the immigrants' hardships were too frequent and vast to be encompassed here. There is a large collection of newspaper clippings in CZA S71.

79. *Yedi'ot 'Aharonot*, April 4, 1949, CZA, S71/192.

80. *Herut*, March 3, 1949, CZA, S71/194.

81. *Ha'olam Hazeh*, June 7, 1951; *Herut*, February 4, 1952, CZA, S 71/1617; *Haaretz*, March 3, 1949, CZA, S71/194.

82. *Kol Ha'am*, October 27, 1950, CZA, S71/51.

83. Quoted in *Yom Yom*, April 4, 1949, CZA, S71/192.

84. *Ma'ariv*, August 23, 1950, CZA, S71/51.

85. *Herut*, December 23, 1948, CZA, S71/194.

86. *Haaretz*, May 25, 1949, June 8, 1949, CZA, S 71/197.

87. *Haaretz*, July 25, 1949, CZA, S 71/197.

88. *Hatsofe*, April 4 1949, CZA, S71/192.

89. *Davar*, April 8, 1949, CZA, S71/192.

90. *Hador*, April 19, 1949, CZA, S71/192.

91. *Yedi'ot 'Aharonot*, April 10, 1949, CZA, S71/192. See also *Hador*, April 19, 1949, CZA, S71/192; *Haaretz*, December 29, 1955.

92. *Yedi'ot 'Aharonot*, August 18, 1950, CZA, S71/195.

93. *Kol Ha'am*, January 18, 1951, CZA, S71/151; *'Al Hamishmar*, September 23, 1953; *Kol Ha'am*, January 23, 1955, CZA, S 71/112 1.

94. *New York Times*, July 18, 1949. See also *Haaretz*, July 19, 1949; *Hamevaser*, July 19, 1949, CZA, S71/192.

95. *Herut*, March 3, 1949, CZA, S71/194; *Yedi'ot 'Aharonot*, January 13, 1954; *Haboker*, July 16, 1953; *Herut*, August 19, 1953, CZA, S71/1749; *Davar*, November 21, 1951, CZA, S71/195; *Ha'olam Hazeh*, November 9, 1950; ISA, MoW, G6161/19, letter, January 7, 1953; ISA, MoJ G8004/14.

96. *Haboker*, June 21, 1953, CZA, S71/1749.

97. *'Al Hamishmar*, June 18 and December 31, 1953; *Ma'ariv*, July 6, 1953; *Herut*, August 15, 1954, CZA, S71/1749. When the political situation in North Africa deteriorated during the summer of 1954, criticism of Israeli immigration policy increased. See, for example, *Haboker*, August 29, 1949.

98. *Haboker*, January 10, 1949, CZA, S71/194.

99. *Hador*, December 29, 1948, CZA, S71/194.

100. S. Chetrit 2004, 93.

101. Pkudat Hamishtara (The police ordinance) (New Version), 5731-1971, DMI NH No. 17 p. 390. In 1979 the British ordinance was still valid. See HCJ 148/79 *Saar v. Ministry of Internal Affairs* 34(2) PD 69.

102. *Haaretz*, February 16, 1949; *Kol Ha'am*, February 21, 1949, CZA, S71/194.

103. *Herut*, April 6, 1949, CZA, S71/192.

104. See Tsoref 2010, 214–19.

105. *Davar*, February 23, April 25, and May 30, 1949; *'Al Hamishmar*, March 2 and 12, 1949, CZA, S71/194; *Kol Ha'am*, April 17 and 25 and June 2, 1949; *Haaretz*, April 25 and 28 and June 30, 1949; *Herut*, April 25, 1949, CZA, S71/192.

106. *Yedi'ot 'Aharonot*, April 25, 1949; *Davar*, April 26, 1949, CZA, S71/192.

107. *Haaretz*, April 26, 1949; *Jerusalem Post*, April 26, 1949, CZA, S71/192.

108. *Kol Ha'am*, May 10, 1949.

109. ISA, OPM, G 334/34, telegram, May 25, 1949. See also ibid., letter, May 26, 1949.

110. *Haaretz*, July 19, 1949; *Haboker*, July 19, 1949; *Herut*, July 17, 1949, CZA, S71/192; ISA, IP, L13/15, letter, July 19, 1949.

111. *Haboker*, July 20, 1949, CZA, S71/192. See also *KM*, 2, August 8, 1949, 1269.

112. *'Al Hamishmar*, July 20, 1949; CZA, S71/192.

113. *Haaretz*, October 19, 1949, CZA, S71/192.

114. *Haaretz*, April 18, 1949, CZA, S71/192; *Kol Ha'am*, December 1, 1949, CZA, S71/195.

115. *Kol Ha'am*, April 21, 1949; *Haboker*, April 21, 1949; *Davar*, April 28, 1949, CZA, S71/192. See also *Kol Ha'am*, January 17, 1950, CZA, S71/196. Part of the shortage was caused by the disparity between the menu and immigrants' tastes and cultural preferences. Yet the shortage was also a result of embezzlement and theft by the managers of the dining rooms. See Lufban 1967, 84–87.

116. *Davar*, April 19, 1949. See also *Yedi'ot-Ma'ariv* (this newspaper soon changed its name to *Ma'ariv*), April 26, 1949, CZA, S71/192.

117. *Kol Ha'am*, April 21, 1949, CZA, S71/192.

118. *Haaretz*, April 24, 1949, CZA, S71/192.

119. *Hatsofe*, September 13, 1949, CZA, S71/192.

120. *Haaretz*, June 21, 1949, CZA, S71/192.

121. *Haboker*, April 11, 1949. See also *Kol Ha'am*, April 11, 1949, CZA, S71/192.

122. *Herut*, May 20, 1949; *'Al Hamishmar*, May 20, 1949; CZA, S71/192.

123. *Haaretz*, May 8, 1949, CZA, S71/192.

124. *Herut*, May 9, 1949, See also *Kol Ha'am*, May 9, 1949; *Haaretz*, May 9, 1949, CZA, S71/192.

125. *Davar*, June 14, 1949, CZA, S71/192.

126. *Haaretz*, July 28, 1949. See also *Davar*, July 28, 1949, CZA, S71/192.

127. *Hatsofe*, August 23, 1949, CZA, S71/192.

128. *Davar*, June 6, 1949; *'Al Hamishmar*, June 6, 1949; *Hamevaser*, June 7, 1949, CZA, S71/192.

129. *Hatsofe*, August 31, 1949, CZA, S71/192.

130. Tsoref 2010, 215.

131. ISA, MoL, G 5444/1639, report, April–June 1949, quoted in Gal 2002, 102, note 39.

132. Tsoref 2010, 215; Gal 2002, 105.

133. ISA, MoW, GL2145/5, letter, July 11, 1949; ibid. G6161/21, letter, June 12, 1951; *'Al Hamishmar*, May 12, 1949; *'Al Hamishmar*, August 29, 1949; CZA, S71/192; *Haboker*, October 9, 1951, CZA, S71/195; *Kol Ha'am*, April 29, June 9, and September 23, 1952; *Herut*, November 26, 1952; *Haaretz*, January 18, 1955; *Haaretz*, January 19, 1955, CZA, S71/1071. For more examples, see CZA, S71/11, S71/51, S71/109, S71/110, S71/112, S71/195, S71/1081, S71/2627; S71/2667, S71/3119,.

134. Goldstein 2012, 297. See also ISA, IP, L17/6.

135. *Ma'ariv*, July 6, 1953, CZA, S71/1749.

136. *Yedi'ot 'Aharonot*, March 2, 1949, CZA, S71/194.

137. Ibid.

138. *Herut*, February 19, 1950; *Haboker*, February 19, 1950; *Davar*, March 10, 1950, CZA, S71/196.

139. *Hayom*, May 12, 1949, CZA, S71/192.

140. Zameret 1997, 148. See also *Yedi'ot 'Aharonot*, January 13, 1951, CZA, S71/1949; Yehudai 2013, 111–12.

141. MSA, 2-2419 49-22, minutes, April 22, 1949, 14. For more about this discussion, see T. Segev 1984, 138–39.

142. MSA, 2-2419 49-22, minutes, April 22, 1949, 10–11. The numbers Dobkin mentions are exaggerated.

143. Ibid., 1–3.

144. Ibid., 17.

145. Ibid., 8–10.

146. Ibid., 15.

147. T. Segev 1984, 106; Hacohen 1994, 61, 109, and 117.

148. MSA, 2-24-1949-22 , minutes, April 22, 1949, 16.

149. Ibid.

150. Ibid., 8.

151. Ibid., 27.

152. MSA, 2-24-1949-21, minutes, April 22, 1949.

153. For a few examples, see *Davar*, February 23 and July 19, 1949, CZA, S71/194; *Haaretz*, June 30, 1949; *Haaretz*, July 19, 1949, CZA, S71/192; *'Al Hamishmar*, February 24, 1954, CZA, S71/109. On immigrants' complaints and positive responses to them, see ISA, MoW, G6161/19, letters, January 7 and July 2, 1953.

154. *Kol Ha'am*, February 17, 1949, CZA, S71/194; *Kol Ha'am*, September 1, 1950,

CZA, S71/195; *Haaretz*, November 27, 1951, CZA, S71/195; *Hatsofe*, February 19, 1951; *Haboker*, February 20, 1951, CZA, S71/51.

155. See, for example, *Kol Ha'am*, October 27, 1950, CZA, S71/51; *Hatsofe*, January 25, 1955, and January 21, 1958; *Yedi'ot 'Aharonot*, January 20, 1958; *Herut*, April 12, 1959, CZA, S71/3120; *Zmanim*, January 25, 1955, CZA, S71/933. On the characteristics of political reactions to immigrants' protests, see Hofnung 2006, 33. See also ISA, IP, L18/11 and L 20/11.

156. For a few examples, see KM, 2:1246–49, August 3, 1949, and August 8, 1949, 1257–69; KM, 14:1525, June 8, 1953; KM, 17:1275, March 24, 1955, KM, 26:2038, May 25, 1959.

157. KM, 2:1137, July 26, 1949.

158. ISA, KR, K91/22, minutes, November 5, 1951. Immigrants' names appeared differently. In the original record, Shaul Hayak was Hayag and Salim Elwya, mentioned below in the text, appeared as Wya Salim. I thank David Khedher Al-Bassoon for his help in locating their names in the listings of Iraqi Jewish immigrants.

159. Ibid.

160. See, for example, *Davar*, October 5, 1953; *Lamerhav*, December 30, 1954, CZA, S71/112(1); *Haboker*, August 3, 1950, CZA, S71/195.

161. Tully 1999, 171.

162. Ibid. On participation in political action, see also Ophir 2004, 178–84.

163. ISA, MoM, G306/94, letters, September 2, 1948; *Herut*, March 23, 1949, CZA, S71/194; *Ma'ariv*, July 5, 1950, CZA, S71/195.

164. *Kol Ha'am*, May 10, 1949.

165. Ibid., September 19, 1949; *Haaretz*, September 19, 1949; *'Al Hamishmar*, September 21, 1949, CZA, S71/192; ISA, OPM, G338/7, telegram, September 18, 1949, and letter, October 12, 1949.

166. *Haboker*, October 27, 1949, CZA, S71/192.

167. Sharon 2012, 149–50. On various forms of resistance, see Scott 1992, 240.

168. *Herut*, September 10, 1951; *Haaretz*, October 30 and 31 and November 26, 1951; *Haboker*, October 31, 1951; *'Al Hamishmar*, November 6 and 12, 1951; *Hatsofe*, November 7, 1951; *Haboker*, November 26, 1951, CZA, S71/229; *Ma'ariv*, January 21, 1951, CZA, S71/48. See also Kemp 2002.

169. Seidelman 2012; Hacohen 1994, 1984; T. Segev 1984, 123 and 134; Don-Yihya 2008, 126–35; YEA, 8–40, minutes, October 28 and November 6, 1951; Lufban 1967, 115–16; Sharon 2012, 120–21; Zameret 2002, 119–21.

170. Smadar Sharon 2012, 119. See also Kemp 2002 and James Tully's diagnosis (1999, 171).

171. For an example of such identity, see Giladi 1990.

172. See, for example, YEA, 8–40, minutes, November 18, 1951. Despite her critical angle, Sharon (2012, 151) shows this too.

173. Sharon 2012, 129–30 and 146–48.

174. *Lamerhav*, September 9, 1960. See also *Haboker*, November 10, 1960; *Haaretz*, November 16, 1960, CZA, S71/3119 .

175. *Haaretz*, March 11, 1951.

176. Ibid. For another example, see Lufban 1967, 152.

177. CZA, S71/192 and S71/194.

178. For a reference to the terms "dignity" and "respect," see Kamir 2004, 27–37.

179. On Shaʻar Haʻaliyah, see Seidelman 2012.

180. Lufban 1967, 162.

181. ʻAl Hamishmar, March 20, 1949, CZA, S71/194.

182. Haʼboker, May 15, 1951, CZA, S71/225.

183. Quoted in Haʻolam Hazeh, June 21, 1951.

184. Eisenstadt 1952, 164; Y. Tsur 2000b, 102, 110, 112, and 117; Lev 2008.

185. Haaretz, March 12, 1951, and October 27, 1953. On various kinds of resistance, see, for instance, Kulick 1996, 3.

186. S. Chetrit 2004, 113.

187. BGA, Minutes Division, "Divrey sofrim," March 27, 1949, 7–8.

188. Eisenstadt 1952, 168. Eisenstadt described the development of what he called an "anti-bureaucratic ideology" (ibid., 145). For a discussion of and literature review about the formation of Israeli bureaucracy and its attitudes toward the immigrants, see Lev 2006, 221–22 and 225–27.

189. Quoted in Shnaton Hamemshalah, 5712, 21–22.

190. BGA, Minutes Division, "Divrey sofrim," March 27, 1949, 5.

191. Davar, December 18, 1950, and January 10, and February 16 and 29, 1951; ʻAl Hamishmar, January 30, 1951.

192. Rozin 2005; Azmon 2001; Stoler-Liss and Shvarts 2004; Sharʻabi and Hadad-Kedem 2013, 266–70; Hacohen 1998, 276–77.

193. Kabalo 2007, 40–45.

194. Avidov 2006, 32; Hacohen 1998, 134–46.

195. PLA, TH, IV 307-1-107, lectures.

196. Levy 1962; Kabalo 2007, 40–45.

197. ISA, PMAA, GL2145/5, letter, September 20, 1949.

198. Kabalo 2007, 44.

199. Z. Drori 2000, 115–19.

200. Kol Haʻam, April 21, 1949, CZA S71/192; KM:1251, 2, August 3, 1949; Goldstein 2012, 295; Koren 1964, 41.

201. Sharʻabi and Hadad-Kedem 2013, 267.

202. Compare Hed Hamizrah, July 29, 1949, and Haboker, November 2, 1949, CZA S71/197.

203. Hatsofe, November 1, 1949; Kol Haʻam, November 6, 1950, CZA S71/197. See also CZA S6/5107, S6/5106; Hatsofe, January 13, 1950, CZA S71/196; Zameret 1993, 145.

204. Kabalo 2007, 44 and 46; Hacohen 1998, 130–33.

205. See, for example, Sharʻabi and Hadad-Kedem 2013, 269–70.

206. IDFA, 435/1953-4, report, February 12, 1950; T. Segev 1984, 130–31 and 134.

207. Hacohen 1998, 262–66; Avidov 2006, 43–45.

208. See, for example, ISA, MoW, G6161/16, letter, October 11, 1951. The workers of the Qaqun transit camp demanded that the transportation service to the camp not be cancelled. Not only did it provide practical assistance to the inhabitants by bringing

workers into the camp and delivering supplies and by evacuating of the camp's patients, but it also provided "a sense of security to the residents of a border settlement, who cannot send out calls for help over the telephone in case of emergency, when attacked" (ISA, MoW, letter, April 15, 1953).

209. IDFA, 50/1953–27, report, November 9, 1951.

210. ISA, MoW, G6161/22, letter, July 29, 1951. On the need for emotional support, see ISA, PMAA, GL2145/5, letter, Nisan 12, 5709.

211. Kabalo 2000, 215–21.

212. *'Al Hamishmar*, January 30, 1951.

213. Hacohen 2001, 122; R. Shapira 1986, 160 and 163–64.

214. Even-Zohar 1980. See also *Shnaton Hamemshalah*, 5712, 8.

215. Y. Maimon 5713, 31–33; NLI, Yaakov Maimon archive, 1530/4, action I 1951–59 (1952), February 18, 1952.

216. Taylor and Gutman 1992, 37–38.

217. Guber 1959.

218. See, for example, CZA S15/9585, letters, May 18, 1951. and July 1, 1953; *KM*, 10, November 28, 1951, 503, and 11, May 14, 1952, 2031–32; YEA, 40–8, report, October 7, 1951.

219. See, for example, *Maslul*, August 14, 1949, and June 16, 1952.

220. ISA, GMA, P811/11, minutes, February 10, 1953, 22. See also MSA, 2–24–1949–22, minutes, April 22, 1949.

221. MSA, 2–11–1950–2, minutes, March 5, 1950.

222. Dayan 1964, 217; Avidov 2006, 45 and 57–58. On the arrangements made to assist those who left the moshavim, see CZA, S92/527, S92/528, S92/529, S92/530, S92/532 and S92/533; PLA, TH, IV 307–1-310, letters, July 8 and December 25, 1959. See also PLA, TH, IV 307–1-271-A; ibid., IV-307-1-275. These files contain many documents indicating that alternative housing was offered to those who asked to leave.

223. *Hed Hamizrah*, July 29, 1949. On the freedom of demonstration, see also KM, 2: 1267, August 8, 1949.

224. Among the protesters were immigrants from Europe, North Africa, and Asia. I have no information about their educational background.

225. Bader 2007, 240.

226. Ouzan 2004; Y. Tsur 2014, 399.

227. See, for example, Kishon 1952, 3. The first edition of this work was published in Tel Aviv in 1951 in Hungarian.

228. For a comparison with France, see Rosenfeld 2011, 327–28.

229. ISA, IP, L25/17 and L42/16.

230. See, for example, ISA, GVM 2, 12, August 14, 1951; ISA, MoJ, G10/5674, letter, January 12, 1951; ISA, MoW, G6170/18 and G 6161/26; *Haboker*, July 3, 1951, CZA S71/225.

231. BGA, Articles and Speeches Division, August 26, 1949, 2–3.

232. Ibid., 15–16.

233. *Haaretz*, March 12, 1951.

234. Lufban 1967, 90–92. See also O'Brien 1996, 31–32.

235. For a theoretical discussion, see Bader 2007, 264.

236. Hirschman 1970, 92–98.

237. Laden 2007, 274. See also Gans 2013, 98–99.

238. On the sense of belonging and its importance, see Calderon 2000, 150–51.

239. For a comprehensive discussion of this point, see Honneth 2008, 143–76.

240. Rosenfeld 2011, 328.

241. Honneth 2008, 143–52.

Conclusion

1. Bareli and Kedar 2011, 23–24.

2. Migdal 2006.

3. Bareli and Kedar 2011, 30.

4. Ozacky-Lazar 1996, 152–56 and 160–61; Robinson 2013, 86–90. In principle, the state recognized the right of families to reunite. See H. Cohen 2006, 119–20.

5. Boimel 2007, 21. See also Harel-Shalev 2010, 60, 62, 84, and 399.

6. Bareli and Kedar 2011, 39–45.

7. See chapter 1. See also Robinson 2013, 33.

8. *Davar*, October 25, 1956.

BIBLIOGRAPHY

· ·

Archives

AHSA · Abba Hillel Silver Archives, Cleveland, Ohio
BGA · Ben Gurion Archives, Sde Boker
   BGAO · Records from Ben-Gurion's time as prime minister
CZA · Central Zionist Archives, Jerusalem
IDFA · Israel Defense Forces and Defense Establishment Archives, Kiryat Ono
ISA · Israel State Archives, Jerusalem
   CR · Chief Rabbinate
   GMA · Golda Meir's private archive
   GoP · Government of Palestine
   GSO · Government Secretary's Office
   GVM · Government Minutes
   IP · Israeli Police
   JCMG · Jerusalem Committee, Military Governor
   KR · Knesset records
      MCLJC · Minutes of the Knesset's Constitution, Law, and Justice Committee
   LAW · Law court records
   MoA · Ministry of Agriculture
   MoH · Ministry of Health
   MoI · Ministry of the Interior
   MoIM · Ministry of Immigration
   MoJ · Ministry of Justice
   MoL · Ministry of Labor
   MoM · Ministry of Minorities
   MoP · Ministry of Police
   MoR · Ministry of Religions
   MoW · Ministry of Welfare
   OPM · Office of the Prime Minister
   PMAA · Prime minister's advisor on Arab affairs
KA · Knesset Archive, Jerusalem
Khan · History Museum, Hadera
MSA · Moshe Sharett Labor Party Archive, Beit Berl
NLI · The National Library of Israel, Jerusalem
PLA · Pinhas Lavon Institute for Labour Movement Research, Tel Aviv
   TH · Tnu'at Hamoshavim Division

TAMA · Tel Aviv–Yafo Municipal Historical Archives, Tel Aviv
YEA · Yad 'Eshkol Archiv, Jerusalem
YTA · Yad Tabenkin — The Research and Documentation Center of the Kibbutz
   Movement Archives, Ramat 'Ef'

Daily Newspapers

'Al Hamishmar
Burlington (NC) Daily Times News
Charleston Gazette
Davar
Haaretz
Haboker
Hador
Hakol
Hamevaser
Hatsofe
Herut

Jerusalem Post
Hayom
Kol Ha'am
Lamerhav
Ma'ariv
New York Times
Palestine Post
Yedi'ot 'Aharonot
Yedi'ot-Ma'ariv
Yom Yom
Zmanim

Periodicals

'Ashmoret
Dvar Hapo'elet
Haahot Beyisrael
Haisha
Haisha Bamdina
Ha'olam Hazeh

Hapo'el Hatsa'ir
Hed Hamizrah
Maslul
Mibifnim
Molad
Time

Government Documents

Halishka Hamerkazit Lestatistika [Central Bureau of Statistics]. 1964. *Hamuslemim,
   hanotsrim vehadruzim beyisrael, pirsumey mifkad haukhlusin vehadiyur.* Vol. 17.
   Jerusalem.
———. 1965. *Nisuin ufiryon* [Part 1] *Pirsumei Mifkad hauhlusin vehadiyur 1961.* M 26.
   Jerusalem.
Hashnaton Hastatisti Leyisrael [Israel Statistical Yearbook].
KM *Divrey Haknesset* [Knesset Minutes].
Official Gazette [of the Israeli Government]
Palestine Gazette

Books, Journal Articles, Theses, and Dissertations

Abramov, Shlomo Zalman. 1995. *Al miflaga shene'elma ve'al liberalism.* Tel Aviv.
Ahrak, Mazal. 1964. "Shalosh pe'amim yatsanu vehazarnu." In *Darki lamoshav,* edited
   by Yosef Rubin, 25–32. Tel Aviv.

Ajzenstadt, Mimi. 2010. "Hitahdut nashim 'ivriyot leshivuy zhuyot beErets Yisrael." In *Huka 'ahat umishpat 'ehad laish velaisha — nashim, zhuyot umishpat bitkufat hamandat*, edited by Eyal Katvan, Margalit Shilo, and Ruth Halperin-Kaddari, 57–86. Ramat Gan.

———— and Jonny Gal. 2001. "Migdar bemedinat harevaha." *Revaha Hevratit* 25 (2): 7–28.

Almog, Oz. 5756. "Dat hilonit beyisrael." *Megamot* 37 (3): 314–39.

Alterman, Nathan. 1973. "Hakoah hasheni bamedina." In *Hatur hashvi'ei*, edited by Menachem Dorman, 3:291–93. Tel Aviv.

Amin, Camron Michael. 2002. *The Making of the Modern Iraninan Woman: Gender, State Policy and Popular Culture, 1865–1946*. Gainesville, FL.

Aronson, Shlomo. 1998. "Huka leyisrael: Hadegem habriti shel David Ben-Gurion." *Politika* 2:9–30.

————. 1999. *David Ben-Gurion manhig harenesans sheshaka*. Sde Boker.

Aschheim, Steven E. 1982. *Brothers and Strangers: The East European Jew in German and German Jewish Consciousness*. Madison, WI.

Avidov, Ofer. 2006. "Yahasey hagomlin bein hamadrihim la'olim hahadashim bemoshavey ha'olim ba'asor harishon." MA thesis, Haifa University.

Avishur, Yitshak. 1990. *Hahatuna hayehudit bebagdad uvnoteha — Minhagim utkasim, mismakhim veshirim, bgadim vetakhshitim*. Vol. 1. Haifa.

Azaryahu, Maoz. 1995. *Pulhaney medina: Hagigot ha'atsmaut vehantsahat hanoflim beyisrael 1948–1956*. Sde Boker.

Azmon, Yael. 2001. "Historia shel kabalat ahrayut." In *Hatishma koli? Yitsugim shel nashim batarbut hayisraelit*, edited by Yael Azmon, 134–52. Jerusalem.

Bader, Veit. 2007. "Misrecognition, Power, and Democracy." In *Recognition and Power: Axel Honneth and the Tradition of Critical Social Theory*, edited by Bert Van Den Brink and David Owen, 238–69. Cambridge.

Baker, Paula. 1990. "The Domestication of Politics: Women and American Political Society, 1780–1920." In *Women, the State, and Welfare*, edited by Linda Gordon, 55–91. Madison, WI.

Barak, Aharon. 1992. "Hahuka shel Yisrael: Avar, hove ve'atid." *Hapraklit* 44 (1–2): 5–23.

Barak-Erez, Daphne. 1999. "Bli politika bebeit-hasefer." In *Beit-hamishpat: Hamishim shnot shfita beyisrael*, edited by David Heshin et al, 34–35. Tel Aviv.

————. 2007. *Outlawed Pigs: Law, Religion and Culture in Israel*. Madison, WI.

Barber, Benjamin R. 2003. *Strong Democracy Participatory Politics for a New Age*. Berkeley, CA.

Bareli, Avi. 2007. *Mapai bereshit ha'atsmaut*. Jerusalem.

————. 2012. "Hadimuy habolsheviki shel mapai." In *Tarbut, zikaron vehistoria, behokara leAnita Shapira*, vol. 2: *Tarbut vezikaron yisraeli*, edited by Meir Chazan and Uri Cohen, 549–61. Jerusalem.

———— and Uri Cohen. 2008. "The Middle Class versus the Ruling Party during the 1950s in Israel: The 'Engine-Coach Car' Dilemma." *Middle Eastern Studies* 44 (3): 489–510.

Bareli, Avi, and Nir Kedar. 2011. *Mamlakhtiyut yisraelit.* Jerusalem.

Barkai, Haim. 1990. *Yemey bereshit shel hameshek hayisraeli.* Jerusalem.

———. 2004. "Ha'alut harealit shel milhemet ha'atsmaut." In *Milhemet ha'atsmaut tashah-tashat: Diyun mehudash*, edited by Alon Kadish, 2:759–92. Tel Aviv.

Bar-On, Mordechai. 1992. *Sha'arey Aza, mediniyut habitahon vehahuts shel medinat Yisrael: 1955–1957.* Tel Aviv.

———. 2001. *Gvulot ashenim.* Jerusalem.

———. 2006. "'Anshei ha'oref, 'anshei hahazit: Dimuyey ha'oref bekerev lohamim." In *Am bemilhama*, edited by Mordechai Bar-On and Meir Chazan, 467-92. Jerusalem.

Bartal, Israel. 1998. "Onut veein onut — Bein masoret vehaskala." In *Eros, erusin veisurim: Miniyut vemishpaha bahistoria*, edited by Israel Bartal and Isaiah Gafni, 225–37. Jerusalem.

Bashan, Eliezer. 2005. *Horim viyladim behagutam shel hahmey Tsfon Afrika.* Tel Aviv.

Basin, Shoshana. 1964. "Hadeaga harishona — Hayeladim." In *Darki lamoshav*, edited by Yosef Rubin, 255–64. Tel Aviv.

Ben-Bassat, Yuval. 2013. "Rural Reactions to Zionist Activity in Palestine before and after the Young Turk Revolution of 1908 as Reflected in Petitions to Istanbul." *Middle Eastern Studies* 49 (3): 349–63.

Ben-Gurion, David. 5711. *Hazon vaderekh.* Vol. 2. Tel Aviv.

Ben-Itto, Hadassah. 2008. *Pninim vrudot miShanghai.* Or Yehuda.

Ben-Porat, Yosef. 1988. *Mahsom latohu: Shanim makhri'ot betoldot mishteret Yisrael.* Tel Aviv.

Berkovitch, Nitza. 1999. "Eshet hayil mi yimtsa — Nashim veezrahut beyisrael." *Sotsyologia Yisraelit* 2 (1): 277–317.

Bhatia, Nandi. 2004. *Acts of Authority/Acts of Resistance: Theater and Politics in Colonial and Post-Colonial India.* Ann Arbor, MI.

Biale, David. 1997. *Eros and the Jews: From Biblical Israel to Contemporary America.* Berkeley, CA.

Bialer, Uri. 2006. *Tslav bemagen david: Ha'olam hanotsri bemediniyut hahuts shel Yisrael 1948–1967.* Jerusalem.

Bilsky, Leora. 1998. "Giving Voice to Women: An Israeli Case Study." *Israel Studies* 3 (2): 47–79.

Boim, Leon. 1975. "Shitat hapasportim bebrit hamo'atsot vehashpa'ata al matzavam shel hayehudim." *Shvut* 3:7–16.

Boimel, Yair. 2007. *Tsel kahol lavan: Mediniyut hamimsad hayisraeli vepe'ulotav bekerev haezrahim ha'aravim, hashanim hame'atsvot 1958–1968.* Haifa.

Boltanski, Luc, and Laurent Thévenot. 2006. *On Justification: Economies of Worth.* Princeton, NJ.

Bondy, Ruth. 1990. *Felix: Pinhas Rosen uzmano.* Tel Aviv.

Braudo, Yael. 2008. "Lo rak imahot — Hanaka berei hamishpat." MA thesis, Tel Aviv University.

Brunner, Jose. 2008. "Mavo." In Axel Honneth, *Zilzul umatan hakara: Likrat teorya bikortit hadasha*, 7–34. Translated by Aya Breuer. Tel Aviv.

Calderon, Nissim. 2000. *Pluralistim be'al korham*. Haifa.

Chazan, Meir. 2014. "Yisrael boheret: Haderekh 'el habhirot laasefa hamekhonenet." In *Politika bemilhama: Kovets mehkarim al hahevra haezrahit bemilhemet ha'atsmaut*, edited by Mordechai Bar-On and Meir Chazan, 88–126. Jerusalem.

Chetrit, Sami Shalom. 2004. *Hamaavak hamizrahi beyisrael 1948–2003*. Tel Aviv.

Chetrit, Yosef, et al. 2003. *Hahatuna hayehudit hamasortit bemaroko: Pirkey iyun veti'ud*. Haifa.

Cohen, Hillel. 2006. *Aravim tovim: Hamodi'in hayisraeli veha'aravim beyisrael: Sokhnim vemaf'ilim, mashtapim vemordim, matarot veshitot*. Jerusalem.

Cohen, Nir. 2010. "From Legalism to Symbolism." *Journal of Historical Geography* 36 (1): 19–28.

Cohen, Tammy. 2005. "Nisuin mukdamim beTeyman: Minkudat mabata shel haisha." In *Halihot kedem bemishkenot Teyman*, edited by Shalom Serri and Yisrael Keisar, 143–55. Tel Aviv.

Cohen, Yinon. 1990. "Hasikhsukh hayehudi-aravi vehayerida min haarets." *Megamot* 32 (4): 433–48.

Cohn, Haim. 2005. *Mavo 'ishi: Otobiografia*. Or Yehuda.

Confino, Alon. 2008. "The Travels of Bettina Humpel: One Stasi File and Narratives of State and Self in East Germany." In *Socialist Modern: East German Everyday Culture and Politics*, edited by Katerine Pence and Paul Betts, 133–54. Ann Arbor, MI.

Cover, Robert M. 1983. "The Supreme Court, 1982 Term — Foreword: Nomos and Narrative." Yale Law School Faculty Scholarship Series. Accessed November 7, 2015. http://digitalcommons.law.yale.edu/cgi/viewcontent.cgi?article=3690&context=fss_papers.

Cunningham, Hugh. 1997. *Children and Childhood in Western Society since 1500*. New York.

Dankner, Amnon, and David Tartakover. 1996. *Eifo hayinu uma asinu: 'Otsar shnot hahamishim vehashishim*. Jerusalem

Darr, Yael. 2013. *Kanon bekama kolot: Sifrut hayeladim shel Tnu'at Hapo'alim 1930–1950*. Jerusalem.

Davis, Natalie Zemon. 1987. *Fiction in the Archives: Pardon Tales and Their Tellers in Sixteenth-Century France*. Stanford, CA.

Dayan, Shmuel. 1964. *Dmuyot basadot*. Tel Aviv.

Daykan (formerly known as Dickstein), Paltiel. 1950. "Hahok al gil hanisuim." *Hapraklit* 7 (7): 437–38.

De Certeau, Michel. 1997. "Hamtsaat hayomyom." Translated by Ariela Azulay. *Teoria uvikoret* 10:15–24.

Din veheshbon shel hava'ada leheker ha'avaryanut bekerev hano'ar. 1956. Jerusalem.

Diskin, Talia. 2011. "Lo iton nashim 'ragil': Degem haisha haezrahit be'ikvot hayarhon haerets yisraeli 'Haisha.'" *Yisrael* 18–19:65–98.

Don-Yihya, Eliezer. 2008. *Mashber utmura bimdina hadasha: Hinukh, dat vepolitika bamaavak al ha'aliya hagdola*. Jerusalem.

Dowty, Alan. 1987. *Closed Borders: The Contemporary Assault on Freedom of Movement*. New Haven, CT.

Drori, Gideon, producer and editor. 1998. "Kibuts galuyot." Episode 4 of *Tekuma*, channel 1 (Israel).

Drori, Zeev. 2000. *'Utopia bemadim*. Jerusalem.

Efrat, Elisha. 1997. "Ayarot hapituah." In *Ha'asor harishon tashah-tashyah*, edited by Zvi Zameret and Hanna Yablonka, 103–12. Jerusalem.

Eisenman, Robert H. 1977. *Islamic Law in Mandate Palestine and Modern Israel: A Study of the Survival and Repeal of Ottoman Legislative Reform*. Ann Arbor, MI.

Eisenstadt, Shmuel Noah. 1952. *Klitat ha'aliya: Mehkar sotsyologi*. Jerusalem.

Eranos Foundation. 2015. "Who We Are: History and Meaning of Eranos." Accessed October 1, 2015. http://www.eranosfoundation.org/history.htm.

Eraqi Klorman, Bat-Zion. 2004. *Yehudey Teyman: Historia, hevra, tarbut*. 2 vols. Ra'anana.

Etz-Hayim, Michael. 5716. "Lehof yam hamavet." In *Sefer hapalmah*, edited by Zerubavel Gilad, 2:354–356. Tel Aviv.

Even-Zohar, Itamar. 1980. "Hatsmiha vehahitgabshut shel tarbut ivrit mekomit veyelidit beErets Yisrael." *Cathedra* 16:165–89.

———. 2010. *Papers in Culture Research*. Tel Aviv. Accessed November 8, 2015. http://www.tau.ac.il/~itamarez/works/books/EZ-CR-2005_2010.pdf.

Ewick, Patricia, and Susan S. Silbey. 1992. "Conformity, Contestation, and Resistance: An Account of Legal Consciousness." *New England Law Review* 26:731–49.

Feldman, Yuval. 2009. "The Expressive Function of Trade Secret Law: Legality, Cost, Intrinsic Motivation, and Consensus." *Journal of Empirical Legal Studies* 6 (1): 177–212.

Fitzpatrick, Sheila. 1996. "Supplicants and Citizens: Public Letter-Writing in Soviet Russia in the 1930s." *Slavic Review* 55 (1): 78–105.

Fleischmann, Ellen. 2003. *The Nation and Its "New" Women: The Palestinian Women's Movement, 1920–1948*. Berkeley, CA.

Flynn, Shila Vera. 2005. "A Complex Portrayal of Social Norms and the Expressive Function of Law." *University of West Los Angeles Law Review* 36:145–248.

Fridrich-Silber, Ilana. 2001. "Sotsiologia bikortit bemivhan habikoret — Misotsiologia pragmatit lesotsiologia tarbutit." *Teoria uvikoret* 19:191–213.

Friedman, Shuki, and Amihai Radzyner. 5767. *Huka shelo ktuva batora*. Jerusalem.

Fulbrook, Mary. 2005. *The People's State: East German Society from Hitler to Honecker*. New Haven, CT.

Gaimani, Aharon. 2006. "Marriage and Divorce Customs in Yemen and Eretz Yisrael." *Nashim* 11 (1): 43–83.

Gal, Johnny. 2002. *Haomnam netel meratson? Sipura shel hahitmodedut im haavtala 1920–1995*. Sde Boker.

Gans, Chaim. 2013. *Teoria politit la'am hayehudi: Shlosha narativim tsiyoniyim*. Tel Aviv.

Gavison, Ruth. 1985. "The Controversy over Israel's Bill of Rights." *Israel Yearbook of Human Rights*. 15:113–54.

———. 5758. *Hamahapekha hahukatit — Teur metsiut 'o nevua hamagshima 'et atsma*. Jerusalem.

Gerber, Noah. 2009. "Hagiluy hatarbuti shel yahadut Teiman: Bein antropologya lefilologya." PhD diss., Hebrew University.

Gil, Binyamin, and Moshe Sicron. 5717. *Rishum hatoshavim, 6 beheshvan 5709*. Jerusalem.

Giladi, Gideon N. 1990. *Discord in Zion: Conflict between Ashkenazi and Sephardi Jews in Israel*. London.

Gluzman, Michael. 2007. *Haguf hatsiyoni — Leumiyut, migdar veminiyut basifrut ha'ivrit hahadasha*. Tel Aviv.

Goitein, Shelomo Dov. 1957. *Hamishpat hamuslemi bemedinat Yisrael*. Jerusalem.

Goldberg, Giora. 5753. "'Kshenot'im etsim 'ein tsorekh behuka' — Al binyan medina vekinun huka." *Medina, mimshal veyahasim beinleumiyim* 38:29–48.

Goldstein, Yossi. 2012. *Golda: Biographia*. Sde Boker.

Gordon, Linda. 1990. "Family Violence, Feminism and Social Control." In *Women, the State and Welfare*, edited by Linda Gordon, 178–98. Madison, WI.

Goyal, R. P. 1988. *Marriage Age in India*. New Delhi.

Green, Nancy L. 2005. "The Politics of Exit: Reversing the Immigration Paradigm." *Journal of Modern History* 77 (2): 263–89.

Greenberg, Ela. 2010. *Preparing the Mothers of Tomorrow: Education and Islam in Mandate Palestine*. Austin, TX.

Greenberg, Itzhak. 2006. "Giyus tsvai shel koah avoda lemif'alim ulesherutim kalkaliyim hiyuniyim bemilhemet ha'atsmaut." In *Am bemilhama*, edited by Mordechai Bar-On and Meir Chazan, 133–54. Jerusalem.

Greene, Graham. 1971. *Travels with My Aunt*. London.

Gross, Eyal. 2000. "Hahuka hayisraelit: Kli letsedek halukati 'o kli negdi?" In *Tsedek halukati beyisrael*, edited by Menachem Mautner, 79–118. Tel Aviv.

Gross, Nahum T. 1997. "Kalkalat Yisrael." In *Ha'asor harishon tashah-tashyah*, edited by Zvi Zameret and Hanna Yablonka, 137-150. Jerusalem.

———. 1999. *Lo al haruah levada: Iyunim behistoria hakalkalit shel 'Erets-Yisrael ba'et hahadasha*. Jerusalem.

Guber, Rivka. 1959. "Mi yilmad mimi?" In *Asor lemoshvei ha'olim*, edited by Yitzhak Koren, 502–4. Tel Aviv.

———. 1962. "Kirhok mizrakh mima'arav." In *Bait bamoshav: Haverot mesaprot*, edited by Hasya Drori and Yosef Margalit, 309–14. Tel Aviv.

Hacohen, Devora. 1994. *Olim bese'ara, ha'aliya hagdola veklitata beyisrael 1948–1953*. Jerusalem.

———. 1998. *Hagar'in veharehaim*. Tel Aviv.

———. 2001. "'Pizur 'ukhlusin' 'u 'mizug galuyot'–mesimot mitnagshot? Hanisayon shel moshvey ha'olim." In *Medina baderekh: Hahevra hayisraelit ba'asorim harishonim*, edited by Anita Shapira, 109–28. Jerusalem.

Hagiladi, Nimrod. 2011. "Hashuk hashahor vehitgabshuta shel hahevra hayisraelit: Mimilhemet ha'olam hashniya ve'ad yemey hatsena." PhD diss., Hebrew University.

Harel-Shalev, Ayelet. 2009. "The Problematic Nature of Religious Autonomy to Minorities in Democracies — The Case of India's Muslims." *Democratization* 16 (6): 1261–81.

———. 2010. *The Challenge of Sustaining Democracy in Deeply Divided Societies: Citizenship, Rights, and Ethnic Conflict in India and Israel*. Lanham, MD.

Har-Even, Yael. 1989. "Hayerida keba'aya hevratit: Hayerida mehaarets kfi shehishtakfa bemikhtavim lema'arekhet *Haaretz 1949–1987*." MA thesis, Tel Aviv University.

Harris, Ron. 1997. "Hamishpat hayisraeli." In *Ha'asor harishon tashah-tashyah*, edited by Zvi Zameret and Hanna Yablonka, 263–80. Jerusalem.

———. 2014. *Hamishpat hayisraeli — Hashanim hame'atsvot 1948–1977*. Tel Aviv.

Heimann, Gadi. 2015. *Sofa shel yedidut muflaa, yahasei Yisrael Tsarfat bitkufat nesiuto shel de Gaulle, 1958–1967*. Jerusalem.

Hendrick, Harry. 1997. *Children, Childhood and English Society, 1880–1990*. Cambridge.

Henry, Eric. n.d. "Excise Taxes and the Airport and Airway Trust Fund, 1970–2002." Accessed November 11, 2015. .

Hermann, Tamar, ed. 1997. *Tnu'ot hevratiyot umehaa politit beyisrael*. 2 vol. Tel Aviv.

Hever, Hannan, Yehuda Shenhav, and Pnina Mutzafi-Haller. 2002. *Mizrahim beyisrael: 'Iyun bikorti mehudash*. Jerusalem.

Higgins, Lesley, and Marie-Christine Leps. 1998. "'Passport, Please: Legal, Literary, and Critical Fictions of Identity." *College Literature* 25 (1): 94–138.

Higginson, Stephen H. 1986. "A Short History of the Right to Petition Government for the Redress of Grievances." *Yale Law Journal* 96 (1): 142–66.

Hirsch, Dafna. 2006. "'Banu hena lehavi 'et hama'arav' — Hanhalat repertuar 'higyeni' bekerev hahevra hayehudit bePalestina bitkufat hamandat." PhD diss., Tel Aviv University.

———. 2011. "Hamedikalizatsia shel ha'imahut — Yahasim 'etniyim vehinukh 'imahot mizrahiyot letipul 'higyeni' batinok bitkufat hamandat." In *Migdar beyisrael: Mehkarim hadashim al migdar beyishuv uvamdina*, edited by Margalit Shilo and Gideon Katz, 1:106–39. Sde Boker.

Hirschman, Albert O. 1970. *Exit, Voice, and Loyalty: Responses to Decline in Firms, Organizations, and States*. Cambridge, MA.

———. 1978. "Exit, Voice, and the State." *World Politics* 31 (1): 90–107.

Hofnung, Menachem. 2006. *Mehaa vehema, hashpa'at hafganot hapanterim hashhorim al taktsivey hevra verevaha*. Srigim-Lion.

Honneth, Axel. 2008. *Zilzul umatan hakara: Likrat teoria bikortit hadasha*. Translated by Aya Breuer. Tel Aviv.

Horowitz, Dan, and Moshe Lissak. 1990. *Metsukot bautopia: Yisrael — hevra be'omes yeter*. Tel Aviv.

Hurwitz, Meir. 1959. "Hayeled vehano'ar bahakika hayisraelit." *Megamot* 10:40–52.

Hyman, Paula. 1989. "The Modern Jewish Family: Image and Reality." In *The Jewish Family: Metaphor and Memory*, edited by David C. Kraemer, 179–93. New York.

Ka'adan, Tagrid. 2013. "Tguvot hatsibur hamuslemi beyisrael klapey hahok leshivuy zkhuyot haisha 1951–1961." MA thesis, Hebrew University.

Kabalo, Paula. 2000. "Ben-Gurion: Ra'ayon hahalutsiyut venosav, tohniyot vemahalahim leshiluv bney hador hatsa'ir betahalihey itsuv hahevra hayisraelit 1949–1956." PhD diss., Tel Aviv University.

———. 2007. *Shurat hamitnadvim: Korotav shel 'irgun 'ezrahim*. Tel Aviv.

———. 2008. "Leadership behind the Curtains: The Case of Israeli Women in 1948." *Modern Judaism* 28 (1): 14–40.

———. 5769. "'Irgunim huts-memshaltiyim bahevra hayehudit beErets Yisrael ubemedinat Yisrael." In *Hazara lapolitika — Hamedina hamodernit, leumiyut veribonut*, edited by Ilan Rachum, 275–307. Jerusalem.

———. 2010a. "Interes veyitsug betashah: 'Ezrahim mitargenim vemegivim lamatsav hamilhamti." In *'Ezrahim bemilhama: Kovets mehkarim al hahevra haezrahit bemilhemet ha'atsmaut*, edited by Mordechai Bar-On and Meir Chazan, 317–42. Jerusalem.

———. 2010b. "'Shurat hamitnadvim' vemisud habikoret hatsiburit beyisrael." In *Tsomtey hakhra'ot veparshiyot merkaziyot beyisrael*, edited by Devora Hacohen and Moshe Lissak, 489–523. Sde Boker.

Kafri, Sarah. 1962. "Leba'ayot hahevra bemoshavey ha'olim." In *Bait bamoshav: haverot mesaprot* edited by Hasya Drori and Yosef Margalit, 271–74. Tel Aviv.

Kamir, Orit. 2004. *Sheela shel kavod: Yisraeliyut ukvod haadam*. Jerusalem.

Kashani-Sabet, Firoozeh. 2011 *Conceiving Citizens: Women and the Politics of Motherhood in Iran*. Oxford.

Katvan, Eyal. 5773. "Refua mona'at (nisuin vegerushin): Bdikot trom-nisuin vehamedikalizatsia shel 'alimut bamishpaha." *Aley mishpat* 10:73–124.

Katzir, Yael. 1984. "Nashim yotsot Teyman kesokhnot tarbut bamoshav." In *Yehudei hamizrah: Iyunim 'antropologiyim al he'avar vehahove*, edited by Shlomo Deshan and Moshe Shokeid, 221–30. Jerusalem.

Kedar, Alexander, and Oren Yiftachel. 2000. "Hakarka'ot hahaklaiyot beyisrael likrat sof haelef." In *Tsedek halukati beyisrael*, edited by Menahem Mautner, 149–201. Tel Aviv.

Kedar, Nir. 2005. "'Tsrikha lihiyot hargasha shel am': Shivyon veshutfut betfisato shel David Ben-Gurion bishnot hahamishim vehashishim." In *Hevra vekalkala beyisrael: Mabat histori ve'ahshavi*, edited by Avi Bareli, Danny Gutwein, and Tuvia Friling, 2:646–70. Jerusalem.

———. 5766. "Al haformalism hamehanekh shel beit hamishpat ha'elyon hamukdam: Iyun mehudash befiskey hadin beparashot Bejerano veShayb." *Mehkarey mishpat* 22 (2):385–423.

———. 2007. "Mabat hadash al hakamat ma'arekhet hamishpat hayisraelit." *Yisrael* 11:1–29.

———. 2009. *Mamlahtiyut: Hatfisa haezrahit shel David Ben-Gurion*. Sde Boker.

———. 2013. "The Roots of Ben-Gurion's Opposition to a Written Constitution." *Journal of Modern Jewish Studies* 12 (1):1–16.

———. 2015. *Ben-Gurion vehahuka: Hukatiyut, mishpat vedemokratia bemishnato shel rosh hamemshala harishon*. Or Yehuda.

Kemp, Adriana. 2002. "'Nedidat amim' 'o 'habe'era hagdola': Shlita medinatit vehitnagdut basfar hayisraeli." In *Mizrahim beyisrael: Iyun bikorti mehudash*, edited by Hannan Hever, Yehuda Shenhav, and Pnina Mutzafi-Haller, 36–67. Jerusalem.

Key, Ellen. 1909. *The Century of the Child*. New York.

Khenin, Dov, and Dani Filc. 1999. "Shvitat hayamaim." In *Hamishim learba'im ushmone: Momentim bikortiyim betoldot medinat Yisrael*, edited by Adi Ophir, 89–97. Jerusalem.

Kimmerling, Baruch, and Joel S. Migdal. 1999. *Falastinim am behivatsruto: Lemin hamered neged Muhamad ve'ad lekhinun harashut haleumit.* Jerusalem.

Kishon, Ephraim. 1952. *Ha'ole hayored lehayeynu.* Translated by Avidgor Hemeiri. Tel Aviv.

Klein, Claude. 1997. "The Right of Return in Israeli Law." *Tel Aviv University Studies in Law* 13:53–62.

Koren, Yitzhak. 1964. *Kibbutz hagaluyot behitnahluto: Letoldot moshvei-ha'olim beyisrael.* Tel Aviv.

Koven, Seth, and Sonya Michel. 1990. "Womanly Duties: Maternalist Politics and the Origins of Welfare States in France, Germany, Great Britain, and the United States, 1880–1920." *American Historical Review* 95 (4): 1076–108.

Kozlov, Denis. 2013. *The Readers of Novyi Mir: Coming to Terms with the Stalinist Past.* Cambridge, MA.

Kozma, Liat. 2011. *Policing Egyptian Women: Sex, Law, and Medicine in Khedival Egypt.* New York.

Krampf, Arie. 2010. "Economic Planning of the Free Market in Israel during the First Decade: The Influence of Don Patinkin on Israeli Policy Discourse." *Science in Context* 23 (4): 507–34.

Kulick, Don. 1996. "Causing a Commotion: Public Scandal as Resistance among Brazilian Transgendered Prostitutes." *Anthropology Today* 12 (6): 3–7.

Kutler, Stanley I. 1982. *The American Inquisition: Justice and Injustice in the Cold War.* New York.

Ladd-Taylor, Molly. 1994. *Mother-Work: Women, Child Welfare, and the State, 1890–1930.* Urbana, IL.

Laden, Anthony Simon. 2007. "Deliberation, Power, and the Struggle for Recognition." In *Recognition and Power: Axel Honneth and the Tradition of Critical Social Theory,* edited by Bert Van Den Brink and David Owen, 270–89. Cambridge.

Lahav, Pnina. 1977. "Al hofesh habituy bifsikat beit-hamishpat ha'elyon." *Mishpatim* 7 (3): 375–422.

———. 1991. "Yad harokem: Yeri'at heruyot haprat al-pi hashofet Agranat." *Iyuney Mishpat* 16 (3): 475–515.

———. 1993. "Kshehapalliative rak mekalkel—Hadiyun bakneset al hok shivuy zhuyot haisha." *Zmanim* 46–47:149–59.

———. 1999. *Yisrael bamishpat: Shimon Agranat vehamea hatsiyonit.* Tel Aviv.

Lamdan, Ruth. 1996. "Child Marriage in Jewish Society in the Eastern Mediterranean during the Sixteenth Century." *Mediterranean Historical Review* 11 (1): 37–58.

Lamdani, Reuven. 1983. "Hayerida miyisrael." *Riv'on lekalkala* 30 (116): 462–78.

Laskier, Michael M. 1983. *The Alliance Israélite Universelle and the Jewish Communities of Morocco, 1862–1962.* Albany, NY.

Layish, Aharon. 5749. "Haisha vehamishpaha." In *Yehudim ve'aravim beyisrael,* edited by Rami Hochman, 135–46. Jerusalem.

———. 2006. *Women and Islamic Law in a Non-Muslim State: A Study Based on Decisions of the Shari'a Courts in Israel.* New Brunswick, NJ.

Lehman-Wilzig, Shmuel. 1992. *Mehaa tsiburit beyisrael, 1949–1992.* Ramat Gan.

Leissner, Omi. 2009. "Ta'asiyat haleyda beyisrael." *Hamishpat* 27:20–33.

———. 2011. "Laledet ve'od eikh: Hukey haleyda haleumiyim bitkufat hamandat." In *Migdar beyisrael: Mehkarim hadashim al migdar bayishuv uvamdina*, edited by Margalit Shilo and Gideon Katz, 1: 336–66. Sde Boker.

Lengborn, Thorbjörn. 1993. "Ellen Key (1849–1926)." Accessed November 9, 2015. http://www.scribd.com/doc/164696328/Ellen-Key-Thorbjorn-Lengborn#scribd. Originally published in *Prospects* 23, nos. 3–4: 825–37.

Lev, Tali. 2006. "Bein humor lekhinun hevra: Shnot hahamishim viytsirato shel 'Efraim Kishon." PhD diss., Tel Aviv University.

———. 2008. "Nimhak 'et avaram shel 'ele sheyesh lahem avar." *Teoria uvikoret* 32:197–226.

Levy, Sarah (written by Ahuva Ron). 1962. "Sipura shel Sarah." In *Bait bamoshav: Haverot mesaprot*, edited by Hasya Drori and Yosef Margalit, 287–302. Tel Aviv.

Lewis, Carolyn Herbst. 2005. "Waking Sleeping Beauty: The Premarital Pelvic Exam and Heterosexuality during the Cold War." *Journal of Women's History* 17 (4): 86–110.

Liebermann, Danna. 2006. "Hashpa'at hamatsav hakalkali vehabitkhoni al yeridat yisraelim mehaarets." MA thesis, Tel Aviv University.

Liebman, Charles S., and Eliezer Don-Yihya. 1983. *Civil Religion in Israel: Traditional Judaism and Political Culture in the Jewish State*. Berkeley, CA.

Likhovski, Assaf. 1999. "Reshita shel hazkhut lehofesh isuk." In *Beit-hamishpat: Hamishim shnot shfita beyisrael*, edited by David Heshin et al., 28–29. Tel Aviv.

———. 2002. "Colonialism, Nationalism and Legal Education: The Case of Mandatory Palestine." In *The History of Law in a Multicultural Society: Israel 1917–1967*, edited by Ron Harris, Alexandre Kedar, Pnina Lahav, and Assaf Likhovski, 75–93. Dartmouth, UK.

———. 2006. *Law and Identity in Mandate Palestine*. Chapel Hill, NC.

———. 2007. "'Training in Citizenship': Tax Compliance and Modernity." *Law and Social Inquiry* 32 (3): 665–700.

———. 2010. "Shfahot, kalot ufo'alot." In *Huka 'ahat umishpat 'ehad laish velaisha— Nashim, zhuyot umishpat bitkufat hamandat*, edited by Eyal Katvan, Margalit Shilo, and Ruth Halperin-Kaddari, 375–404. Ramat Gan.

Lindenmeyer, Kriste. 1997. *A Right to Childhood: The U.S. Children's Bureau and Child Welfare, 1912–1946*. Urbana, IL.

Lissak, Moshe. 1999. *Ha'aliya hagdola bishnot hahamishim: Kishlono shel kur hahitukh*. Jerusalem.

Lotan, Nissim. 1995. "Mediniyut haklita shel ha'aliya haTsfon 'Afrikanit bahityashvut, nokhah hade-kolonizatsia beMaroko uveTunisya, 1954–1956." MA thesis, Tel Aviv University.

Lufban, Hezi. 1967. *'Ish yotse 'el 'ahiv*. Tel Aviv.

Maccoby, Hyam. 1986. "The Wandering Jew as Sacred Executioner." In *The Wandering Jew*, edited by Galit Hasan-Rokem and Alan Dundes, 236–60. Bloomington, IN.

Mahony, Joan. 1989. "Civil Liberties in Britain during the Cold War: The Role of the Central Government." *American Journal of Legal History* 33 (1): 53–100.

Maimon, Ada. 5718. *Hamishim shnot Tnu'at Hapo'a lot beErets Yisrael 1904–1954.* Tel Aviv.

Maimon, Yaacov. 5713. "Morim mitnadvim bama'abarot." *Megamot* 4 (1): 27–36.

Margalit-Stern, Bat-Sheva. 5766. "'Haverot lamofet': Yotsot Teyman bein migdar, ma'amad ve'eda bitnu'at ha'avoda." *Cathedra* 118:115–44.

———. 2006. *Geula bikvalim tnuat hapo'a lot haeretz yisraelit 1920–1939.* Jerusalem.

———. 2011. "Bein 'hok hateva' le'din hatnu'a': 'Imahut veal-'imahut bahevra hatsiyonit beErets Yisrael (1920–1925)." In *Mehkarim hadashim al migdar bayishuv uvamdina,* edited by Margalit Shilo and Gideon Katz, 1:170–97. Sde Boker.

———. 2014. "Bishlihut hatsibur: Hamaavak leshivyon nashim uleshiluvan bemosdot hamedina 1947–1949." In *'Ezrahim bemilhama,* edited by Mordechai Bar-On and Meir Chazan, 453–83. Jerusalem.

Margolin, Jacob, and Eliezer Witztum. 2014. "Hatnu'a lehigyena ruhanit beErets Yisrael." *Iyunim bitkumat Yisrael* 24:283–305.

Mark, Gregory A. 1998. "The Vestigial Constitution: The History and Significance of the Right to Petition." *Fordham Law Review* 66 (6): 2153–31.

Mark, Maya. 2010. "Kshehadin lo nokev 'et hahar: Batey hadin haminhaliyim veyahasey harashuyot bithumey kitsuv hamazon vehagbalat dmey hashirut bashanim haformativiyot shel hamedina." LL.M. thesis, Tel Aviv University.

Markovitsky, Yaacov. 2005. "Hagakhal — Giyus hutz-laaretz bemilkhemet ha'atzma'ut." In *Milhemet ha'atzma'ut tashah — tashat,* edited by Alon Kadish, 525–38. Tel Aviv.

Mautner, Menahem. 2008. *Mishpat vetarbut beyisrael befetah hamea ha'esrim veahat.* Tel Aviv.

———. 5768. *Mishpat vetarbut.* Ramat Gan.

———. 2013. "Petah davar: Liberalism beyisrael — 'haadam hatov,' 'haezrah har'a' vehasigsug haishi vehahevrati." *Iyuney Mishpat* 36: 7–79.

Mayo, Katherine. 1998. *Mother India.* Edited and with an introduction by Mrinalini Sinha. New Delhi.

McAdams, Richard H. 2000. "An Attitudinal Theory of Expressive Law." *Oregon Law Review* 79 (2): 339–90.

McCarthy, Justin. 1990. *The Population of Palestine: Population History and Statistics of the Late Ottoman Period and the Mandate.* New York.

Meir-Glitzenstein, Esther. 2009. *Bein Bagdad leRamat Gan: Yotsei Irak beyisrael.* Jerusalem.

———. 2012. *Yetsiat yehudey Teyman: Mivtsa koshel umitos mekhonen.* Tel Aviv.

Melamed, Shoham. 2004. "'Ka'avor asrot shanim mu'atot nihiye kulanu bney adot hamizrah . . .': 'Imahut, piryon vehavnayato shel 'haiyum hademografi' behok gil hanisuin." *Teoria uvikoret* 25:69–96.

——— and Yehuda Shenhav. 2008. "Me'ever laleumiyut: Al mishtar hahatsdaka haneo-maltusyani ve'al gibusha shel mediniyut hapiryon beyisrael 1950–1966." In *Pe'arey 'Ezrahut: Hagira, piryon vezehut beyisrael.* edited by Yossi Yonah and Adriana Kemp, 125–66. Tel Aviv.

Melman, Billie. 1998. "'Re'alot shkufot': Kolonyalism vegender—likrat diyun histori hadash." *Zmanim* 62: 84–103.

Michael, Sami. 1974. *Shavim veshavim yoter.* Tel Aviv.

Migdal, Joel S. 2001a. *State in Society: Studying how States and Societies Transform One Another.* Cambridge.

———. 2001b. *Through the Lens of Israel: Explorations in State and Society.* Albany, NY.

———. 2006. "Whose State Is It, Anyway? Exclusion and the Construction of Graduated Citizenship in Yisrael." *Israel Studies Forum* 21 (2): 3–27.

Molcho, Avner. 2009. "Shinuy vehemshekhiyut bahevra hayisraelit ba'asor harishon berei hahinukh ha'al-yesodi." PhD diss., Tel Aviv University.

Moors, Annelies. 1995. *Women, Property and Islam: Palestinian Experiences, 1920–1990.* Cambridge.

Morris, Benny. 1996. *Milhamot hagvul shel Yisrael.* Tel Aviv.

———. 2010. *1948—Toldot hamilhama ha'aravit–hayisraelit harishona.* Tel Aviv.

Moyn, Samuel. 2010. *The Last Utopia.* Cambridge, MA.

Nair, Janaki. 1996. *Women and Law in Colonial India: A Social History.* Bangalore, India.

Naor, Moshe. 2009. *Bahazit ha'oref: Tel Aviv vehitgaysut hayishuv bemilhemet ha'atsmaut.* Jerusalem.

Negbi, Moshe. 1987. *Me'al lahok.* Tel Aviv.

———. 1995. *Hofesh ha'itonut beyisrael: Arakhim biri hamishpat.* Jerusalem.

Neuberger, Binyamin. 1997. *Sugiyat hahuka beyisrael.* Tel Aviv.

Nofech-Mozes, Hemda. 1967. *Besvakh hamishpat.* Tel Aviv.

O'Brien, Kevin J. 1996. "Rightful Resistance." *World Politics* 49 (1): 31–55.

Oliver, F. R. 1971. "The Effectiveness of the U.K. Travel Allowance." *Applied Economics* 3 (3): 219–26.

Olshan, Yitzhak. 1978. *Din udvarim: Zikhronot.* Jerusalem.

Ophir, Adi. 2004. "Rashut rabim vesheelat hashilton: Al hamahshava hapolitit shel Arendt." In *Hannah Arendt—Hatsi mea shel pulmus,* edited by Idith Zartal and Moshe Zukerman, 171–98. Tel Aviv.

Ouzan, Françoise. 2004. "Rebuilding Jewish Identities in Displaced Persons Camps in Germany 1945–1957." *Bulletin du Centre de recherche français à Jérusalem* 14:98–111.

Ozacky-Lazar, Sarah. 1996. "Hitgabshut yahasey hagomlin bein yehudim le'aravim bimedinat Yisrael, ha'asor harishon 1948–1958." PhD diss., Haifa University.

———. 2002. "Hamimshal hatsvai kemanganon shlita baezrahim ha'aravim 1948–1958." *Hamizrah Hahadash* 43:103–32.

Parker, Reginald. 1954. "The Right to Go Abroad: To Have and to Hold a Passport." *Virginia Law Review* 40 (7): 853–73.

"The Passport Puzzle." 1956. *University of Chicago Law Review* 23 (2): 260–89.

"Passport Refusals for Political Reasons: Constitutional Issues and Judicial Review." 1952. *Yale Law Journal* 61 (2): 171–203.

Peled, Yoav, and Gershon Shafir. 2005. *Mihu Yisraeli: Hadinamika shel 'ezrahut murkevet.* Tel Aviv.

Peleg, Ilan. 1998. "Israel's Constitutional Order and Kulturkampf: The Role of Ben-Gurion." *Israel Studies* 3 (1): 230–50.

Penslar, Derek J. 2013. *Jews and the Military: A History*. Princeton, NJ.

Picard, Avi. 2004. "Mediniyut ha'aliya vehaklita shel yehudey Tsfon 'Africa 1951–1956." PhD diss., Ben-Gurion University.

———. 2009. "'Mi vami haholhim': Ikhlusan shel ayarot hapituah." In *Ayarot hapituah*, edited by Zvi Tzameret, Avivah Halamish, and Esther Meir-Glitzenstein, 195–214. Jerusalem.

———. 2013. *Olim bimsura, mediniyut Yisrael klapey aliyatam shel yehudey Tsfon 'Afrika 1951–1956*. Sde Boker.

Pinchevski, Amit. 2006. "Bizkhut hashtika: Hofesh habituy vehaahrayut leaherut." In *Sheket medabrim, hatarbut hamishpatit shel hofesh habituy beyisrael*, edited by Michael Birnhack, 395–424. Tel Aviv.

Pinkus, Hasia. 1971. *Mearb'a ruhot: Shikumo shel no'ar ole*. Jerusalem.

Poole, Deborah. 2007. "The Right to Be Heard." *Socialism and Democracy* 21 (2): 113–16.

Portugese, Jacqueline. 1998. *Fertility Policy in Israel: The Politics of Religion, Gender, and Nation*. Westport, CT.

Priver, Ida. 1962a. "Ronit." In *Bait bamoshav: Haverot mesaprot*, edited by Hasya Drori and Yosef Margalit, 327–29. Tel Aviv.

———. 1962b. "Peh lailemet. . . ." In *Bait bamoshav: Haverot mesaprot*, edited by Hasya Drori and Yosef Margalit, 277–79. Tel Aviv.

Procacia, Gualtiero. "Hok gil hanisuin." 1951. *Megamot* 2 (3): 385–93.

Radzyner, Amihai. 2010. "Milhamot hayehudim: Itsuvo shel 'isur habigamiya leyehudim beErets Yisrael hamandatorit." In *Huka 'ahat umishpat 'ehad laish velaisha — Nashim, zhuyot umishpat bitkufat hamandat*, edited by Eyal Katvan, Margalit Shilo, and Ruth Halperin-Kaddari, 151–98. Ramat Gan.

Ram, Uri, ed. 1993. *Hahevra hayisraelit: Hebetim bikortiyim*. Tel Aviv.

Razi, Tami. 2009. *Yaldey hahefker, hahatser haahorit shel Tel Aviv hamandatorit*. Tel Aviv.

———. 2010. "Reuya hamishpaha sheyivnuha mehadash." In *Huka 'ahat umishpat 'ehad laish velaisha — Nashim, zhuyot umishpat bitkufat hamandat*, edited by Eyal Katvan, Margalit Shilo, and Ruth Halperin-Kaddari, 21–56. Ramat Gan.

Reifen, David. 1961. *No'ar bamishpat*. Tel Aviv.

———. 1978. *Hakatin uveit hamishpat leno'ar*. Tel Aviv.

Resnik, Julia, and Michal Frenkel. 2000. "Misotsyologia bikortit lesotsyologia shel habikoret: Hasotsyologia hapragmatistit shel Luc Boltanski." *Teoria uvikoret* 17:101–22.

Rigger, Hagit. 1952. "Leba'ayat hahit'arut shel hano'ar haTeymani baarets." *Megamot* 3 (3): 259–91.

Rimerman, Yehuda, and Menahem Amir.1971. *Hitabduyot venisyonot hitabdut shel ktinim ad gil 18 bashanim 1963–1966*. Jerusalem.

Robinson, Shira. 2013. *Citizen Strangers: Palestinians and the Birth of Israel's Liberal Settler State*. Stanford, CA.

Rosenfeld, Sophia. 2011. "On Being Heard: A Case for Paying Attention to the Historical Ear." *American Historical Review* 116 (2): 316–34.

Rosenthal, Ruvik. 2009. *Milon Hatserufim: Nivim umatbeot lashon ba'ivrit hahadasha, gilgulim, mekorot, shimushim.* Jerusalem.

Rozin, Orit. 2002a. "Miguf rishon rabim leguf rishon yahid: Tahalikhey 'individualizatsia bahevra hayisraelit bereshit ha'asor harishon lamedina." PhD diss., Tel Aviv University.

———. 2002b. "Tnaim shel slida: higyena vehorut shel olim meartsot haislam be'eyney vatikim bishnot hahamishim." *Iyunim bitkumat Yisrael* 12:195–238.

———. 2005. "Nashim koltot nashim — Tafkidan shel nashim vatikot biklitat ha'aliya hagdola bishnot hahamishim: Historia veteoria." In *Hevra vekalkala beyisrael: mabat histori ve'ahshavi*, edited by Avi Bareli, Danny Gutwein, and Tuvia Friling, 2:646–70. Jerusalem.

———. 2006a. "Food, Identity and Nation-Building in Israel's Formative Years." *Israel Studies Forum* 21 (1): 52–80.

———. 2006b. "Kol ha'am beheksherey tkufato." In *Sheket medabrim, hatarbut hamishpatit shel hofesh habituy beyisrael*, edited by Michael Birnhack, 71–128. Tel Aviv.

———. 2007. "Forming a Collective Identity: The Debate over the Proposed Constitution, 1948–1950." *Journal of Israeli History* 26 (2): 251–71.

———. 2008. *Hovat haahava hakasha: Yahid vekolektiv beyisrael bishnot hahamishim.* Tel Aviv.

———. 2011. *The Rise of the Individual in 1950s Israel: A Challenge to Collectivism.* Waltham, MA.

———. 2012. "Austerity Tel-Aviv: Everyday Life, Supervision, Compliance, and Respectability." In *Tel-Aviv: The First Century: Visions, Designs, Actualities*, edited by Maoz Azaryahu and S. Ilan Troen, 165–87. Bloomington, IN.

——— and Nadav Davidovitch. 2009. "Hahistadrut harefuit beyisrael bishnot hahamishim uvishnot haalpayim." *Iyunim bitkumat Yisrael* 19:56–92.

———. 5772. "Nashiyut uvinyan 'uma besirtey hasbara yisraeliyim mishnot hahamishim — Dyokanan shel olot meartsot haislam." *Te'uda* 24:261–300.

Rubinstein, Amnon, and Barak Medina. 1996. *Hamishpat hakonstitutsyoni shel medinat Yisrael.* 2 vols. 5th ed. Jerusalem.

Salter, Mark B. 2003. *Rights of Passage: The Passport in International Relations.* Boulder, CO.

Scott, James C. 1990. *Domination and the Arts of Resistance: Hidden Transcripts.* New Haven, CT.

———. 1992. *Seeing Like a State: How Certain Schemes to Improve the Human Condition Have Failed.* New Haven, CT.

Segev, Tom. 1984. *1949—Hayisraelim harishonim.* Jerusalem.

———. 1991. *Hamilyon hashvi'ei: Hayisraelim vehashoa.* Jerusalem.

Segev, Zohar. 2004. "The Jewish State in Abba Hillel Silver's Over-All World View." *American Jewish Archives* 1–2:94–127.

Seidelman, Rhona. 2012. "Conflicts of Quarantine: The Case of Jewish Immigrants to the Jewish State." *American Journal of Public Health* 102 (2): 243–52.

Sela-Sheffy, Rakefet. 2003. "'Ha'yekim' bisde hamishpat vedfusim shel tarbut burganit bitkufat hamandat." *Iyunim bitkumat Yisrael* 13:295–322.

Shachar, Yoram. 5763. "Hatyutot hamukdamot shel hakhrazat ha'atsmaut." *Iyuney mishpat* 26:523–600.

Shaked, Gershon. 5758. "Shavim, shavim yoter, shavim: Al 'adot hamizrah basiporet ha'ivrit." In *Kibbutz Galuyot, aliya leErets Yisrael—Mitos umetsiut*, edited by Devora Hacohen, 363–98. Jerusalem.

Shaked, Michal. 2012. *Moshe Landau: Shofet*. Tel Aviv.

Shamir, Ronen. 2000. *The Colonies of Law: Colonialism, Zionism, and Law in Early Mandate Palestine*. Cambridge, MA.

Shapira, Anita. 1992. *Herev hayona: Hatsiyonut vehakoah 1881–1948*. Tel Aviv.

———. 5757. "Bein yishuv lemedina: hamarkivim shelo avru." In *Leumiyut vepolitika Yehudit: Perspektivot hadashot*, edited by Jehuda Reinharz, Yosef Salmon, and Gideon Shimoni, 253–71. Jerusalem.

———. 2014. *Ben-Gurion: Father of Modern Israel*. New Haven, CT.

Shapira, Rina. 1986. "Hamora Rina vetalmideha bema'aberet Talpiyot (symposium)." In *Olim uma'abarot 1948–1952*, edited by Mordechai Naor, 157–68. Jerusalem.

———. 2011. *"Mora Rina 'amra sheanakhnu yeholim": Hamas'a she'asinu talmidai veani bishnot hahamishim baderech leyisrael*. Jerusalem.

Shapira, Yonatan. 1977. *Hademokratia beyisrael*. Ramat Gan.

———. 1996. *Hevra bishvi hapolitikaim*. Tel Aviv.

Shar'abi, Rachel. 2002. *Sinkretism vehistaglut: Hamifgash bein kehila masortit uvein hevra sotsyalistit*. Tel Aviv.

———. 2005. "Hitmodedut olot miTeyman im misgeret hevratit." In *'Isha bamizrah, 'isha mimizrah: Sipura shel hayehudiya bat hamizrah*, edited by Tova Cohen and Shaul Regev, 207-231. Ramat Gan.

———. and Naama Hadad-Kedem. 2013. "Hahalutsot mimoshvey ha'olim: Sipuran shel olot mizrahiyot bemoshvey prozdor Yerushalaim." In *Bein haprati latsiburi —Nashim bakibuts uvamoshav*, edited by Sylvie Fogiel-Bijaoui and Rachel Shar'abi, 251–83. Jerusalem.

Sharfman, Daphna. 1993. *Living without a Consitution: Civil Rights in Israel*. New York.

Sharon, Smadar. 2012. "Lo mityashvim 'ela meyushavim—Dfusei hagira, tihnun vehityashvut beezor lakhish beemtz'a shnot hahamishim." PhD diss., Tel Aviv University.

Shavit, Yaacov. 1992. "Meshihiyut 'utopia vepesimiyut bishnot hahamishim: Iyun bavikoret al hamedina haBen-Gurionit.'" *Iyunim bitkumat Yisrael* 2:56–78.

Shilo, Margalit. 2001. *Nesikha 'o shvuya, hahavaya hanashit shel hayishuv hayashan biYerushalayim*. Haifa.

———. 2010. "Kolot nashiyim bidvar shivyon migdari vetovat hauma bamaavak al zkhut habhira bayishuv." In *Huka 'ahat umishpat 'ehad laish velaisha—Nashim, zkhuyot umishpat bitkufat hamandat*, edited by Eyal Katvan, Margalit Shilo, and Ruth Halperin-Kaddari, 221–49. Ramat Gan.

———. 2013. *Hamaavak al hakol: Neshot hayishuv vizkhut habbira 1917–1926.* Jerusalem.

Shvarts, Shifra. 2000. "The Development of Mother and Infant Welfare Centers in Israel, 1854–1954." *Journal of the History of Medicine* 55 (4):398–425.

Sicron, Moshe. 1986. "'Ha'aliya hahamonit' — Memadeyha, meafyeneha vehashpa'oteha." In *Olim vema'abarot 1948–1952*, edited by Mordechai Naor, 31–52. Jerusalem.

Silber, Marcos. 2008. "'Immigrants from Poland Want to Go Back': The Politics of Return Migration and Nation Building in 1950s Israel." *Journal of Israeli History* 27 (2): 201–19.

Simon, Rachel. 1992. *Changes within Tradition among Jewish Women in Libya.* Seattle, WA.

Sinha, Mrinalini. 1993. "Refashioning Mother India: Feminism and Nationalism in Late-Colonial India." *Feminist Studies* 26 (3): 623–44.

Sivan, Emmanuel. 1991. *Dor tashah: Mitos, dyokan vezikaron.* Tel Aviv.

Sofri, Tsiyona. N.d. *Tsiyunyuney haderekh.* Printed by author.

Spanbauer, Julie M. 1993. "The First Amendment Right to Petition Government for a Redress of Grievances: Cut from a Different Cloth." *Hastings Constitututional Law Quarterly* 21 (1): 15–70.

Spivak, Gayatri Chakravorty. 1995. "Klum yeholim hamukhpafim ledaber?" *Teoriya uvikoret* 7:31–66.

Sprinzak, Ehud. 1986. *'Ish hayashar be'eynav: 'I-legalism bahevra hayisraelit.* Tel Aviv.

Stahl, Avraham. 1993. *Mishpaha vegidul yeladim beyahadut hamizrah: Mekorot, hafnayot, hashvaot.* Jerusalem.

Stampfer, Shaul. 5747. "Hamashma'ut hahevratit shel nisuey boser beMizrah Europa bameah hayud-tet." In *Kovets mehkarim al Yehudey Polin — Lezikhro shel Paul Glickson*, edited by Ezra Mendelsohn and Chone Shmeruk, 65–77. Jerusalem.

Stoler-Liss, Sachlav, and Shifra Shvarts. 2004. "'Nilhamot baba'arut ubehergelim nehshalim': Tfisot vepraktikot shel 'ahayot verofim klapey olim ba'aliya hagdola shel shnot hahamishim." *Yisrael* 6:31-62.

———. 2011. "'Hahigyena shel haisha litkufoteha': Migdar, leumiyut va'avoda bikhtaveha shel rofat hanashim Dr. Miriam 'Aharonova (1889–1967)." In *Migdar beyisrael*, edited by Margalit Shilo and Gideon Katz, 1:85–105. Sde Boker.

Straughn, Jeremy Brooke. 2005. "'Taking the State at Its Word': The Arts of Consentful Contention in the German Democratic Republic." *American Journal of Sociology* 110 (6): 1598–650.

Sunstein, Cass R. 1996. "On the Expressive Function of Law." *University of Pennsylvania Law Review* 144 (5): 2021–53.

Tadmor-Shimony, Tali. 2007. "Hamorim ha'olim kesokhney klita." *Dor ledor* 31:97–116.

Tal, David. 1994. "Pe'ulot hagmul: Mimakhshir bitahon shotef lemakhshir bitahon yesodi." In *'Hets shahor' — Pe'ulat Aza umediniyut hagmul shel Yisrael bishnot hahamishim*, edited by Motti Golani, 65–90. Tel Aviv.

———. 1998. *Tfisat habitahon hashotef shel Yisrael, mekoroteha vehitpathuta 1949–1956.* Sde Boker.

Taylor, Charles. 1994. "Examining the Politics of Recognition." In *Multiculturalism*, edited by Amy Gutmann, 25–73. Princeton, NJ.

——— and Amy Gutmann. 1992. *Multiculturalism and the Politics of Recognition*. Princeton, NJ.

Tene, Ofra. 2005. "'Kakh nevashel' bait beyisrael — Kria besifrey bishul mishnot hashloshim ad shnot hashmonim." In *Beten melea: Mabat 'aher al 'okhel vehevra*, edited by Aviad Kleinberg, 92–130. Jerusalem.

Terri, Ora. 5754. "Shinuyim bema'amada shel bat-Teyman im aliyata 'artsa." In *Bat-Teyman: Olama shel haisha hayehudiya*, edited by Shalom Serri, 311–22. Tel Aviv.

Thompson, Elizabeth. 2000. *Colonial Citizens: Republican Rights, Paternal Privilege, and Gender in French Syria and Lebanon*. New York.

Tivoni, Shlomo. 1982. *'Ahavat Hadassah: Sipuran shel mishpahat Nadav miTeyman umishpahat Basin meRusia*. Tel Aviv.

Torpey, John. 2000. *The Invention of the Passport: Surveillance, Citizenship and the State*. Cambridge.

Trattner, Walter I. 1999. *From Poor Law to Welfare State: A History of Social Welfare in America*. 6th ed. New York.

Treitel, Andrew. 1994. "Conflicting Traditions: Muslim *Shari'a* Courts and Marriage Age Regulation in Israel." *Columbia Human Rights Law Review* 26 (2): 403–38.

Tsoref, Hagai. 2010. "Meafyeney mediniyuta shel Golda Meyerson (Meir) bemisrad ha'avoda, 1949–1956: Leor tfisat olama hahevratit-kalkalit." PhD diss., Haifa University.

Tsur, Michal. 1999. *Takanot hahagana (she'at herum) 1945*. Jerusalem.

Tsur, Yaron. 2000a. "'Eimat hakarnaval — 'HaMarokanim' vehatmura babe'aya ha'adatit beyisrael hatse'ira." *'Alpayim* 19:126–64.

———. 2000b. "Haba'aya ha'adatit." In *Ha'asor hasheni tashyah-tashkah*, edited by Zvi Zameret and Hanna Yablonka, 101–25. Jerusalem.

———. 2001. *Kehila Kru'a: Yehudei Marocco vehaleumiyut 1943-1954*. Tel Aviv.

———. 2002. "Haba'aya ha'adatit bediyuney hanhalat hasokhnut beshilhey tkufat ha'aliya hahamonit." *Yisrael* 2: 81–106.

———. 2014. "Hakaryera haktsara shel Prosper Cohen: Mi'migzar' koloniali le'ma'amad' beyisrael hatse'ira 1948–1949." In *Marei makom: Zehuyot mishtanot vemikumim hevratiyim beyisrael*, edited by Zeev Shavit, Orna Sasson-Levy, and Guy Porart, 383–415. Tel Aviv.

Tully, James. 1999. "The Agonic Freedom of Citizens." *Economy and Society* 28 (2): 161–82.

Turack, Daniel C. 1972. *The Passport in International Law*. Lexington, MA.

Ury, Scott. 2012. *Barricades and Banners: The Revolution of 1905 and the Transformation of Warsaw Jewry*. Stanford, CA.

Van Den Brink, Bert. 2011. "Recognition, Pluralism and the Expectation of Harmony: Against the Ideal of an Ethical Life 'Free from Pain.'" In *Axel Honneth: Critical Essays with a reply by Axel Honneth*, edited by Danielle Petherbridge, 155–76. Leiden.

Viola, Lynn. 1996. *Peasant Rebels under Stalin: Collectivization and the Culture of Peasant Resistance*. Oxford.

Vorm, Shalom. 1963. *The Life and Work of Giyora Yoseftal*. Tel Aviv.

Wasserstein, Bernard. 2003. *Israel and Palestine: Why They Fight and Can They Stop?* London.

Weiss, Yfaat. 2001. "Hagolem veyotsro, 'o 'eikh hafakh hok hashvut 'et Yisrael lemedina multi-etnit." *Teoria uvikoret* 19:45–69.

Weitz, Yechiam. 1995. "Miflaga mitmodedet im kishlona — Mapai lenokhah totsot habhirot laknesset hashlishit." *Catedra* 77: 24–38.

Whelan, Frederick G. 1981. "Citizenship and the Right to Leave." *American Political Science Review* 75 (3): 636–53.

Williams, David W. 1974. "British Passports and the Right to Travel." *International and Comparative Law Quarterly* 23 (3): 642–56.

Yablonka, Hanna. 1994. *'Ahim zarim*. Jerusalem.

Yanai, Natan. 1990. "Hama'avar lemedinat Yisrael lelo huka." In *Hama'avar miyishuv lemedina 1947–1949: Retsifut utmurot*, edited by Varda Pilowski, 23–35. Haifa.

Yehudai, Ori. 2013. "Forth from Zion: Jewish Emigration from Palestine and Israel: 1945–1960." PhD diss., University of Chicago.

Zalashik, Rakefet. 2006. "Hitpathut hapsikhiatria bepalestina vebeyisrael 1892–1960." PhD diss., Tel Aviv University.

———. 2008. *Ad nefesh: Mehagrim, olim, plitim vehamimsad hapsikhiatri beyisrael*. Tel Aviv.

Zalkin, Mordechai. 1998. "Hamishpacha hamaskilit vemekoma behitpathut tnu'at hahaskala hayehudit." In *'Eros, 'erusin veisurim: Miniyut vemishpaha bahistoria*, edited by Israel Bartal and Isaiah Gafni, 239–51. Jerusalem.

Zameret, Zvi. 1993. *Yemey kur hahitukh: Va'adat hakira al hinukh yaldey ha'olim (1950)*. Sde Boker.

———. 1997. *Aley gesher tsar*. Sde Boker.

———. 2002. *The Melting Pot in Israel: The Commission of Inquiry Concerning the Education of Immigrant Children during the Early Years of the State*. Albany, NY.

Zamir, Yitzhak. 1994. "Likhvod hashofet Zvi Bernson." *Mishpat vemimshal* 2 (2): 325–37.

Zelizer. Viviana A. 1994. *Pricing the Priceless Child: The Changing Social Value of Children*. Princeton, NJ.

Zerubavel, Eviatar. 2003. *Time Maps: Collective Memory and the Social Shape of the Past*. Chicago.

Zidon, Asher. 1966. *Beit hanivharim*. Jerusalem.

Zilbershatz, Yafa. 994. "Zkhut hayetsia mimedina." *Mishpatim* 23 (69): 90–95.

Zurn, Christopher F. 2005. "Recognition, Redistribution, and Democracy: Dilemmas of Honneth's Critical Social Theory." *European Journal of Philosophy* 13 (1): 89–126.

INDEX

. . . .

Note: Page numbers in *italics* indicate figures and tables; page numbers with 'n' indicate endnotes.

absorption: belonging, 127, 131; contradictions, 156–59; of Holocaust refugees, 6; of immigrants, 18, 118–26, 131; Jewish Agency, 31, 122–23, 125, 140, 152, 154; meeting policymakers, 150–51; and resources, 124; responsibility for, 27, 117, 153–54; Zionism, 94

active resistance, 145–48

Adiv, Rachel, 168–69

Age of Marriage Law (1950): age determination, 48; Chief Rabbinate, 26–32; circumvention of, 45, 47–49, 56, 58, 180n166, 180n169, 182n205; current scholarship, 17–18; enactment, 32–35; enforcement, 45–47, 50–57; inculcating values, 61–66; Jewish Agency, 32, 62; Knesset debates, 35–42, 45, 61, 65, 178n117, 184n253; Maimon's crusade to establish, 15–16, 18–20, 32–38, 43–45, 48, 179n126; minorities, 164; Mizrahi Jews, 18, 60, 63; 1960 amendment, 17, 44, 46, 52, 58, 63, 65; Orthodox community, 55–58; overview, 12–13; penal code reform, 20–25; perceptions of, 64–65; petition for amendment, 59; position of the courts, 50–55; religious communities' response, 55–58; right to childhood, 18–20; and women's status, 25–26, 55, 57, 66; Yemenites, 32, 36, 41, 59–62

Agron, Gershon, 78, 96

'Agudat Yisrael, 23, 55, 58

Aharonova, Miriam, 40

Aharonowitz, Ziama, 39, 139

Ahrak, Mazal, 183n229

'Al Hamishmar (newspaper), 31–32, 149

Amidar (state-owned housing company), 122

Anerkennung. See recognition

"anti-bureaucratic ideology," 199n188

Arab citizens of Israel: citizenship, 13, 163–64; demographic anxiety, 36; discrimination against, 4, 70, 163–64; enforcement of marriage law, 45–47; former citizens, 123–24, 134–35, 140, 145; gender equality, 26; growing population, 17; identity cards, 47–48; marriage age, 17, 46–49, 57–58; women, 18, 22, 42, 60

Aran, Zalman. *See* Aharonowitz, Ziama

arranged marriages, 22, 43, 49.

See also child marriage

Ashkenazi Jews, 22, 27–28, 40, 44, 53, 126, 163

austerity program, 5–6, 79–80, 84, 99, 101, 113–14, 124

Avtalyon, Avraham, 116–17, 148–49, 157

Ayanot (school), 36

Bachi, Roberto, 179n122

Barak, Aharon, 53–55

Bar-Rav-Hai, David, 28, 38–39

Bar-Yehuda, Israel, 84–87, 90, 92–93

Basin, Shoshana, 61, 183n229

Bedouin community, 24, 180–81n170

Beersheva Labor Bureau, 138–39

overview, 4–7; scholarly portrayals,
9–12; shifting policies, 7–9, 76–88,
109–10
Govrin, Akiva, 142–44
Great Britain, 7, 20, 23, 185n13, 185n39
Guber, Rivka, 155

Haaretz (newspaper), 47–48, 137, 147, 158
Haboker (newspaper), 30, 49, 137, 149
Hacohen, David, 114
Hadassah, 27, 175n16
Hador (newspaper), 116–18, 132–33
Hakol (newspaper), 55–56
Halakhah, 28–29
halitzah, 101
Ha'olam Hazeh (weekly), 49, 51
Hapo'el Hamizrahi party, 37, 56
Harari, Yizhar, 82–83, 85, 92–93
Haskalah, 16
Hatsofe (newspaper), 55–56, 138
Hayak, Shaul, 143
health: maternalism of government,
18–20, 64; provision in marriage law
for, 34–35, 41, 45, 56, 58; as reason for
travel, 93, 100–105; reform, 18; right
to, 9; services, 122–24, 126, 154, 163;
women's organizations, 152
Hebron district, 23–24
Hed Hamizrah (periodical), 41, 156
Herut (newspaper), 131–32
Herut party, 40, 86
Herzog, Yizhak HaLevi, 28
Hirschman, Albert, 159–60
Histadrut, 1, 15, 83, 100, 125, 130, 136–37,
142, 158
Histadrut Executive Committee, 143, 145
Holocaust refugees: absorption, 6; educational level, 125–26; as immigrants,
3, 71, 119–20, 132; military service, 127;
perception of, 126–27; protests by, 6,
135, 139; travel policies, 104–7
Honneth, Axel, 117, 160
Horowitz, Dan, 65
housing, 122–23, 131

hunger strikes, 136, 149, 155, 166
hutz la'aretz (outside the land), 95

Idelson, Beba, 37, 39, 63, 140–41, 153
identity, 2–5, 60, 114–15, 134, 154, 160, 165
identity cards, 47–48, 164
'Im ha'Oleh (with the immigrant), 152
immigrant camps: demand for dignity,
148–50; illegal marriage, 29–31, 62;
living conditions, 139–40; Mapai
Party, 155; meeting policymakers,
142–43; network of listeners, 152–56;
placement, 96, 123–25; protests,
131–37; restrictions on freedom, 146
immigrants: absorption, 118–26, 131;
active resistance, 145–48; belonging,
107, 110, 115, 117; Ben-Gurion on, 126,
138, 140–41; citizenship, 160–61;
countries of origin, 119–20, *121*; education, 122–23, 154, 163; emigration,
83, 90–92; establishment response,
139–42, 155–57; exit permits, 82; experience of, 116–18; financial burden,
80, 96; Histadrut, 130; Holocaust refugees, 3, 71, 119–20, 132; Jewish, 28–29,
48–49; marriage age, 50–55, 56–57;
means of expression, 128–29; meeting
policymakers, 142–45; network
of listeners, 150–55; perception of,
126–27, 184n247; polarization, 157–59;
population growth, 118–20; protests,
92, 134–39, 167; rate of arrival, 71;
representation, 129–31; resources
provided for, 31, 122–23, 127, 131–32,
143–44; right to childhood, 2, 59–60,
63; treatment of, 131–34, 148–50;
values, 55; women's organizations, 25,
61–66. *See also* Islamic world
individual freedoms, 88, 91–92
infant mortality, 18, 124
Interior Ministry, 48, 56, 67, 80, 83, 85–87
intermarriage, 174n15
International Women's Suffrage Alliance,
21

Iraqi immigrants, 119–20, *121*, 125, 142, 150
"iron curtain," 81, 91, 92, 111
Islamic world: absorption, 118–26;
    immigrants from, 3, 9, 13, 16, 18, 42,
    71, 126–27, 155; Orientalism, 64;
    Palestinian Arabs, 3–4, 171n10. *See also*
    Arab citizens of Israel; North African
    immigrants; *specific countries by name*
isolation, 9, 114, 144, 153, 154
Israel Bar Association, 81
Israel Defense Forces, 5, 18, 88, 106, 141,
    153
Israeli Exit Policy, 1948–1961, 67–70,
    79–80, 196n97
Israel Medical Association, 81

Jarjora, Amin-Salim, 38–39, 45
Jerusalem Post (newspaper), 78, 112
Jewish Agency: absorption, 31, 122–23,
    125, 140, 152, 154; Age of Marriage Law,
    32, 62; and centralized government,
    129; defined, 26–27; emigration,
    73; exit permits, 76, 109; immigrant
    settlements, 145–47; protests, 137–39,
    140–42, 149–50; travel applications, 83
Jewish National Fund, 99
Jews. *See* Ashkenazi Jews; Mizrahi Jews

Kaplan, Eliezer, 80–81, 137, 192n214
Kasztner affair, 84
Kaufman, Haya, 82
Key, Ellen, 18–19
kibbutzim, 61, 106, 122
Klorman, Bat-Zion Eraqui, 29
Klugman, Shabtai. *See* Shabtai, K.
Knesset: age of marriage debates, 35–42,
    45, 61, 65, 178n117, 184n253; Chief
    Rabbinate, 27–32; First Knesset, 5,
    25, 52, 130; immigrant rights, 153, 166;
    Maimon's age of marriage bill, 15–16,
    32–38; protests, 135, 140, 142–44, 149,
    165; representative of Muslims, 45–46;
    travel policies, 73, 82, 85–86, 89, 111–13
Kol Ha'am (newspaper), 62, 132, 135, 137

labor service, 77
laissez-passer (limited travel document),
    67, 70, 76
Lamerhav (newspaper), 147
Lamm, Yosef, 15, 39, 52
Landau, Haim, 86
Landesberg, Bruno, 195n75
Landsberg, Avraham, 105
landsmanschaften (immigrant organiza-
    tions), 83, 129–31
Layish, Aharon, 17, 180n169
League of Nations, 20–23
letters, 95–110, 115
Libyan Jews, 120, *121*, 137
liquidated property, 71
living conditions: camps, 139–40;
    immigrant voices, 127, 130; infant
    mortality, 18, 124; media, 155–57;
    political support, 130, 169; protests,
    136, 147; during World War II, 5
loopholes, 22, 28, 49, 85
loyalty, 91, 104, 106–8, 115, 160
Luke, Harry Charles, 22

ma'abarot (transit camps), 123–24, 131–32,
    142, 149, 154
Ma'ariv (newspaper), 49, 138
Maimon, Ada, 15–16, 18–20, 28, 32–38,
    41–44, 48, 63–66, 173n3
mamlahtiyut principle, 65
Mapai Party: education, 33; elections,
    26; immigration challenge, 139–40;
    Kasztner affair, 84; against liberal
    capitalist values, 8; marriage age, 38;
    media, 1, 168; political role, 92–93;
    representatives, 15, 28, 30, 41–45, 52,
    112, 114, 142, 155; travel policies, 86–87
Mapam party, 39
Marcus, Yoel, 84
Marima, Dizi, 51–52
marriage age. *See* Age of Marriage Law
    (1950)
mass immigration, 16, 90, 119, 125, 141
maternalism, 18–20, 64, 175n32

Matmon, Tehila, 62
media: access to, 155–57; child marriage, 29, 33, 52, 62–63, 65; discrimination, 116–18; emigration, 73; living conditions, 155–57; Mapai party, 1, 168; middle class, 30; protests, 128, 131, 135, 146, 159; right to travel, 70, 90; United States, 141; vilification of authorities, 139, 145; women's status, 25–26
medical treatment, 5, 71, 96, 102, 106. *See also* health
Meir, Golda, 57, 136, 138, 155–56
Melamed, Shoham, 17–18, 36, 41, 179n122
mental hygiene movement, 35, 45, 60, 64
middle class: children, 19; media, 30; recognition, 111, 167; right to travel, 2, 13, 71, 93; women's organizations, 15, 21
military service, 18, 48, 77, 103, 107, 109, 114, 117, 127, 137–38
minimum marriage age, 17, 23, 26, 28, 34–35, 39–40, 45, 56–58. *See also* Age of Marriage Law (1950)
Ministerial Committee on Interior Affairs and Services, 56
Ministerial Committee on Legislation, 34, 57–58
Ministries of Justice, Health, Religions, and Welfare, 56
Ministry of Defense, 77, 84, 85, 99, 108
Ministry of Finance, 76, 80, 81, 84, 87, 111
Ministry of Foreign Affairs, 78
Ministry of Health, 34, 56
Ministry of Immigration, 67, 76, 78, 80, 101, 105, 108, 185n31
Ministry of Internal Affairs, 99
Ministry of Justice, 31, 33, 34, 56, 78
Ministry of Labor (also Labor and Construction), 76–77, 135
Ministry of Minorities, 47
Ministry of Religions (also Religious Affairs), 28, 46, 56–57, 97, 101
Ministry of War Victims, 103
Ministry of Welfare, 29, 31–32, 48, 56
Mizrahi Jews: Age of Marriage Law, 18,

60, 63; children, 44; demographic anxiety, 17–18, 36, 41–42; intermarriage, 174n15; marriage age, 27, 40, 57–58; perception of, 64, 126–27; women, 22. *See also* Yemenites
Morocco, 120, *121*, 127
moshavim (communal villages), 60–61, 122, 124, 146, 153, 155–56
Moshavim Movement, 152–53, 155
motherhood, 17–19, 42–45
Muslim countries. *See* Islamic world
Muslims. *See* Arab citizens of Israel
Myerson, Golda. *See* Meir, Golda

Naor, Esther Raziel, 40
National Council, 15, 27, 77, 107
national identity, 2–5, 7–9, 14, 55, 163–64
nation building, 4, 93–94
negative freedoms, 8, 68, 118
network of listeners, 150–55
Neumann, Erich and Julia, 98–99
New York Times (newspaper), 133
Nixon, Margaret, 21, 23–25
non-Jews, 71–73, 160
North African immigrants, 16, 42, 122, 124, 126–27, 133–34, 138, 194n56

old-timers, 126, 158, 162, 195n75
Organization of Working Mothers, 27
Orientalism, 22, 40, 64, 126, 153, 179n122
Orthodox-Zionist National Religious Party, 58
Ostern, Dr., 34–36, 41
Ottoman family law, 21–22, 24

Palestine, 20–25. *See also* British Mandate period
Palestine Post (newspaper), 78, 96
Palestinian Arabs, 3–4, 171n10
Palestinian guerrillas, 85, 90
parental consent, 20–25, 34, 38, 40, 54, 57
patriarchal culture, 39, 42–43, 54, 66, 164
penal code reform, 20–25
petitions, 97, 128, 138, 189n150

Pinkas, David-Zvi, 38
Po'alei 'Agudat Yisrael Party, 55, 58
Polish immigrants, 81, 119, 120, *121*
politics, 92–93. See also *individual parties by name*
polygamy, 27
population growth, 118–20
Portugese, Jacqueline, 17
positive rights, 68, 118
press. *See* media
privacy, 100
protests: active resistance, 145–48; camps, 131–37; citizenship, 164–65; Histadrut, 136–37, 142; historical context, 128, 134; Holocaust refugees, 6, 135, 139; at Knesset, 135, 140, 142–44, 149, 165; living conditions, 131–37, 147; media perspective, 128, 131, 135, 146, 159; nonverbal, 157; response to, 139–42, 149–50, 167; violent, 137–39; by women, 132; Yemenites, 147
"pseudo-patriotism," 86
public opinion, 23, 70, 128
public works, 125, 135, 136

qadi (Muslim cleric), 22

Ramla, 123, 132–33, 135–36, 140–41, 156, 158
recognition: belonging, 150, 157; historical context, 130–31; ideological, 160; immigrant demand for, 116–18, 127, 159; meeting policymakers, 142–45; middle class, 111, 167; network of listeners, 150–55; overview, 12–13; Yishuv, 2. *See also* protests
reform movement, 18–20, 178n114
registration of marriage, 47, 181n172
Reifen, David, 53
relatives abroad. *See* travel
religious education, 33, 146
religious versus secular law, 9, 28–29, 37–38, 40, 45, 50, 55–58
Remez, David, 81

reparations, 6, 190n178
representation issue, 25–27, 126, 129–31
Riftin, Yaakov, 86
Rigger, Hagit, 60
right to be heard, 2, 12–13, 103, 118. *See also* protests
right to childhood. *See* children
right to education. *See* education
right to petition, 193n9
right to travel. *See* travel
Rokach, Israel, 41–42, 82, 89, 111
Romanian immigrants, 81, 119, 120, *121*, 134
Rosen, Pinhas, 35–36, 42–44, 58, 61, 79–81, 98–99, 105–6, 111–12, 184n253
Rosetti, Moshe, 142–43

Salameh (immigrant settlement), 131
Samuel, Edwin, 22
Samuel, Lady Beatrice and Lord Herbert, 21
Schoken, Gershom, 90
secular education, 33, 146
secular versus religious law, 9, 28–29, 37–38, 40, 45, 50, 55–58
security issues, 6–7, 19, 68, 79, 82–89, 113–14, 165, 166, 200n208
Segev, Tom, 127
Sha'ar Ha'Aliyah camp, 123, 148
Shabtai, K., 110
Shag, Avraham-Haim, 41
Shapira, Haim-Moshe, 56–58, 79–81, 111–12, 184n253, 185n31
Shapira, Yaacov Shimshon, 67
Sharett, Moshe, 78, 80, 84, 112
Shari'a Courts, 17, 46, 48–49
sharia law, 22
Sharon, Smadar, 146
Shazar, Zalman, 81, 92, 111
Shazuri, Shmuel 'Aharon, 30–32
Sheetrit, Bechor-Shalom, 79, 179n136
Shenhav, Yehuda, 17–18, 36, 41, 179n122
Shilo, Margalit, 176n69
Shilo, Yitzhak, 54–55

132; rights of, 20, 36; status, 18–19, 25–26, 35–42; Zionism, 15, 22, 25, 27, 37, 175n16

Women's International Zionist Organization (WIZO), 15, 20, 25, 37

women's organizations: child marriage, 21; citizenship, 25; education, 27, 35, 61; health, 152; Histadrut, 15; immigrants, 25, 61–66; international connections, 175n16; middle class, 15, 21; Yemenites, 27; Yishuv, 15, 25, 63

World War II, 17, 69, 76, 79, 118, 185n39

Yedi'ot 'Aharonot (newspaper), 131, 133

Yemenites: Age of Marriage Law, 32, 36, 41, 59–62; child marriage, 16, 29, 49, 55, 183n238; complaints from, 131–32; culture, 15–17; as immigrants, 120, *121*, 173n2, 173n6; Maimon on children, 36; protests, 147; women's organizations, 27

yibum, 27

Yishuv: belonging, 107; children, 168; ethnic parsing, 22; national identity, 3–4, 154, 165; obligation to immigrants, 116–17; recognition, 2; representation issue, 25–27, 126; sovereignty, 1, 20–21; suffrage, 20; Western influence, 7; women's organizations, 15, 25, 63

Yosef, Dov, 81, 93

Yoseftal, Giora, 140

Youth Aliyah, 27, 31, 123

Za'arur, Yosef, 51–52

Zimmerman, Zvi, 88

Zionism: absorption, 94, 126; children, 168; Diaspora, 3, 94–95, 160; exit permit justification, 107; ideology, 93–95, 101–3, 106, 110, 159–60; Jewish National Fund, 99; values, 7, 20, 44; women, 15, 22, 25, 27, 37, 175n16. *See also* General Zionist Party

Zmanim (daily), 63